CRIMINAL PSYCHOLOGY

CRIMINAL PSYCHOLOGY

edited by

RICHARD W. NICE

*Clinical Psychologist on the Treatment Staff of the
New Jersey State Reformatory for Men
at Bordentown, New Jersey*

PHILOSOPHICAL LIBRARY

New York

© Copyright, 1962,

by Philosophical Library, Inc.

15 East 40th Street, New York

Library of Congress Catalog
Card No. 60-53158

Printed in the United States of America

To: Dr. Ralph B. Winn
Psychologist, Professor, Friend

CONTENTS

CONTENTS

CRIMINAL PSYCHOLOGY

CRITICAL INFRASTRUCTURE

I

INTRODUCTION

It is not difficult to understand the modern use of Psychology in our courts of law as an adjunct to legal procedure when one understands that man is a socio-biological, mind-body unit. In previous times the body and the mind were thought to exist independently of each other. The materialists vehemently denied that the mind even existed; the idealists maintained that only the mind was real. Still later the interactionists stated that both existed, but they could not come to any agreement as to their relationship to each other. Modern medicine postulates a mind-body unity each interacting upon the other.

All disease, whether mental or physical, is regarded as the result of the interplay between the individual and his environment. Thus the personality make-up of the individual will frequently determine his somatic response to disease. For example although the germ causing typhoid or infantile paralysis is present the disease may not necessarily develop. Other factors will influence the result, the physical resistance of the body, whether the individual is otherwise healthy, whether he is well-adjusted, whether he seeks to escape from emotional difficulty by falling ill.

1

The environment encompasses not only food and shelter, but happiness, contentment, and other emotional factors as well. The neurotic is in conflict with his environment, sometimes because he is faced with a really difficult situation, sometimes because some hereditary factor prevents him from resolving his troubles, and sometimes because of faulty upbringing which has made him react in an unhealthy way. All diseases must be looked upon as a reaction of the total person to his environment.

Man is a part of his environment and his environment is a part of him. He reacts with what he is, to what he is not, which makes him other than he was, and grows physically and emotionally by this process. He attempts to mould his world and to resist being moulded by it.

Man also responds to stress, accident, and disease as a body-mind unit. What affects his body affects his mind. and vice versa. Starvation, fever, alcoholism, thirst, accidents, pneumonia, hardening of the arteries, diseases of the heart, rheumatism, drug addiction give rise to disturbances in the mind as well as in the body. In the same way, anxiety, fear, anger, worry and hatred may in time give rise to actual physical changes in the heart, the stomach, the lungs, the blood vessels. A feeling of disgust may lead to nausea and vomiting. The peristaltic movements of the intestines are reversed in direction and this is accompanied by congestion of the blood vessels supplying the intestines and stomach. With frequent repetition, the lining of the intestines and stomach becomes irritated and ulcerated. These anatomical changes may be temporary at first, but if the stress continues they will become permanent.

Emotions and thought processes are never purely psychological, for the psyche is an organic agent. Nor does an organic ailment ever remain wholly organic. It affects the very core of the personality.

Mental conflict becomes understandable only in relation to the individual's social development in his culture. Social maladjustment is the expression of the conflict of the individual with his cultural pattern.

No one actually knows where the physical reaction stops and the mental reaction begins. Grief and gaiety, failure and success, disappointment and surprise are not mere states of feeling but states of being. They involve the heart, the lungs, the stomach and blood vessels, the brain and nerves. A cramp in the stomach may give rise to a fear to eat—a fear to eat may lead to the pain of hunger. Loss of memory may be due to a severe emotional conflict, to a tumor of the brain, to hardening of the arteries of the brain. Laughter may arise from a sense of the incongruous or from an organic disturbance of the power inhabiting the laughter center in the brain. Symptoms of disease represent not only the disease process, but also the reaction of the personality afflicted to the physical condition. The reaction of fear or rage, despair, a desire for death, a determination to live affect the body's power to recuperate.

Man's unity lies in his capacity to function on physical, intellectual, emotional, social and spiritual planes. Limitations may exist upon one plane and impair progress upon other planes, or deficiencies in total organization may impede development upon all or any of the planes.

Mental health has been defined as personal adjustment to one's self and the world, with a maximum of personal and social effectiveness and satisfaction. Social responsibility is a vital component of this adjustment. Complete isolation of human actions is impossible. The human machine exists in close relationship to the industrial machine, the economic machine, the social machine. They all work together to mould the world in which we live.

Man cannot exist by himself alone. He exists in

3

close relatedness with those about him and with his surroundings. A person's existence is not enclosed in the boundaries of his physical body. In his actions, feelings, intentions, thoughts, memories, the individual reaches out beyond himself into the surrounding world, and the world reaches into his existence. Existence is with others. Man's actions affect everyone and everything around him. By the same token, the world's actions affect him, and he reacts to these influences as a total personality. His effectiveness as a human being depends upon his capacity to react to these influences.

The natural history of human behavior, in psychoanalytic terms and concepts, is approximately as follows: The pre-oedipal mother relationship in the early months of life is shattered because of its aggressive contradictions. Hatred of the mother, the same mother upon whom the child nevertheless depends for food and care becomes unbearable. The boy then shifts his hatred onto his father, his passive feelings remaining with his mother, whom he now conceives of as passive-feminine and loving. The father becomes the recipient of his hatred as a solution of the boy's unbearable conflict concerning his mother and because the boy takes cognizance of the father's existence as a competitor for his mother. In this manner the transition between the pre-oedipal and oedipal phases is established. According to Edmund Bergler, failure to reach the oedipal stage and consequent fixation at the oral level, is at the root of criminal activity.

Dr. Bergler compares the criminal to the orally repressed neurotic, who must constantly unconsciously formulate the same triad:

1. Unconsciously they create situations in which they are rejected and disappointed.
2. Then they throw themselves, full of aggression

4

and seemingly in self-defense against their fancied enemies and combat them with all sorts of devices.

3. As a final act, they indulge in masochistic self-pity.

In this triad, which Dr. Bergler has called the mechanism of orality, the initial provocation and masochistic pleasure are completely repressed; only the righteous indignation and self-commiseration are conscious.

The mechanism of orality is the key to all neuroses. However, despite the similarity between the mechanism of orality and that of criminal behaviour, they are not identical. The neurotic exhausts himself in the constant unconscious construction of situations in which he is rejected, giving him the right to indulge in defensive aggression, and producing the unconscious pleasure of self-pity. The mechanism of criminality, according to Dr. Bergler differs in the following respects:

1. Despite the fact that the starting point—feeling of being unjustly treated by the pre-oedipal mother —is identical in both the oral and criminal mechanism, it lends to different reactions. The oral neurotic created the triad outlined above. This feeling of helplessness is overcome by two devices. First, he repeats actively what he originally experienced passively, using the "unconscious repetition compulsion" (Freud), which restores his mortified narcissism. Second, he seems to overcome his feelings of helplessness toward the pre-oedipal mother by feeling consciously that he is aggressive in self-defence, despite the fact that unconsciously he enjoys psychic masochistic pleasure. The criminal suffers similarly to begin with, but apparently his feeling of helplessness is not

5

successfully overcome. The motor action in criminality is based on the inner feeling of being incapable of making the mother feel that he seeks revenge on her. Feelings of passivity and of being unmanly and aggression in defense against them are experienced, as Drs. Schilder and Keiser have shown.

Herostratos, in 346 B.C., burned the famous temple of Artemis in Ephonos in order to gain great fame. There is something herostratic about many criminal actions. Criminals perform similar deeds with another purpose: to force the mother to acknowledge that they are at least capable of taking revenge on her. The deepest core of the criminal's conflict is the pre-oedipal helplessness and the feeling that the mother and her successive representatives do not believe that the child can help himself even in revenge.

2. The disproportion between the underlying reason for a criminal act and the nature of the act itself is understandable when we take into account the fact that the unconscious motive is the herostratic compensation for a deep feeling of helplessness, leading to revenge.

3. The unconscious expectation of punishment to appease the superego is an essential prerequisite of every criminal action.

4. The criminal's sense of self-preservation leads him to attempt to conceal his crime. However, his typical self-betraying mistakes are determined not only by an unconscious need for punishment, but also by an unconscious need to exhibit his helplessness.

Dr. Bergler sums up as follows: The criminal commits his specific crime for two reasons; he is confronted with an unconscious conflict (variable factor) and solves this conflict by committing a herostratic

6

motor act (constant factor), motivated by an infantile pre-oedipal pattern, also unconscious. It is, therefore, not true that everyone is a potential criminal. Criminality presupposes specific childhood conflicts and their unsolubility. By the same token it is not true that unfavorable social factors alone can explain criminality. In many instances the social factor in criminal actions is either an excuse or a rationalization for hidden unconscious motives. The focal point of the criminal act is the repetition of injustices experienced in reality or phantasy in the child-mother (later, father) relationship, projected and perpetuated masochistically upon society.

The question has been raised as to whether the aggression shown in the motor act is a defense mechanism. Dr. Bergler, in agreement with Drs. Schilder and Keiser, and Drs. Alexander and Healy, believes that it is a defense mechanism. Drs. Alexander and Healy lay great stress on an inner prestige motive. They regard stealing, for example, as "an attempt to regain the lost self-esteem by a kind of pseudo-masculinity, as well as an attempt to repair oral damage." Drs. Schilder and Keiser state: "We conclude that in many instances aggressive action (in criminals) is a reactive state resulting from a sense of passivity. The passivity is frequently felt as identical with homosexual trends."

What part does the superego play in criminal activity? The core of the superego consists of the introjected educational authority (mother, father, and their successive representatives.) What is introjected, however, is by no means the attitudes of the real mother or father, but of the mother and father as the child sees them. When, therefore, the child projects a great deal of his own aggression upon his parents, he later introjects them as cruel and malicious, even though in reality they may be mild and benevolent.

The superego makes itself clinically visible in its

7

effects: feelings of guilt, need for punishment, sense of depression.

To what degree are feelings of guilt the simple consequences of a criminal act? There are several divergent views on this point. Drs. Schilder and Keiser state: "We have no definite reason to believe that the wish for punishment, although present, is one of the outstanding factors. Most criminals want to be punished. but not too severely. It is the attitude of the child, who regains the love of his parents after punishment."

According to Dr. Gregory Zilboorg: "As soon as the impulse is discharged and the special Id drives are thus temporarily gratified and silenced, the Super Ego re-establishes itself and asserts its demands. Even the hard, defiant criminal then feels unconsciously repentant. His challenging, snarling, boisterous defiance of the law, or his sullen, apparently indifferent emotionless attitude is, in most cases, but an automatic covering, boastful or humbled, of the sense of guilt. Many criminals, as a result of this inner penance, kill themselves soon after the crime."

Dr. Bergler believes that the unconscious feeling of guilt has a place of pivotal importance in criminal deeds. If the criminal did not know unconsciously that he would be punished, if he did not project his expected punishment upon the judicial and penal authorities, making them the executive organ of his own superego, his feelings of guilt would prevent his deed in the first place. Only because he projects this expectation of punishment, does he often appear detached and sometimes without penance. Dr. Bergler is of the opinion that crime is not an outburst of an id-wish but a defense against it, executed by highly complicated means. The feeling of guilt does not appear *post facto*, but is embedded in the deed itself.

8

Let us explore the drives in the psychological make up of an individual that lead to homicide. In general, there is the impression that for the potential murderer, whether he is of high or low intelligence homicide is a fundamental desire which has been frustrated at some period in life. Under sufficient provocation his emotional maladjustment leads to violent behavior. The murderer is not able to compensate for frustrations and rejections by socially approved modes of conduct.

According to John Lewis Gillen (*The Wisconsin Murderer*. Madison. The University of Wisconsin Press, 1946), common to all murderers' histories are an incapacity to adjust normally to life situations; harmful emotional experiences in early life; a crisis too severe for an unstable person to cope with adequately and sanely. In a study of the life histories of murderers Gillen has come to the following conclusions as to causative factors:

1. The murderer through heredity, disease, or accident is defective in physical vigor, nervous stability, or mental and emotional capacity required to meet the demands of life.

2. His social environment has failed to prepare for his self-support, limited his cultural opportunities and choice of associates, and engendered the undesirable attitudes and habits that prevail in certain poorly paid, rough occupations.

3. His family environment has produced a sense of inferiority and of economic, emotional, or social insecurity: there is resistance to established authority; deep-seated resentment; misguided efforts to compensate for frustrations; and an irritable nature that breaks bounds in the face of a crisis.

4. The educational experience of the murderer has been inadequate, either because it was too short or because it was unsuited to the moulding of a well-

9

adjusted personality. The boy whose education is prematurely cut short is deprived of the socializing influences of the school.

5. The murderer has been subjected to community influences which created a pattern of responses and attitudes condemned by the larger society—excessive drinking, sexual promiscuity, and violent methods of achieving desired ends. The home, the school, the community—these form the complex of influences which largely determine the personality that will develop from natural endowments.

6. He is excessively frustrated, from whatever cause, with regard to his fundamental desire for security, ego satisfaction, peer recognition, and new experiences. Such frustration may cause serious emotional disturbances, destroy ambition, undermine the desire for social status and foster anti-social and even criminal methods of satisfying the ego.

7. Love relationships have been disrupted. The emotions attending love are among the strongest that govern the individual, and the threat to their satisfaction may create a serious emotional upheaval.

8. A sudden unexpected event or the culmination of a series of unfortunate events threatens one of the fundamental drives of the individual.

Murder finds expression in a variety of ways and outlets, such as murders of passion. There may be a common denominator in all such crimes, but each is a highly individual case, which requires detailed study in order to arrive at a unified conception. However, it is quite evident that the true motivation in murders of passion is frequently unconscious. At the root of some apparently trivial overt motive lie years of unconscious hostility. The victim may represent a reproach to the murderer; he may be a sacrifice for the murderer's sins, or the murderer's guilt may be projected upon the victim. Premeditated murders may appear carefully planned, but often the unconscious driving forces stem from deeper sources of the personality. The capacity for murder seems to vary in individuals. The murderer is apparently lacking in some inhibitory quality which is present in others, who react differently under similar circumstances.

Psychoanalytic study attempts to probe the murderer's mind. Among other findings, psychoanalysis postulates the victim often represents the murderer in the latter's unconscious. The psychopathic or psychotic individual projects his own castration fears and guilt-directed punishment tendencies to someone in the environment who has, in the offender's mind, come symbolically to represent himself.

The attitude towards death is a fertile field of investigation, according to the psychoanalytic view. A study of the attitudes toward death on the part of murderers and among normal individuals demonstrates the ubiquity of representations of the love object in unconscious mentation. There are various unconscious meanings of death for self or others; death can be an equivalent for the final sexual union with an incest object; a state of final narcissistic perfection of the body image granting eternal satisfaction; a gratification of masochistic tendencies toward self and others, etc.

Alcohol and drugs, when used excessively have resulted in homicide. Body image perceptions altered by the toxic effects of alcohol evoke anxieties visible in the frequent castration and dismemberment fears of acute alcoholic psychotics. These reactions dip into the infantile psychic organization of the patient (anal levels), but also reflect current anxieties. Guilt from unconscious passive impulses aids regression to an earlier level where dismemberment represents destruction of the body image. The psychopathology and physiopathology of alcoholic psychosis (castration and dismemberment fears, disorders of equilibrium and time sense) indicate the intermixture of body

11

image perception disorder and psychosexual disturbances that assail the ego. When the defenses against this catastrophic series of injuries to the alcoholic's ego fail, aggressive acts such as murder occur.

It appears valid to state in general terms that aggressive behaviour will ensue when ego strength is insufficient to combat the destructive forces derived from early oral aggression. Whether suicide will occur in a given case depends upon the degree of integrity which the ego can maintain as it attempts to withstand the exacting pressure of id and superego. Whether murder will occur depends upon the strength of the revenge motive against the mother-figure, which itself is conditioned by the capacity for projection and introjection, and of feelings of helplessness on the part of the infant who becomes the psychic masochist in later life.

Perhaps the only conclusion tenable is that an estimate of the relative strength of early oral tendencies as compared with ego strength would furnish material for prognosticating violent crime. It may well be that no all-inclusive formula will ever be devised to foretell the response of an ego to the unconscious forces bombarding it. Experience may prove that analysis of each childhood or adolescent neurosis (or pre-psychopathic individual), may be required to enable society to anticipate and prevent violent crime.

II

THE PSYCHIATRIST'S ROLE IN THE ADMINISTRATION OF CRIMINAL JUSTICE *

Dr. Henry A. Davidson
*Superintendent, Overbrook Hospital,
Cedar Grove, N. J.*

The criminal is a deviate from the average, hence —in a broad sense—must have some sort of psychiatric abnormality. If you believe that psychiatric patients are not accountable for their acts, you may find yourself, in effect, subscribing to the doctrine that no criminal defendant is ever responsible. Obviously society is not prepared to accept, nor are psychiatrists ready to promote, any such conclusion.

What are these psychiatric disorders? They fall into two broad classes. In the first group are disorders of *thought and feeling;* in the second are disorders of *will and character.* The first includes the insanities, the psychoneuroses, certain organic disorders, and the various forms of mental deficiency. Most defendants, however, fall into the second class: disorders of will and character.

Some insist that this is a spurious distinction. However, as a practical matter we must assume that there *is* such a thing as free will, and that there *is* such a thing as character. To deny the existence of free will would be to embrace the doctrine that no one is ever responsible for what he does, since every man is then assumed to be a helpless product of

13

environment and heredity. On purely theoretical grounds it is possible to say that character traits are merely the mechanical result of a battery of reflexes. But such a doctrine is unworkable. It happens to be a fact that some people are kindly and others are selfish; some are greedy and others are undemanding; some behave as if they are controlled by a conscience and some act as if they had no conscience. Regardless of the origin of these drives, they do exist, and in the aggregate they constitute character. We recognize that there *is* a group of disorders which, as an operational concept at least, seem to be disorders of will and character. Included in this group would be alcoholics, certain sexual psychopaths, the rage reactions of poorly controlled individuals, and that strange actor in the arena of crime, the psychopath.

This distinction between the two major groups of psychiatric disorders is literally of vital importance; for a defendant's life may depend on whether he has a disorder of thought and feeling or whether he has a disorder of character or will.

Consider an insane person who perpetrates an assault because he has a delusion that his victim is trying to influence him with radio waves. If he is irresponsible, it is because he doesn't realize that his assault is wrong. Compare this with a man who is drunk, and who knows he should not assault people, but who, in his drunken defiance, just doesn't care.

Let us return to the first group—disorders of thinking and feeling. This includes *mental deficiency* which means a marked limitation of intelligence, usually from birth. Mental deficiency is measured by tests which determine mental age. Thus, an adult may have the intelligence of an 8-year old: that is, his mental age is eight. Low grade mental defectives usually cannot realize that the act is wrong. An idiot might gleefully push his friend out of a 4th story

14

window, knowing that it was naughty but not really appreciating how wrong it was. A higher grade mental defective—say one with a mental age over nine or ten—would be technically responsible because he would know that the act is wrong, though he would not be intelligent enough to advise counsel, cooperate in his defense, or understand the nature of a plea.[1]

A second set of diseases in this group of "thought and feeling disorder," is *insanity*. The word "psychosis" is a synonym for insanity. Do not confuse this with the word "psychopath" which is very different. A psychotic or insane person is one who has lost a large degree of contact with reality. Not all insane persons are irresponsible; and insanity is not the only cause of irresponsibility. Hence the phrase "insanity defense" is incorrect. It is a defense of "irresponsibility," not a defense of "insanity." Dementia praecox is one psychosis; melancholia is another, and senile dementia a third, and so on.

Then we have a group of very different entities called in the aggregate, the *neuroses* or psychoneuroses. Here we find an attempted compromise with the harshness of reality, rather than a flight from reality. These neuroses include hysteria, neurasthenia, anxiety states, phobias, compulsions, and various ways of expressing emotional conflict through physical symptoms. Neurotics do not have hallucinations, though they frequently have obsessions. True compulsions fall into this category. Another neurotic symptom of forensic interest is amnesia [2] which occurs episodically in certain forms of hysteria. Apart from these two symptoms (compulsion and amnesias) the psychoneuroses do not play a large role in criminal justice.

We now turn to the second group: disorders of will and character. One of these is *alcoholism*. As physicians, we say that alcoholism is a sickness; but we doctors use the word "sickness" in a specialized sense. The doctor uses a word like "sickness" to mean "anything unhealthy," and in that sense alcoholism *is* a sickness. But the general statement that alcoholism is an illness is misleading because the layman makes the analogy to other illnesses like pneumonia or diabetes. For forensic purposes, alcoholism is not a sickness but a bad habit. If psychiatrists keep repeating that alcoholics are sick people, some day judges may begin to believe us. Then a person will be able to get away with murder by the simple process of fortifying himself with enough whiskey to allow him to commit the crime. Since by that time you will have classed alcoholism with pneumonia, you will be no more able to hold him responsible for murder than you would be able to hold responsible a man who commits an assault during the delirium of pneumonia. This would be the logical result of classifying alcoholism as a disease. Until we are ready for this innovation in criminal law, we will have to adhere to the concept that alcoholism is a disorder of character or will, not a disease.[3]

Rage reactions in otherwise normal people would also fall into this category of disorders of will. Many people, at times, have a brief urge to kill. Certainly any bridge player will recognize it. But most of us do control the impulse. Failure to restrain such an urge is evidence of defect in will, not defect in the thought process. Unless we are prepared to accept the doctrine of universal irresponsibility, we must exclude these reactions from the category of mental disease. Otherwise, we place a premium on loss of self control. Most people do hold these rage reactions in check for fear of consequences.

The commonest, and by all odds the most troublesome, of our defendants is the *psychopath*. A psychopath may be anything else, but he is *not* insane. A psychopath is a person who lacks a conscience. He is a rebellious, antisocial individual who gets that way because of some personality quirk not because of any mental disease. He is a psychopath not by reason of what he says or thinks but by reason of what he does. He is unreliable, and amazingly inconsiderate of others. He may be of superior intelligence, and may make a good first impression. He often commits crimes for astonishingly low stakes. His record is studded with examples of recklessness, folly, impulsiveness and antisocial behavior. Under pressure he is explosive, and sometimes displays brief tantrums of nearly psychotic behavior. He seems to learn nothing by experience, except some added craft in evading detection. He has weak inhibitions rather than strong drives. The psychopath knows that his acts are wrong. He seeks to explain or escape by evasions, flight or the piling up of ingenious prevarications—actions which mean that he knows he has done something wrong. When closely watched he commits no crime—which indicates that he is not in the grip of any irresistible impulse.

Sexual misconduct by itself does not constitute a psychiatric category. The sex offender may be insane, or mentally defective, or a psychopath or a neurotic, and that will be the primary psychiatric classification. If none of these categories applies, we may speak of a primary sexual psychopath.[4] His act is compulsive, repetitive and traumatizing. It is compulsive in that the defendant is driven to it because of some mounting inner tension which can be relieved in no other way. It is repetitive in that it is one of a cycle of similar acts. It is traumatizing in that it inflicts mental anguish or physical hurt on the victim. If, as so often happens, the defendant seeks to perform the act in secret, conceals his identity, or tries to flee, then he must know that the act is wrong. If, as often happens, he hunts for or waits for a favorable opportunity, then obviously he *can*, for a time at least,

17

resist the impulse; therefore it does not represent an irresistible impulse.

The actual appraisal of the defendant's responsibility consists in matching the psychiatric findings with the M'Naghten rule. Thus, it must first be determined whether the defendant has a mental disorder; second, whether because of that he does not know the nature of the act, or does not know its quality, or does not know that the act is wrong. The "mental disorders" contemplated here are disorders of "thinking and feeling," and not disorders of "will or character." I know of no case where an appellant court reversed a guilty verdict because a defendant was suffering from a disorder of character or will. Juries sometimes acquit an alcoholic or a psychopath, but these acquittals are blind alleys; they are not likely to get into the reports or establish new laws. If the defendant does not have a psychosis, a psychoneurosis, mental deficiency or an organic brain disease, the rest of M'Naghten's rule is of no relevance.

If the accused does have a disorder of "thought or feeling," the next step is to determine whether it impairs his knowledge of the nature, quality or wrongfulness of the act. Almost any one above the mental age of six or seven knows the nature of his acts, though occasionally a defendant is so violent that he obviously does not know what he is doing. Extreme cases like that present no problem. The "quality of the act" is a vague term which, in practice tends to boil down to an understanding of the wrongfulness of the act.[5] In most cases, the defense turns on whether the accused knew that the act was wrong. This is the core of the plea. Sometimes there is an added element—irresistible impulse, and in at least one jurisdiction (U.S. military law) the "nature and quality" clauses are omitted.

Analysis of the concept of "knowing an act is

wrong" is the key item in an irresponsibility plea.
The test is whether the defendant knows that this
specific act is wrong. Sometimes an attorney asks
the psychiatrist: "Is he able to distinguish right from
wrong?" The general capacity to distinguish right
from wrong is an abstract ethical concept, which is
not very material.[6]

How does the psychiatrist determine whether the
defendant knew that the act was wrong? Experts
disagree and by their disagreements reveal an honest
and profound cleavage of opinion. One group approaches it this way. If the defendant tried to escape,
evaded arrest, denied his guilt, voluntarily surren-
dered,[7] or planned to commit his crime in privacy,
then he must have known that he was doing something wrong, no matter how sick he might be mentally. From this point of view, so long as the M'Naghten rule is the law of the land, this is the only
honest way to look at it. Other experts say this: a
man cannot really grasp how wrong his act is by
normal standards unless he is a free agent. An insane
person using distorted standards of reasoning must
not be judged by the same formula as a sane person.
The weakness of this position is that the law does
not say that the accused must know *how wrong* the
act is, it says simply that if he knows it is *wrong*, he
is culpable. Let us hypothecate a case. A paranoiac
with well preserved intelligence believes that a really
harmless person named Elmer is constantly spreading malicious gossip about him, so he craftily kills
Elmer. His plan of escape [8] fails and he is detected.
Now it can be argued that no matter how paranoid
this defendant is, he must know that the spreading
of malicious gossip is no justification of murder. Therefore he knows the act is wrong and is culpable. Or
it could be argued, that in his diseased mind, he
thought that killing was a proper retaliation for slan-
der. Therefore he did not know that the act was

wrong. Doctors can disagree without either expert being guilty of perjury or venality.

For all its imperfections the M'Naghten formula has lasted more than a hundred years and shows no signs of being abandoned. To understand how a century-old rule can survive unchanged in the face of the progress in psychiatry, consider some of the proposed alternatives. It has been suggested that the true test ought to be this: if the accused would not have done the act *but for* his mental disorder, he should be acquitted. This "but-for" formula is very popular with psychiatrists. It has one great weakness. Nobody does anything except as a manifestation of his mental processes, so that if a person has any mental disorder at all, it can be said that, *but for* that disorder, he would not have behaved thus.

An even simpler test has been proposed; that is the formula that insanity should be a bar to conviction; if a defendant was psychotic when he committed the crime, he should be exculpated. This has a certain superficial plausibility. But many crimes are committed in states of anger, and if this formula were written into the law, it would free defendants who could demonstrate that they had a temporary loss of control which might fit a formal definition of a transient insanity.

Ever since the M'Naghten formula was adopted, attempts have been made to change it. But all courts of last resort have come back to the rule. This is not due to any mystic reverence for 19th century law. It is due to the fact that after all the oratory has evaporated, one stark fact remains. Unless a man is held answerable for doing what he knows he should not do, there will be no enforceable sanction against criminal behavior. Even very psychotic patients can be influenced by fears, hopes and promises. A mental hospital today is not a Bedlam, precisely because so many of its insane patients try hard to conform

20

to hospital rules in the hope of early release or transfer to a better ward. Not all patients are responsive to external social pressures; but many are. And it is not unreasonable to hold even a lunatic accountable for doing something that he really knows is wrong. They do it every day in mental hospitals.

Let us examine a case which stretches the M'-Naghten rule to its extreme. I refer to the trial of Albert Fish in New York in 1934. Here the formula is pulled to the end of the line. If its application rendered substantial justice in this case, it will do so in any case. Albert Fish was insane. He would perpetrate assaults and kill little children after a sexual orgy. He said he would cook their flesh with carrots, onions and strips of bacon, and eat it. He derived an orgiastic joy out of inflicting pain. He would normally wear overalls over his naked body and hunt for children in slum areas. The purpose of the overalls, he explained, was two-fold. First, people would think he was a janitor or painter and not notice as he prowled around basements and backyards. Second, he could strip himself naked by loosening a few buttons, and thus saved time and trouble. He moved constantly, seldom returning to the same area. He usually kidnapped and assaulted colored children because, he said, authorities paid less attention when they were missing. He tried to beat children in a place where their screams would not be overheard, but if other people were near he would gag them first to silence their cries. He told how on one occasion, he miscalculated how near his place was to a highway, so that he had to restrain himself from mutilating the little boy he had with him, because he was afraid some passing motorists would hear the screams. Fish showed that he knew he was doing something wrong. Otherwise, why would he gag children only when he could be overheard? Why did he refrain the time he was too near a highway?

Why did he seldom return to the same area? Why did he prefer children whose absence would raise less disturbance? Why did he want to prowl unnoticed? All of these facts indicate that he knew he was doing something wrong; and the court thought so too.

The case raised two questions with reference to the M'Naghten formula. First, did he have *mens rea* under the rule? Second, does application of the rule result in substantial justice? Everything indicated that he knew the nature and quality of his acts, and that they were wrong. The defense psychiatrist argued that he could not realize how wrong his acts were because he was profoundly diseased mentally. But we have to deal with operational concepts, not abstractions. This man was doing something that he knew he ought not do. Suppose Fish had been released by a decision of the Court of Appeals that he was irresponsible. What then? Even the defense psychiatrist said he was untreatable. Had he been committed to a mental hospital, the best they could offer would be custody. But no mental hospital is a maximum security institution in the sense that a prison is. And a few years later he would have demanded another day in court on a writ to show that he had regained his reason. He might be released, and would be free to prey on society again. Here you have a direct conflict between the concept of duty to the individual sufferer which is the function of the doctor, and the duty to protect society which is the function of the court. There are those who say that his conviction was an injustice, because he was a sick man. Yet no more satisfactory alternative is offered by these people, nor do they consider the question of justice to his future victims whose lives were spared because the state took the defendant's life. This kind of case admittedly stretches the M'Naghten rule almost to the breaking point. But it does not break. Even in this extreme situation, it seems to lead to substantial justice.[9]

One of the appendices to the M'Naghten rule is the doctrine of irresistible impulse.[10] This is an acceptable defense in 21 states, though it is seldom worded exactly that way. It is called "deprivation of the power to choose" or "inability to adhere to the right" or "loss of free agency" and various other terms.

Three kinds of irresistible impulse pleas correspond to three psychiatric disorders, and represent three expanding degrees of juridical generosity. (A) The narrowest concept is the irresistible impulse sometimes generated within insane persons—sudden explosive reactions powered by some urge within the person. (B) A slightly wider concept would include the impulses of the compulsive neurotic. For example in certain compulsive neuroses there is an impulse to steal, in others an impulse to step on cracks in the sidewalk or to count fence posts or to repeat a certain verbal formula. There is a well-recognized neurosis in which so-called "pyromania" is a symptom—that is compulsive setting of fires. Where irresistible impulse is a defense, it is usually large enough to include these cases, though in some jurisdictions, only the impulses associated with true insanity are grounds for exculpation. (C) Finally, the concept might be broadened to include the kind of impulse which occurs to all of us from time to time, usually in response to rage or frustration. It might seem inequitable to hold a person accountable for doing that which he could not refrain from doing. But there are good reasons for this. When the doctrine is accepted with reference to insane impulses, it is logical for defense counsel to insist that it apply with equal force to neurotic compulsions. For these too are the result of psychiatric disorder. Then comes the plea that it should cover impulsive acts committed while drunk, for intoxication is also a form of mental sickness. One step further carries us to the point where it furnishes a shield to any one who commits a crime in a fit of rage, pique or frustration.

Time was when the chief objection to this defense was that it was hard to prove and easy to malinger. However any psychiatrist, given sufficient time with the patient and an adequate history, can recognize a psychosis. and if the doctrine be limited to psychotic impulses, there is no serious probative difficulty. If the defense is expanded to include neurotic impulses, modern psychiatric science can still meet the challenge. The competent psychiatrist knows that a neurosis is a way of life, not a transient reaction, so he looks for a neurotic history. He knows that in true compulsive neuroses, there is a typical pattern of mounting tension, internal conflict, abashed yielding to the impulse, brief relief from tension, subsequent recrimination and guilt-feeling leading to more tension with a repetition of the cycle. The psychiatrist is suspicious of an irresistible impulse with no past history that began five minutes before the commission of the crime.

One of the chief points of dispute in connection with irresistible impulse is the old query: "Would the person have yielded to that impulse had there been a policeman at his elbow?" In true neurotic compulsiveness the patient is ashamed of his impulses and tries to yield to them only in privacy. One argument runs that this test is faulty because it does not prove the spuriousness of the impulse. However, the opposite point of view presents a logically irrefutable answer. If an impulse can be resisted in the presence of a policeman then the impulse is obviously not irresistible.

A person with an irresistible impulse to commit a crime is more dangerous to the community than one

24

who purposefully commits a crime after due deliberation. The very force of the irresistible impulse must make our ordinary safeguards against it ineffective. Assume a jurisdiction where neurotic irresistible impulse is a valid defense, and a situation where a defendant escapes a murder conviction because he proves an irresistible neurotic impulse to kill. He cannot be confined in a mental hospital because he has no psychosis. A psychiatrist who is willing to help free such a person by testifying as to the reality of the impulse, has a duty to call attention to the hazard the defendant presents to the community. A doctor's duty to society transcends his obligation to the individual patient. The code of ethics of the American Medical Association makes it clear that a doctor has a primary duty to the community with respect to the reporting of contagious diseases, but is silent about the situation presented by dangerous mental disorders.

Irresistible impulse is frequently pleaded in cases associated with sexual perversion, most often as a defense in charges of sodomy, or of murder secondary to perverted sex acts. A man with a very powerful sexual urge, which he seeks to gratify through normal channels, is held accountable: he is expected to check that urge until he gets into a situation which is both private and voluntary. The same restraint can be expected of a man with a strong sexual urge which he seeks to gratify through abnormal channels. He too can be held accountable for restraining himself until he gets into a private, adult and voluntary relationship. If he is to be exculpated, say of the charge of practicing sodomy on children, then the man with a normally channeled sex urge could ask to be freed of a rape charge because his biologic urge also mounted to an irresistible impulse.

The psychiatrist has a useful role in the administration of justice. He can give the clinical diagnosis, he can tell the court whether the defendant was able to recognize that his act was wrong, he can determine whether an irresistible impulse existed, and if so whether it was part of a psychosis, part of a compulsive neurosis, or whether it was a normal reaction to rage or frustration. He can tell whether the defendant had sufficient mentality to deliberate, plan or premeditate. He can contribute not only to the guilt-finding but also to the sentencing function of the court. As part of a pre-sentence investigation he can list any psychiatric factors which the court should know in possible mitigation of guilt or lessening of sentence. He can give some kind of prognosis with respect to the possibilities of rehabilitating the offender.

But can the psychiatrist ask the courts to surrender to him the custody of psychiatric offenders generally and psychopaths in particular? Before we ask you to turn such cases over to us, we ought to be able to give some assurance that we can keep the offender in safe custody as protection against his preying on society while he is still dangerous. However hospitals are not prisons; even in hospitals for the insane, attendants are not armed. By comparison with a prison, a hospital is not a maximum security institution; escapes are commoner from hospitals than from prisons. And unless a patient is specifically found insane, he cannot be kept in a hospital against his will. Most of your problem cases will be psychopaths, sex offenders, alcoholics and others in the "not insane" category. Unless you place a detainer, such a person cannot be kept in a hospital, if he insists on his release. But to place a detainer, you must first find the defendant guilty. All this seems too obvious to labor here, but I have been asked—sometimes by judges—whether we could not admit a defendant to a hospital in lieu of having him stand trial. This might be a man who committed an assault while

26

drunk, or one who repeatedly set fires, or seduced little boys into submitting to sodomy. I was once asked to hospitalize a young man who had perpetrated a series of forgeries. The prosecutor said that the boy came from a good family and would not be forging checks unless something was the matter with him, and if we could hospitalize him, the office would *nolle prosse*. There was no suggestion that any of these defendants was insane. It was just assumed that the pyromaniac, the forger, the drunkard and the homosexual would voluntarily remain in the hospital. Sometimes we are told: he needs treatment, not punishment. This is a worthy sentiment, but if we took such patients into our hospitals, they would walk out as soon as the legal pressure was off. Cures in all these cases are extremely rare, and it is certain that most of these defendants will soon be back in the community and continue their antisocial behavior. Indeed, this time they would be more dangerous, because with a mental hospital record, they could bolster their pleas of irresponsibility, so that the cycle would be repeated. As doctors we have no objection to accepting such patients in our institutions. But let it be clearly understood that we cannot. through hospital or clinic, furnish the custodial security which protection of society requires.[11] Courts and prosecutors should be made more aware of this limitation.

Psychopaths and homosexuals are hardly ever cured. I have never known of a homosexual who was reconverted to normal sexual channels. I have never seen a single reliable report of a cured psychopath. Alcoholism offers a better chance. The group known as "Alcoholics Anonymous" has an astonishing record of rehabilitation. With the insane, our batting average is somewhat better. There is enough chance of recovery to make treatment worth while. Deeply entrenched or deteriorated psychotics rarely reach the criminal courts, and with early psychotics

27

the outlook is more promising. To be sure, the well preserved paranoiac is resistant to treatment, but other early psychotics may improve considerably under modern mental hospital therapy. In round numbers, ratio of recovery in early psychotics runs from 30 to 50 per cent—which is pretty good considering that insanity has traditionally been considered "incurable." Among neurotics, the recovery potential is even higher. Our problem is not so much one of finding a method as it is one of finding a doctor. Relatively few persons can afford private and intensive psychotherapy. Even in our more progressive states, the public mental hygiene clinics are swamped with applications. State hospitals are overcrowded and understaffed, and by and large, they do not offer good facilities for ambulatory neurotics. Psychiatry knows how to handle successfully a large proportion of our psychoneurotics. We still have to work out a method of making our manpower available to those who need it most.

The psychiatrist can be a help: and wants to be a help, in the administration of criminal justice. But he is neither Mr. Know-It-All nor Mr. Fixit. We can tell you about a defendant's intelligence, sanity, intent, and prospects for rehabilitation. Ours is a highly individualized orientation which may sometimes blur our focus with respect to the overall social picture. We will try to tell you how the defendant got that way. But crime is socially defined; it is largely socially determined; and to a great extent it must be dealt with by social instruments.

NOTES

*Reprinted with the permission of the Rutgers Law Review, Rutgers University School of Law.

1. It has been suggested that a mentally defective defendant be judged by his mental age rather than by his actual age. Since the law imposes on the state the burden of proving mental capacity when the defendant is under the age of 14, it might seem logical to throw a similar protection around adults whose mental ages are under 14. One excellent reason for rejecting this thesis was presented by the court in *State v. Schilling*, 95 N.J.L. 145,112 Atl. 400 (1920). The Justice there wrote: "The precise question is whether at the age of 28 he had sufficient mentality to distinguish right from wrong . . . The jury found that he had . . . There is a vast difference between a child at the age of 11 (the defendant's mental age was 11) and a man of 28 . . . When a man reaches manhood the presumption is that he possesses the ordinary mental capacity and it is for him to overcome that presumption. The presumption of the lack of capacity in favor of a child is due more to the number of years he has lived than to the development of his mind."

There are two other reasons for rejecting the use of mental age as a legal yardstick of responsibility.

29

First, the average mental age of adults is only 14, so that if the rule were changed, it would have the net effect of imposing the burden of proving responsibility on the prosecution in the "average" case. While to the psychiatrist this sounds like a good idea, it would require a radical change in some fundamental legal presumptions. Second, an adult with a mental age of 12 is *not* the same as a normal 12 year old boy. The adult has lived longer, has acquired more experience and more experiences, has greater shrewdness and judgment, and is presumed to have an emotional maturity consonant with his chronologic rather than his intellectual age. This may be rebutted in individual cases, but it seems only fair to impose the burden of such refutation on the defense, since these things are easier to prove than to disprove.

2. Sometimes a defendant says that "everything went black" or persists in his contention that he remembers nothing from a short time before the act until a short time after it. Faced with this allegation, the psychiatrist considers six possible explanations: (a) Insanity, (b) Hysterical amnesia, (c) An epileptic clouded state, (d) Malingering, (e) Head injury, or (f) Alcoholic intoxication. Given an adequate personal history, and sufficient time to observe and examine the patient, he is ordinarily able to confirm or rule out each of these six possibilities and reach a clinically correct diagnosis.

3. Alcoholism of course may strip the offense of some element, such as willfulness, premeditation or deliberation, and thus reduce the degree of the crime.

4. Sex offenders and sex psychopaths are variously defined. Thus, in *Michigan* (Public Acts 1939, Number 165), the definition is as follows:

> "Any person suffering from a mental disorder who is not insane nor feeble minded, whose men-

tal disorder has existed for not less than one year, and whose mental disorder is coupled with propensities to the commission of sex offenses, is hereby declared to be a criminal sexual psychopathic person."

In *Minnesota*, section 526.09 of the 1945 statutes, gives the following definitions:

". . . the existence in any person of such conditions of emotional instability, impulsiveness, lack of good judgment, failure to appreciate the consequences of his act or a combination of any such conditions, as to render such a person irresponsible for his conduct with respect to sexual matters, and thereby dangerous to other persons."

In the *District of Columbia*, the sexual psychopath is defined by Public Law 615, 80th Congress, in the following terms:

". . . a person not insane who by a course of repeated misconduct in sexual impulses is found to be dangerous to others because he is likely to attack or otherwise inflict injury, loss, pain or other evil on the object of his desire."

California, (chapter 447 of the Laws of 1939), lays down two alternative criteria: (a) that the defendant has a psychopathic personality, mental disease, or mental disorder, or (b) that he exhibits marked departures from normal mentality in a form predisposing to commission of sexual offenses, to a degree constituting a menace to the health and safety of others.

In *New York*, Senate bill 2790 (1947 session) which was vetoed, included this definition:

". . . in such a state of mental aberration that he cannot control his impulses towards the commission of sex offenses."

Perhaps the most flexible statute is chapter 20, Laws of 1949, *New Jersey*. This first recites the sexual offenses—sodomy, indecent exposure, et cetera, requires a mental examination of all persons *convicted* of such acts, and then requires commitment to a special institution if as a result of examination, the defendant is found suffering from "any form of abnormal illness which resulted in the commission of any of the sex offenses enumerated."

5. Originally "nature and quality of the act" were bracketed together as a single concept. In the original M'Naghten case, certain questions were put by the House of Lords to the Judges. The consolidated answer to question 2 and 3 included the following phrases which have become the basis for the irresponsibility test in all our civilian jurisdictions:

". . . that the accused was labouring under such a defect of reason from disease of the mind, as not to know the nature and quality of the act he was doing, or if he did know *it*, that he did not know that he was doing what was wrong."

The use of the singular pronoun *it* can mean only that the Judges considered "nature and quality" to represent a single unitary concept. In some American jurisdictions the word "quality" has been replaced with "consequences." The entire phrase "if he did not know it" is generally omitted in our statutes, codes and decisions, so that "nature and quality" has come to imply two different entities. On this basis the "nature" of an act is presumably its physical characteristics. The "quality" of an act means either its "moral" characteristic (in which case it becomes identical with the concept that "he was doing what was wrong") or it means the long range implications ("consequences") of the act. I have treated this point in more detail in previous publications: 1 *New Jersey Law Review* 123 (May 1935) and again in 57 *Archives of Neurology and Psychiatry* 730 (June 1947).

6. As recently as May 1949, a New Jersey Supreme Court Justice disapproved of a charge because "the jury understood this to mean that *general capacity* to distinguish right from wrong . . . rather than *actual deliberation* constituted the standard of guilt . . ." (Dissenting in opinion in State v. Cordasco 2, N. J. 189, 66 A. 2d 27 (1949.) Italics mine).

7. Too little attention has been paid to the probative meaning of the methods of apprehension. When a person with mental disorder is accused, there are four possible routes of apprehension (a) He may have gone to the police and demanded punishment, (b) He may have committed the crime so openly that it was obvious he was not avoiding identification, (c) He may have used every means to avoid arrest, or (d) He may have done nothing to lead to his arrest and nothing to conceal himself from apprehension.

The psychiatrist ought to be told of the circumstances of the apprehension since this may throw considerable light on the offender's general state of mind and on his evaluation of the wrongfulness of his acts.

Where an offender used every method to avoid detection, it would appear that he was conscious that he was doing something wrong. When, without pressure, a mentally disturbed person proclaims his guilt and demands punishment, that is *prima facie* psychologic evidence that he knew he was doing a legal wrong, but that he considered it morally righteous or that he acted under the influence of an irresistible impulse. Some observers say that this behavior (open insistence on punishment) is inconsistent with responsibility. This is tantamount to saying that the only time you can be sure the offender does not know he did something wrong, is the time when he says he did something wrong.

That a person commits a crime in public has no consistent significance. If irresistible impulse is offered as a defense, this does meet the "policeman at the elbow test": but there are two limitations to that. The fact that the crime was committed publicly, does not by itself, *establish* irresistible impulse, though it supports such a contention if there is other evidence of it. And in most jurisdictions, acceptable irresistible impulse must be part of a disorder of "thinking or feeling" and not part of a disorder of "will or character."

For the cognate problem of "planning," see note 8.

8. A favorite prosecution argument is that an offender must have known he was doing something wrong if, in advance, he elaborated a plan. This is an oversimplification. Many psychotic persons are capable of crafty planning. Indeed, their singleness of purpose often leads to extraordinary shrewdness and perseverance. It is necessary to distinguish: (a) planning aimed at certainty that the crime will be committed; and (b) planning to avoid detection. Where (a) exists and (b) does not, this suggests that the defendant—if psychotic—did *not* know he was doing something wrong. If a paranoid person buys a gun, registering it under a false name, we want to know: was his purpose in using the alias, to confuse his imaginary persecutors, or to escape apprehension?

9. That the outcome of the Fish case represented substantial justice is my own opinion, but I cannot speak for the entire profession. As a matter of fact, Dr. Frederic Wertham, one of the country's top psychiatrists and a witness of unquestionable integrity, believed that Fish should have been acquitted even under a strict application of the M'Naghten rule. Dr.

34

Wertham knew more about Fish than any other psychiatrist. After the Court of Appeals refused to disturb the judgment, Dr. Wertham joined with the Fish family in an application for executive clemency. In his book *Show of Violence* (Doubleday 1949) Dr. Wertham summarizes his statement to the Governor as follows: "I was not appealing on behalf of Mr. Fish who didn't mind the electric chair anyway in his distorted ideas of atonement. He was, in my opinion, a man not only incurable and unreformable, but also unpunishable. I was appealing on behalf of his many child victims. I was appealing on account of the many victims past and future of such men as Fish."

On the face of it, this seems like an illogical statement, since it is hard to see how the execution of Fish could hurt future potential victims, or how sending him to a state hospital would have been an act "on behalf of his many child victims." Dr. Wertham's point, however, was this. The finding of guilt and the execution carried with it an "implication" of sanity, since it is the general (but false) idea that an insane person is neither convicted nor executed. Therefore the Governor was, in effect, declaring that Fish was sane.

The weakness of Dr. Wertham's position, it seems to me, is this: incarcerating Fish in a state hospital would not contribute one iota to the apprehension and confinement of others like him. Since escape or release from a hospital is easier than escape or release from a prison, there would be a possibility of his subsequent return to the community. Dr. Wertham states that this defendant is "incurable and unreformable" so that placement in a state hospital would be frankly a custodial measure and nothing more. In view of the serious hazard he presents to the community, he should be in a place of maximum custodial security (a prison) rather than a hospital—especially since he is untreatable. But to confine him to a prison would mean (which Dr. Wertham denies) that Fish was "guilty" of a crime.

10. Irresistible impulse has no official standing in most states. In Pennsylvania there is an old decision (Commonwealth v. DeMarzo, 223 Penna. 573; 1909) in which power of self control is accepted as an essential of *mens rea*.

". . . sufficient will power to choose whether he would do the act or refrain from doing it." According to Sheldon Glueck, other jurisdictions which accept irresistible impulse as a defense are: Alabama, Arkansas, Colorado, Connecticut, District of Columbia, Georgia, Illinois, Indiana, Iowa, Kentucky, Louisiana, Massachusetts, Michigan, Montana, New Hampshire, New Mexico, Ohio, Vermont, Virginia and Wyoming. (Glueck, S. Sheldon, *Mental Disorder and the Criminal Law;* Little, Brown, Boston, 1925).

Acceptance of the doctrine is wider than this list suggests. A jury may be sufficiently impressed by evidence of an uncontrollable impulse to free the defendant even when this is not a sound defense. They may misunderstand or ignore the Judge's charge. Of course such verdicts would not enter the law reports. Yet if the jury accurately reflected public opinion, we would have, in practice, an acceptable irresistible impulse defense in a state which does not recognize it.

11. Disposition of sex offenders poses a special problem. Most definitions exclude insane defendants, so ordinary commitment to a mental hospital is impossible without special legislation. See note 4 for definitions and citations.

There are substantial variations on the basis for jurisdiction in sex cases. In New Jersey and Ohio, conviction of a sex crime is essential before the rest of the statute can operate. In Illinois, Michigan, and California, a criminal charge (but not necessarily a conviction) is required before the court can dispose of the offender as a sex psychopath. In Wisconsin,

Minnesota, Massachusetts and the District of Columbia, no formal criminal charge is necessary.

The method of determining whether the accused is a sex psychopath also varies. Psychiatric examination (usually by two experts) is required in all jurisdictions. A jury is optional in the District of Columbia, Michigan, California, Wisconsin and Massachusetts; in the latter state, at the discretion of the court, in the others, at the demand of the defendant. A jury is mandatory in Illinois. In the Ohio and Minnesota statutes, there is no provision for a jury.

While all the laws provide for the admission of the sex offender to state hospitals, there is considerable variation in the methods for effecting the patient's release. In the District of Columbia, California, Minnesota and Wisconsin, release is accomplished on recommendation of the hospital, usually with provision for a court hearing if the hospital, on demand of the patient, declines to transmit such a recommendation. In New Jersey, the patient cannot be retained in the hospital longer than the maximum sentence period for his crime. In Illinois, Ohio and Massachusetts, another court hearing is required to effect release from the hospital.

In the District of Columbia, Illinois and California, a finding that the offender is a "sex psychopath" has the effect of staying the criminal action. In other states, such a finding is no defense to the criminal charge.

12. If a defendant does not willingly submit to psychiatric examination, would the findings be barred on the basis of compulsory self-incrimination? Apparently not. "An examination to ascertain mental condition is not a deprivation of constitutional rights; nor does such an examination require him to give evidence against himself." Blocker v. State, 110 South. 547 (Fla. 1926). If the accused does not want to have the psychiatric examination, the doctor will still be

able to assemble data about his patient's appearance, gestures, postures, gait, speech and mood,—items which form part of a psychiatric study. Courts consistently admit finger prints, presence of scars and the confusion of other reactions shown by a suspect when interviewed. It is hard to see why these should be admitted and psychiatric observations excluded.

It would, of course, be unethical for the examiner to imply that the interview was confidential and then to disclose it to the prosecutor or court. An experienced prosecutor's psychiatrist usually explains to the defendant that notes are being taken, that a report will be sent to the probation office, that if the patient would not want some items included in the report, he should tell the doctor that he'd rather not answer that question. I have never seen a defendant become mute because of this warning. Usually he says he has nothing to conceal and is glad of the opportunity of telling his side of the story freely to a prosecutor's representative. Generally speaking, the accused cannot see how anything he tells the psychiatrist can hurt his case. Some schizophrenics are persistently mute but that is because of their psychosis, not because of the warning given by the examiner. And such obvious psychotics do not present a serious problem in appraising responsibility.

In jurisdictions where doctor-patient communications are privileged, it is probable that these psychiatric findings would be admitted in evidence because the psychiatrist is not a *bona fide* treating physician, under these special circumstances.

In England, it seems to be unsporting, if not positively un-British, for the examiner to discuss the circumstances surrounding the crime. Mercier (page 233 of *Criminal Responsibility* by Charles Mercier, Physicians and Surgeons Book Company, New York 1926) writes: ". . . the examiner is warned against questioning a prisoner—as to the circumstances of the crime.

I have heard caustic comments from the bench on this practice."

American psychiatrists, however, find it impossible to conduct a psychiatric examination aimed at measuring criminal responsibility without touching on "the circumstances surrounding the crime."

III

INSANITY AS A DEFENSE TO A CRIMINAL ACT

RICHARD W. NICE, M.A.
Clinical Psychologist
New Jersey State Reformatory for Men
at Bordentown, New Jersey

It was argued by counsel for the now famous Durham case that the existing tests in the District of Columbia for determining criminal responsibility, *i.e.*, the so-called right and wrong test supplemented by the irresistible impulse test, are not satisfactory criteria for determining criminal responsibility. This contention has behind it nearly a century of agitation for reform.

The right-wrong test was approved in the District of Columbia in 1882,[1] and was the exclusive test of criminal responsibility until 1929 when the irresistible impulse test was approved as a supplementary test in *Smith* v. *United States*.[2] The right-wrong test has its roots in England. There, by the first quarter of the eighteenth century, an accused escaped punishment if he could not distinguish between "good and evil," *i.e.*, if he "doth not know what he is doing, no more than . . . a wild beast." [3]

Later in the same century, the "wild beast" test was abandoned and "right and wrong" was substituted for "good and evil." [4] And toward the middle of the nineteenth century, the House of Lords in the famous M'Naghten case restates what had become the accepted "right-wrong" test in a form which has since been followed, not only in England but in most American jurisdictions [5] as an exclusive test of criminal responsibility.

As early as 1838, Isaac Ray, one of the founders of the American Psychiatric Association, in his now classic Medical Jurisprudence of Insanity, called knowledge of right and wrong a "fallacious" test of criminal responsibility.[6] This view has long since been substantiated by enormous developments in knowledge of mental life. In 1928 Mr. Justice Cardozo said to the New York Academy of Medicine: "Everyone concedes that the present (legal) definition of insanity has little relation to the truths of mental life." [7]

Medico-legal writers in large numbers, THE REPORT OF THE ROYAL COMMISSION ON CAPITAL PUNISHMENT 1949-1953, and THE PRELIMINARY REPORT BY THE COMMITTEE ON FORENSIC PSYCHIATRY OF THE GROUP FOR THE ADVANCEMENT OF PSYCHIATRY AND THE AMERICAN LAW INSTITUTE, present convincing evidence that the right and wrong test is "based on an entirely obsolete and misleading conception of the nature of insanity." [8] The science of psychiatry now recognizes that a man is an integrated personality, and that reason, which is only one element in that personality, is not the sole determinant of his conduct. The right and wrong test, which considers knowledge or reason alone, is therefore an inadequate guide to mental responsibility for criminal behavior. As Professor Herbert Wechsler, Professor of Law at Columbia University and Chief Reporter of the American Law Institute, states in his article, THE AMERICAN LAW INSTITUTE: SOME OBSERVATIONS ON ITS MODEL PENAL CODE: "The problem is when a punitive correctional disposition is appropriate and when a medical-custodial commitment is the only kind the law should allow. The traditional M'Naghten rule resolves this problem solely in regard to the

41

capacity of the individual to know what he was doing and to know that it was wrong. Absent these minimal elements of rationality, condemnation and punishment are obviously futile and unjust. They are unjust because the individual could not, by hypothesis, have employed the act; he did not and he could not know the facts essential to bring reason into play. A madman, who chokes his wife believing that he is squeezing lemons or is fighting off a murderous attack or that homicide is the command of God is plainly beyond reach of the restraining influence of law; he needs restraint but condemnation is entirely meaningless and ineffective."

The fundamental objection to the right-wrong test, however, is not that criminal irresponsibility is made to rest upon an inadequate, invalid or indeterminable symptom or manifestation, but that it is made to rest upon *any* particular symptom. In attempting to define insanity in terms of symptoms the courts have assumed an almost impossible role. As the Royal Commission emphasizes, it is dangerous "to abstract particular faculties, and to lay it down that unless these particular faculties are destroyed or gravely impaired, an accused person, whatever the nature of his mental disease, must be held to be criminally responsible." [9]

Up to the turn of the century despite demands in scientific advancement the Washington, D.C. court refused to alter the right-wrong test, but in 1929 the irresistible impulse test was added as a supplementary test for determining criminal responsibility. In Smith v. United States this test was "to be the law of this District, (Washington, D.C.) that, in cases where insanity is interposed as a defense, and the facts are sufficient to call for the application of the rule of irresistible impulse, the jury should be so charged."

Although the *Smith* case did not abandon the right-wrong test it did liberate the fact finder from exclusive reliance upon that discredited criterion by

42

allowing the jury to inquire also whether the accused suffered from an undefined "diseased condition, which deprived him of the will-power to resist the insane impulse. . . ."

The term "irresistible impulse," however carries the misleading implication that "diseased mental conditions" produce only sudden, momentary or spontaneous inclinations to commit unlawful acts. As the Royal Commission found:

". . . In many cases . . . this is not true at all. The sufferer experiences a change of mood which alters the whole of his existence. He may believe, for instance, that a future of such degradation and misery awaits both him and his family, that death for all is a less dreadful alternative. Even the thought that the act he contemplates are murder and suicide pales into insignificance in contrast with what he otherwise expects. The criminal act, in such circumstances, may be the reverse of impulsive. It may be coolly and carefully prepared; yet it is still the act of a madman. This is merely an illustration; similar states of mind are likely to lie behind the criminal act when murders are committed by persons suffering from schizophrenia or paranoid psychosis due to disease of the brain." [10]

In a report formulated by The Committee on Psychiatry and Law of the Group for the Advancement of Psychiatry written in May, 1954 there was this statement in regard to the use of the M'Naghten Rule: [11]

"Many dangerous persons are essentially undeterrable and it is the business of psychiatry to supply the law with such knowledge as is necessary to detect such persons among whom may be counted several classes of mentally disordered offenders. In the trial, the M'Naghten formula does not determine realistically who such persons are. Many undeterrable offenders are treated as if they are "sane" and sent to prison to be released at the termination of sentence, free to repeat the cycle. As matters stand, as a device of criminal law administration the Rules touch only a fraction of undeterrable mentally ill. In this there is no security for the law-abiding community."

On appeal to the United States Court of Appeals for the District of Columbia on March 19, 1954, Durham's judgment and conviction by the District Court was reversed, and the case was remanded for a new trial. The U. S. Attorney, on November 9, acting pursuant to the Court of Appeals' decision in *Gunther v United States*,[12] filed a petition to determine the mental competency of Durham. Attached to this petition was a copy of a letter from the Acting Superintendent of St. Elizabeths Hospital, dated February 12, 1953, (see Appendix No. 3 and 4) advising the Attorney General that Durham was then competent to stand trial. As a result of the mental examination "Monte W. Durham is at present found mentally competent to enable him to understand the proceedings against him and properly assist in his own defense."

Thus on February 25, 1955, a new trial resulted before a jury with the Honorable David A. Pine presiding. At the beginning of the trial the charge of grand larceny was reduced to a charge of petit larceny. Again the principle of defense was that Durham was insane at the time the alleged crime took place. On March 1, 1955, the jury returned a verdict of guilty and Durham was again convicted of housebreaking and petit larceny. The judgment was entered on March 28, 1955, and on the same day Durham was sentenced to imprisonment for a period of one to four years.

Because of two points of error by the lower court, there again followed an appeal to the District Court of Appeals. These two major points are: 1. That the evidence to the effect that Durham was suffering from a mental disease which was the cause of the crime in question, was so compelling that reasonable jurymen must necessarily have a reasonable doubt as to his sanity at the time of the crime. The trial judge, therefore, erred in denying the defense counsel's motion for a judgment of acquittal by reason of insanity. 2. The trial court's instruction to the jury that Durham would be released by St. Elizabeth's Hospital very shortly if they acquitted him by reason of insanity was not based on any evidence in the record, but rather on the court's own misconception regarding the procedure governing the trial and commitment of the criminally insane in the District of Columbia.

Even if the letter from the Acting Director of St. Elizabeth's, on which the court had based their instruction, had been received in evidence, the inference which the court drew was false, since it does not follow from the fact that St. Elizabeth's has released a person as competent to stand trial under 18 USC section 4244 that they will release him into the community in the event that he is returned there upon acquittal by reason of insanity.

The three statutes involved in the Durham case are: Title 18, section 4244 and 4246 of the United States Code, 1946 Edition, and Title 24, section 301, of the District of Columbia Code, 1951 Edition.

Section 4244. Mental incompetency after arrests and before trial.

Whenever after arrests and before or prior to the imposition of sentence or prior to the expiration of any period of probation the United States Attorney has reasonable cause to believe that a person charged with an offense against the United States may be presently insane or otherwise so mentally incompetent as not to be able to understand the proceedings against him or properly to assist in his own defense, he shall file a motion for a judicial determination of such mental competency of the accused, setting forth the ground for such belief with the trial court in which proceedings are pending. Upon such a motion or upon a similar motion in behalf of the accused, or upon its own motion, the court shall cause the accused, whether or not previously admitted to bail, to be examined as to his mental condition by at least one qualified psychiatrist, who shall report to the court. For the purpose of the examination the court may order the accused committed for such a reasonable period as the court may determine to a suitable hospital or other facility to be designated by the court. If the report of the psychiatrist indicates a state of present insanity or such mental incompetency in the accused, the court shall hold a hearing, upon due notice, at which evidence as to the mental condition of the accused may be submitted, including that of the reporting psychiatrist, and make a finding with respect thereto. No statement made by the accused in the course of any examination into his sanity or mental competency provided for by this section, whether the examination shall be without or with the consent of the accused, shall be admitted in evidence against the accused on the issue of guilt in any criminal proceeding. A finding by the judge that the accused is mentally competent to stand trial shall in no way prejudice the accused in a plea of insanity as a defense to the crime charged; such finding shall not be introduced in evidence on that issue nor otherwise be brought to the notice of the jury.

Section 4246. Procedure upon finding of mental incompetency.

Whenever the trial court shall determine in accordance with sections 4244 and 4245 of this title that an accused is or was mentally incompetent, the court may commit the accused to the custody of the Attorney General or his authorized representative, until the accused shall be mentally competent to stand trial or until the pending charges against him are disposed of according to law. And if the court after hearing as provided in the preceding sections 4244 and 4245 shall determine that the conditions specified in the following section 4247 exist, the commitment shall be governed by section 4248 as herein provided.

Title 24, Section 301, District of Columbia Code, 1951 Edition:

Section 24-301 (6:374). Commitment of insane criminals to the Gallinger Municipal Hospital—Certification to the Federal Security Administrator—Confinement—Expense—Right to appeal.
When any person tried upon an indictment or information for an offense or tried in the juvenile court of the District of Columbia for an offense, is acquitted on the sole ground that he was insane at the time of its commission, that fact shall be set forth by the jury in their verdict; and whenever a person is indicted or is charged by an information for an offense, or is charged in the juvenile court of the District of Columbia with an offense, and before trial or after a verdict of guilty, it shall appear to the court, from the evidence adduced at the trial, that the accused is then of unsound mind, the court may order the accused committed to the Gallinger Municipal Hospital for

47

a period not exceeding thirty days, which period may be extended by the court for good cause shown, for examination and observation by the psychiatric staff of said hospital. If, after examination and observation, the said psychiatric staff shall report that in their opinion the accused is insane, the court may cause a jury to be impaneled from the jurors then in attendance on the court or, if the regular jurors have been discharged, may cause a sufficient number of jurors to be drawn to inquire into the sanity of the accused, and said inquiry shall be conducted in the presence and under the direction of the court. If the jury shall find the accused to be then insane, or if an accused person shall be acquitted by the jury solely on the ground of insanity, the court may certify the fact to the Federal Security Administrator, who may order such person to be confined in the hospital for the insane, and said person and his estate shall be charged with the expense of his support in the said hospital. The person whose sanity is in question shall be entitled to his bill of exceptions and an appeal as in other cases.

PSYCHOLOGICAL HISTORY

A better understanding of the Durham case will be obtained if we digress for a moment and discuss the psychological aspects of the case. In three admissions to St. Elizabeth's Hospital, Durham was twice found to be without mental disorder, although he was considered to be suffering from a non-psychotic illness in the form of psychopathic personality. What of this psychopathic personality, and its effect upon the mental condition and actions of Durham?

Dr. Joseph L. Gilbert testified that Durham was of unsound mind on July 13, 1951 and, "even prior to that date" there was a "definite causal relation" between the crime which Durham committed and the mental disease from which he was suffering at the time. Dr. Gilbert based this opinion on an examination in September and October of 1951 and his having examined Durham *nine* times previous to that date.

The Navy discharged Durham in 1945, after having had him in an observation ward at Bethesda Naval Hospital, stating that he "suffers from a profound personality disorder."

What of these personality disorders and their effect upon Durham, or any individual for that matter? Had his intelligence, which had been measured at I. Q. 85, any bearing on the Durham case, or was his mental ability or deficiency a remote factor and not to be considered here?

Alfred Binet, the Father of intelligence testing formulated a description of intelligence as "the tendency to take and maintain a definite direction; the capacity to make adaptations for the purpose of attaining a desired end; and the power of auto-criticism." [13] The other end of the scale, which is mental deficiency, is defined by The American Association on Mental Deficiency as follows:

"The term is used generally to include all degrees of mental defects due to alleged or imperfect mental development, as the result of which the person so affected is incapable of competing on equal terms with his normal fellows, or of managing himself or his affairs with ordinary prudence." [14]

It is not meant by this statement to convey to the reader that Durham was mentally defective, nor was any such idea brought out at his trial, however, his I. Q. of 85 places him in the dull normal category of mental ability.

Psychologists have set a classification based on

49

the intelligence quotient, which is obtained by the administration of formalized standard tests. The reader should remember that the mark of 100, given as an I.Q., is not a perfect score, rather it is supposed to represent the average performance of the population on which the original tests were standardized. These tests are constructed and scored so that the average I.Q. for anyone is 100. The results measured in I. Q., then fall into these groupings: [15]

> Above 135 — Genius
> 125-135 — Very superior
> 115-125 — Superior
> 105-115 — High normal
> 95-105 — Normal
> 80-95 — Dull normal
> (This was the grouping in which
> Durham fell, with an I. Q. of 85).
> 70-80 — Borderline
> 50-70 — Moron or feeble-minded
> 30-50 — Imbecile
> 0-30 — Idiot

The I.Q. of 85 which Durham possessed was a contributing factor toward criminal behavior. It has been established, by psychologists and psychiatrists, that there is a definite correlation between the I. Q. of an individual and the tendency toward crime. Page, in his book on Abnormal Psychology, states that "the intelligence of apprehended criminals and delinquents is slightly lower than that for the general population. Especially among youthful offenders, there is usually a higher percentage of mental defectives and a smaller percentage of mentally superior individuals than in the general population." [16] There are several reasons for this condition. The first is the background of the criminal. Many would-be criminals are of poor sociological background, with broken homes, poor living conditions, and inadequate up-bringing, they are unable to cope with everyday problems, and so choose the easy way out, crime. Another factor is that criminals with high intelligence tend to plan their crimes so that detection will be slow in coming if not absent altogether.

It is interesting to consider the relationship between mental defect and the type of crime committed. Defectives, presumably, would be incapable of certain kinds of crimes requiring considerable planning and insight and would be more inclined to commit offenses in which it was a matter of acting on a momentary impulse. The first offense for which delinquents come in contact with the law is generally truancy.

It appears that the mental defectives are more inclined to get into impulsive crimes, such as sex offenses, destroying property, or committing acts of violence, than they are to be involved in crimes demanding insight and planning.

A consideration of the diagnosis given by St. Elizabeth's Hospital in August 1947 and April 1948 shows that Durham had been found to be "without psychosis, psychopathic personality," and "psychosis with psychopathic personality." Dr. Hirsch found, in July 1951, that Durham was a psychotic. Let us now consider these mental conditions and their relationship, if any, with Durham in particular, and crime in general.

There are several groupings which can, for convenience, be used in order to classify the mentally ill, they are:

1. The mentally defective
2. Psychopathic personality
3. The psychoneurotic or neurotic.
4. The psychotic.

A brief discussion of the mentally defective has been presented and so we shall now consider the second group, that of the psychopathic personality.

In order to better understand this classification, the basic concept of personality itself must first be discussed.

Personality is the result of biological factors and psychological experiences. It seems that the general feeling among psychiatrists is that psychopathic personality is due to very early traumatic psychological experiences, rather than to biological factors, however, there is no definite evidence to support this belief.[17]

There is some clinical evidence to substantiate the theory that the very early emotional patterns of responses that the child develops in the first months of his life have much to do with the development of this phase of his personality. When the history of childhood of psychopaths can be obtained, it is startling to note how often the child was unwanted, in the way, or seriously handicapped by disease or malnutrition, neglected in his suffering or had no mother-substitute.

The only child, the first, or the last born child in the family seems more frequently to develop this rigid, selfish type of reaction which is found in the psychopath. Also it is interesting to note that very few psychopaths think they have had a happy childhood, and perhaps they are right. For even if their home was otherwise normal, their early development difficulties in adjustment spoiled it for themselves and often for the other members of the family. Again there is a similarity between this example and the early childhood and home-life of Durham.

Individuals of average intelligence who are neither psychotic nor neurotic but yet are social misfits and borderline cases are thus called psychopathic personalities or constitutional psychopathic inferiors. It is a general classification which includes pathological liars, sexual perverts, tramps, misanthropes, eccentric and amoral individuals, all to different degrees in need of treatment. Their lives lack stability, direction and tenacity of purpose. They also lead nomadic existences by changing jobs frequently and moving from place to place.[18] Notice again the similarity between the tendency to change jobs and Durham's quitting his job at the People's Drug Store in 1951. Also his many trips to Georgia and the mid-west, all of which follow the pattern found in psychopathic personalities.

The direct pursuit of pleasure, which is expressed by an immediate gratification motive of needs and desires, regardless of the consequences to himself or others, is the main drive in life and thus, in many respects, they resemble spoiled children.

There is an interesting paradox in the present medicolegal definition of the psychopathic personality.

The psychopath is capable of distinguishing right from wrong and therefore may be held responsible for their acts. However, on the other hand, it is recognized that most of these individuals are incurable and that threats of imprisonment and punishment have little if any effect in deterring them from criminal and antisocial acts.

In April 1948 Durham was diagnosed by St. Elizabeth's Hospital as suffering from psychosis with psychopathic personality.

Psychoses are major personality disorders with marked mental and emotional disorganization which renders the individual incapable of self-management and adjustment to society. Two terms associated with psychosis are insanity, which is the legal term, and dementia, which was applied to many disorders but which is now accepted as synonymous with major mental deterioration.

There are many types of psychosis, each with its

own symptomology and pattern. However, when symptoms are classified on the basis of their social importance, it is found that 99 per cent of patients at sometime engage in behavior which is peculiar, annoying or bizarre. Three-fourths of hospitalized cases exhibit traits of detrimental or dangerous actions to themselves or others, in the form of disoriented or suicidal behavior.[19]

The individual symptoms generally center around delusions of a persecutory nature. This condition is found in 46 per cent of the cases. Mental confusion, with a frequency rate of 43 per cent, is the next most common trait. One-third exhibit characteristics of depression, incoherent speech, loss of memory and disorientation.[20]

Psychoses are generally classified in two general groups. The first are mental disorders which are not associated with any organic or toxic pathology on the part of the patient. These are called functional or constitutional psychoses. In this group are schizophrenia, manic-depressive psychosis, paranoia and involutional melancholia.

In the second group are those cases which *are* associated with, and due to, organic and toxic pathology. These are known as toxic-organic psychoses and include senile dementia, psychosis with cerebral arteriosclerosis, general paresis, and alcoholic psychosis.

Each one of these forms of psychosis is responsible, each year, for approximately one-third of the admissions to hospitals. The remaining one-third is difficult to classify.

There is, no doubt, a direct connection between Durham's behavior in May 1951, and the diagnosis of psychosis. Perhaps this was of the paranoid type. If we consider the testimony of Mrs. Durham during the first trial when she answered the question; "Did you notice anything unusual about his (Monte Durham) behavior after his release from St. Elizabeth's Hospital in May 1951?"

A. "Well, the very first day, the very first night he was home he wanted me to have a steel door put up at the bedroom door and bars at his windows; that he saw people looking in at him and checking up on him, and he didn't want that, and said, 'Mother, if you don't do it I am going to ask the janitor if he won't have it done for me'."

This same paranoid condition existed when Durham worked for the People's Drug Store during 1951. At this time he left his job after about a month's employment because "people were spying" on him. These ideas of persecution lasted throughout Durham's psychiatric history and are mentioned several times in the Court Record by different witnesses.

The probability of Durham simulating insanity or malingering was brought up by the prosecution. It is not uncommon, and it is understandably a natural reaction, for an individual who is facing a problem, or in this case a criminal charge, to simulate insanity in order to escape punishment.

According to W. Lindesay Neustatter, in his book, "The Mind of the Murderer," simulated insanity may take two forms: "there is a crude variety, akin to malingering, in which the patient deliberately puts on an act which he thinks represents lunacy; or there is a type of reaction that is known as a prison psychosis or the 'Ganser syndrome'." [21]

In the latter condition the patient has an exaggerated mood and highly emotional feeling. There is a tendency to "let himself go." He is uncooperative, will not obey orders, and refuses to answer questions or in any way help in his own rehabilitation. Although the prisoner is not insane there is a real anxiety and suffering underlying these actions. These are especially prevalent when the full impact of his sentence or crime becomes a realization to him.

The quality of the simulation, of insanity, depends upon the ability and skill of the patient and his knowledge of psychiatric disorders. Fortunately for the psychologist this ability is usually limited. It is my personal belief that Durham was not malingering and that he did not have this ability to simulate insanity.

In a recent decision concerning the release, unconditionally, of Milton T. Rosenfield, a man acquitted of housebreaking by reason of insanity in the District of Columbia, Judge Alexander Holtzoff of the District Court stated that the Durham case was a case where the insanity plea was "misused."

Judge Holtzoff felt that Durham's plea of guilty at his third trial was an example of using the insanity plea as an escape since this plea meant that he (Durham) was admitting that he was sane at the time of the crime charged.

Judge Holtzoff also wrote, in this first formal interpretation of a statute which requires hospital commitment of all those acquitted of crimes by reason of insanity, describing the Durham decision as "general, indefinite and puzzling as to practical application."

The difficulties it presents to local courts, he added, have been multiplied by the requirement of the Court of Appeals that the Government prove a defendant is sane once "a mere scintilla of evidence" of insanity is introduced.

Against this sharp criticism by a Judge who first tried Durham in 1953, we have the backing of other equally concerned legal authorities such as Professor Henry Weihofen, Professor of Law at the University of New Mexico Law School and author of many books and articles on the subject of mental disease as a criminal defense.

Professor Weihofen has this to say concerning the need and recommended use of a new rule, as opposed to the older M'Naghten rule:

"In deciding what changes to make, we should bear in mind the main defects of the old rule that we are trying to remedy. We have said that the main defect with the right and wrong test is that it does not accord with modern psychiatric thinking. The law simply does not talk the same language as the psychiatrist.

"The primary requisite for any new rule therefore, is that it bridge this gap between legal and psychiatric thinking. Any revision of the legal rule should be aimed at providing a formula that does not run counter to current psychiatric concepts, a formula that will permit the expert witness to give the jury the fullest and clearest picture possible of what the defendant's mental condition actually is.

"I submit that the formulation that best accomplishes this objective is that adopted by the Court of Appeals for the District of Columbia in 1954 in *Durham v. United States. . . .*" [22]

Consider also this excerpt from an article written by the Honorable Simon E. Sobeloff, past Solicitor General of the United States, in his article, "From M'Naghten to Durham and Beyond."

"The New Hampshire or Durham approach seems preferable. It makes the causes of abnormality matters of fact for the juries to determine in each case upon the basis of explanations furnished them by the psychiatric expert witness." [23]

And so the eternal conflict goes on between the legal interpretation of criminal responsibility or right-wrong tests and the practicable usage of the terms as viewed by the medical and psychiatric professions. In order to ever reach a common ground there must be some understanding between these two factions as to what the other half is trying to do, and why.

Perhaps, on this problem of defining criminal insanity, the proposed method of the American Law Institute should be considered. It states that: "A person is not responsible for criminal conduct if at the time of such conduct he lacks substantial capacity either to appreciate the criminality of his conduct or to conform his conduct to the requirements of law." [24]

The differences do not stop just with this one aspect of determining criminal responsibility. Should, for example, psychopaths be considered in determining criminal responsibility? What also of drug addicts and crime committed under the influence of alcohol? The New Jersey Courts held recently that drug addiction and crime committed while under the influence of drugs is not a defense.

These problems as well as the all important problem of sex offenders have been considered and some steps taken to curb the tide of professional disagreement and lay prejudice in recent years.

Along with the American Law Institute's work revising the present outdated laws and preparing a "model penal code" we have legislation by different states to revise and aid their own systems of dealing with the mental and sexual offender.

The Massachusetts Briggs Law was a step in the right direction when it was enacted in 1921, for it introduced a new principle in the investigation of persons accused of crime by the routine examination of them by the Department of Mental Health. This examination, before trial, makes it possible to discover any existing mental disorders that might have gone unnoticed otherwise.

Another means of having access to the criminal, for determining his mental condition, is through court attached clinics. Such a clinic is that of Cook County, Illinois, under the direction of Dr. William H. Haines. "The purpose," according to Dr. Haines, "is to give the Court impartial, expert assistance and especially to protect the defendants who are unable to pay for expert testimony." [25] Before its establishment in 1931, if the defense had three psychiatrists, or even five, it was necessary that the State use a similar number in rebuttal. Since 1931, defense psychiatrists have been rare, as either side may call the Behavior Clinic psychiatrists to testify on their examination findings. This provides the most impoverished defendant with the same impartial psychiatric examination as the most wealthy could receive.

Other clinics are found in Baltimore, Cleveland, Detroit, New York and Pittsburgh.

Of these clinics attached to the court system Professor Henry Weihofen, in his book, *Mental Disorder as a Criminal Defense,* has this to say: "The court clinic is unique in that it is an integral part of the court administration. The professional staff has daily contact with the prosecutors and judges as well as with defense counsel. The staff of the clinic are looked upon by the judges as team-mates rather than outsiders. This makes possible the exchange on an informal basis of ideas and attitudes about specific cases and general problems." [26]

If the general public's peace of mind requires that they be assured that persons acquitted by reason of insanity shall be institutionalized, it is even more essential to the peace of mind of the juryman whose immediate and primary responsibility is to determine the disposition of an accused who has pleaded insanity. The new law thus represents in part a recognition by Congress of the need pointed out by the District Court of Appeals in the *Durham* and *Taylor* cases for relieving any fears the jury may have that the defendant will be let loose in society if they should acquit him by reason of insanity.

In the *Taylor* case, the appellant argued that the judge told the jury in effect that if appellant were acquitted he would go free. The Court of Appeals found that the trial judge had not in fact conveyed to the jury "that erroneous idea." In the *Durham* case, however, "that erroneous idea" was conveyed to the jury not once, but twice. By instructing the jury that St. Elizabeth's would release the defendant very shortly, the trial judge completely vitiated the purpose and effect of the prior statement that if acquitted by reason of insanity the defendant would be sent to St. Elizabeth's Hospital for confinement until it is determined that he is of sound mind.

In the *Taylor* case the Court of Appeals held that to inform the jury that the defendant had been released by St. Elizabeth's as competent to stand trial was an error which prejudiced the defense of insanity. "The fair meaning of section 18 U.S.C. section 4244 is that the jury shall not be told that the accused has been found competent to stand trial." This statute provides that "A finding by the judge that the accused is mentally competent to stand trial shall in no way prejudice the accused in a plea of insanity as a defense to the crime charged; such finding shall not be introduced in evidence on that issue nor otherwise be brought to the notice of the jury."

In Durham's case not only was the finding of his competency to stand trial admitted in evidence, but a letter from St. Elizabeth's to the same effect which was not received in evidence was described to the jury in the Court's instructions and was used as the basis for the Court's comment that if the defendant were acquitted and sent back to St. Elizabeth's, he would soon be released. As if it were not damaging enough to bring the finding of competency to stand trial to the jury's attention, the Court proceeded to draw the inference from the fact that St. Elizabeth's had released the defendant into the custody of the Attorney General as competent to stand trial in 1953 that they would release him into society in 1955.

The advisability of submitting the defense of insanity to the jury without telling the jury that the accused would be committed to a mental institution in the event of acquittal on such grounds was questioned as early as 1909 in the State of Oregon. In *State* v. *Daley*,[27] defense counsel requested that the jury be instructed that:

> "The defense of insanity having been interposed by the defendant in this case, you are instructed that if you find him not guilty on that ground, to state the fact in your verdict and the court must thereupon, if it deems his being at large dangerous to the public peace or safety, order him to be committed to any lunatic asylum authorized by the state to receive and keep such persons until he becomes sane, or be otherwise discharged therefrom, by authority of the law."

While in 1909, the majority of the Oregon Court would not go so far as to say, as the Court did in the Taylor case, that the jury should be instructed that the defendant would be committed in the event of acquittal by reason of insanity, the effect of telling the jury that the defendant would be *released* in that event was not considered in that case.

Several recent cases have been found in which the latter comment was made to the jury by the prosecuting attorney and in every instance it has been held to be a reversible error unless corrected by the trial judge. No case has been found in which the judge himself instructed the jury that the defendant would be released if acquitted by reason of insanity.[28]

In most cases the mentally ill are recognized by the courts, and the disposition of them for treatment is a good one, having all the humane and just motives which society can provide. However, as in all other human endeavors, mistakes are made, as in the case of a particularly horrible crime in which the public is emotionally involved. The jury may, over expert psychiatric advice, bring a verdict of guilty and the defendant be unjustly committed to a state prison. These miscarriages of justice do occur, but we hope that with the advancement of medical science and the educating of the public in the problems of mental illness that they can be minimized.

There has been endless literature written on the problem of insanity as a defense to a criminal act, each having a set of conclusions which is aimed at the betterment of the present situation. If we take a few of these diverse opinions the reader can soon see the problem which is facing the judiciary in their effort to modernize the present outdated system of insanity laws.

The states themselves have different opinions of what should be done with the individual who has been acquitted by reason of insanity. In ten states, the court is required to order the defendant committed to the proper mental institution without any further inquiry as to whether he still continues to be insane or not. This applies to Georgia, Kansas, Massachusetts (for murder and manslaughter cases), Michigan (for murder), Minnesota, Nebraska, Nevada, Ohio, Oklahoma, and Wisconsin.

In these ten states, the jury shall, by their verdict, state that the defendant is not guilty by reason of insanity or irresponsibility at the time of the commission of the offense. In Minnesota, the verdict must also state whether the defendant at the date of the offense had homicidal tendencies, and, if so, he is committed to the hospital for the dangerously insane.

After the finding of "not guilty by reason of insanity" in six of the ten states, commitment to a proper hospital is by order of the court; in three upon order of the judge; and in one, Michigan, it is not clear just who does order the commitment. In Massachusetts and Michigan the individual is committed for life. Release varies in these different states, as well as in the other states that I have not mentioned. In Massachusetts and Michigan the governor is permitted to order the release; in others, with the exception of Georgia, Nebraska, Nevada, and Oklahoma, it is by order of the committing Court. In these four states it seems that insane persons are released the same way as other inmates in a mental hospital.

In Kansas, a person committed may be granted convalescent leave or discharged as any other committed patient after thirty days' notice to the county attorney and the sheriff. The authority to discharge patients is in the Department of Social Welfare which may be delegated to the superintendent of the hospital.

In Minnesota, such person shall be liberated upon the order of the court which committed him, whenever the superintendent of the hospital certifies to the court in writing that in his opinion the patient is fully recovered and that no person will be endangered by his discharge. If the superintendent fails or refuses to furnish such a certificate, a petition may be addressed to the court and the question decided by the Court without regard to the superintendent's opinion.

In Wisconsin, a re-examination of the patient's sanity may be had upon a petition to the committing Court. The Court then must appoint two qualified physicians to examine the person. A jury may be demanded. This procedure is available to all patients including those committed on "acquittal of crime by reason of insanity," but the latter are not to be discharged unless the judge or jury trying the issue of recovery determines that he is not only sane and mentally responsible, but also that he is not likely to have a recurrence of insanity or mental irresponsibility as would result in acts which, before such condition, would constitute crime.

In Ohio, such persons shall not be released from confinement in the hospital until the judge of the Court of Common Pleas of Allen County; the superintendent of Lima State Hospital; and an alienist to be designated by the judge and the superintendent or a majority of them, after a notice and hearing find and determine that the defendant's sanity has been restored and that his release will not be dangerous. The defendant may be given a fibal or conditional release or he may be paroled.

Maryland and seven other states have laws that permit an individual to be found not guilty because of insanity at the time of the commission of the offense and recovery at the time of the trial. When this is the case the defendant may walk out of the courtroom a free man without further examination.

From these brief examples the reader can see the confusion and diverse positions held by the different states. I believe, as so many psychiatrists and psychologists do, that there should be a set standard of rules governing the plea of insanity in our country. Dr. William H. Haines, Director of The Behavior Clinic of Cook County in Chicago, says in an article that: "We are in need of a uniform definition of insanity which would apply in the forty-eight states and the District of Columbia. This should be recognized by the Army, Navy, United States Health Service, and the Veteran's Administration. In other words, we need a uniform criminal code and commitment law." [29]

What of the psychiatrist as an expert witness in our court-rooms? Should not their testimony and reports be available to both the defense and the prosecution? Dr. Manfred S. Guttmacher, Chief Medical Officer of the Supreme Bench of Baltimore, has this to say in regard to the psychiatrist as an expert witness.[30] "Second only to being used as a partisan, is the psychiatrist's objection to the way in which he is generally forced to present his opinion testimony. He is dependent almost entirely on the knowledge and skill, or lack of it, possessed by the lawyer who employs him. He is admonished repeatedly to give "Yes or No answers" to questions, which rarely can be adequately answered in this way. This is particularly true of psychiatry which is as complex as human behavior itself, which is its essence."

I also feel that the hypothetical question should, in cases of insanity or when expert witnesses are testifying, be abolished. For a doctor, who has sworn to "tell the truth," to feel that his answers are creating the right impression and an accurate account of the patient's illness, he must be able to elaborate on his diagnosis. A doctor may be required to reach an opinion on a hypothetical statement of facts which he convinced gives a distorted picture of the case and, yet he is not, in many cases, allowed to elaborate or amend his opinion. The opinion of an expert witness as to whether a person may, in the next ten years, again have a mental illness is a remote question and requires more consideration than can be given to a hypothetical question put to him while he is on the witness stand.

The American Law Institute recognizing the need for better understanding between the law court and the medical profession included in their Model Penal code a section dealing with this point of expert testimony:

When a psychiatrist who has examined the defendant testifies concerning his mental condition, he shall be permitted to make a statement as to the nature of his examination, his diagnosis of the mental condition of the defendant at the time of the commission of the offense charged and his opinion as to the extent, if any, to which the capacity of the defendant to appreciate the criminality of his conduct or to conform his conduct to the requirements of law or to have a particular state of mind which is an element of the offense charged was impaired as a result of mental disease or defect at that time. He shall be permitted to make any explanation reasonably serving to clarify his diagnosis and opinion and may be cross-examined as to any matter bearing on his competency or credibility or the validity of his diagnosis or opinion.[31]

Judge Bazelon's opinion on the Durham case has been hailed by psychiatrists everywhere as a noteworthy advance toward a better understanding of the problem. The major dilemma, as it has existed for hundreds of years, is how to bring together the demands of exactness of law, and the humanitarianism and treatment demanded by the medical profession. There are two aspects to this problem; to recognize the sick criminals and second to treat them. The first, with the help of modern science is relatively easy, the second is difficult and in some cases impossible, under the present system of handling the insanity plea.

The problem of responsibility, which seems relatively simple as an operational concept when used in the treatment of psychiatric patients, becomes more complicated when it is tied up with the idea of punishment. This problem becomes especially important in cases of capital punishment, since an "insanity" plea rarely is used in other cases. The accused, in noncapital cases, seems to recognize the implications of pleading mental illness, and seems to shun the prospect of commitment to a mental hospital. The advantage, in a capital crime, arises in part out of the gap in the law, a gap by which there is one set of standards for acquittal because of lack of "criminal responsibility" and another set of standards for commitment to a mental hospital because of mental illness. If this gap were plugged, and conviction to a mental hospital made mandatory as well as the other basic reforms suggested, a large part of the existing problem could be solved.

NOTES

1. 12 D.C. Sup. Ct. (1 Mackey) 498, 550 (1882). The right-wrong test was reaffirmed in United States v. Lee, 15 D.C. Sup. Ct. (4 Mackey) 489, 496 (1886).

2. 59 App. D.C. 144, 36 F. 2d 548 (1929).

3. Glueck, *Mental Disorder and the Criminal Law,* 138-39 (1925), citing Rex v. Arnold, 16 How. St. 695, 764 (1724).

4. *Id.* at 142-52, citing Earl Ferrer's case, 19 How. St. Ter. 886 (1760). One writer has stated that these tests originated in England in the 13th or 14th century, when the law began to define insanity in terms of intellect for purposes of determining capacity to manage feudal estates. *Comment, Lunacy and Idiocy —The Old Law and Its Incubus,* 18 U. of Chi. L. Rev. 361 (1951).

5. Weihofen, *The M'Naghten Rule in its Present Day Setting,* FEDERAL PROBATION 8 (Sept. 1953); Weihofen, *Insanity as a Defense in Criminal Law* 15, 64-68, 109-47 (1933); Leland v. Oregon, 343 U. S. 790, 800 (1952).

6. Ray, *Medical Jurisprudence of Insanity* 47 and 34 *et seq.* (1st ed. 1838). "That the insane mind is not entirely deprived of this power of moral discernment, but in many subjects is perfectly rational, and displays the exercise of a sound and well balanced mind is one of those facts now so well established,

that to question it would only betray the height of ignorance and presumption." *Id.* 32.

7. Cardozo, *What Medicine Can Do For the Law,* 32, 1930).

8. ROYAL COMMISSION REPORT 80.

9. ROYAL COMMISSION REPORT 114. And see State v. Jones, 50 N. H. (2 Shirley) 369, 392-93 (1871).

10. ROYAL COMMISSION REPORT 110; for additional comment on the irresistible impulse test see: Davidson, *Irresistible Impulse and Criminal Responsibility* (1954); Guttmacher & Weihofen, *Psychiatry and the Law,* 410-12, 1952).

11. *Criminal Responsibility and Psychiatric Expert Testimony,* formulated by The Committee on Psychiatry and Law of the Group for the Advancement of Psychiatry, Topeka, Kansas, May, 1954.

12. U. S. App. D. C., 215 F. 2d 493 (July 1, 1954).

13. Cronbach, Lee J., *Essentials of Psychological Testing,* p. 103, Harper & Brothers, New York, 1949.

14. Burtt, Harold E., Applied Psychology, Prentice-Hall, Inc., New York, 1950.

15. Barr, M. W., *Types of Mental Defectives,* P. Blakiston Son and Company, Philadelphia, 1920.

16. Page, James D., *Abnormal Psychology,* p. 394, McGraw-Hill Book Company, Inc., New York, 1947.

17. *See* Kahn, E., Psychopathic Personalities, Yale University Press, New Haven, 1931.

18. *See* Prue, P. W., The Concept of Psychopathic Personality, in *Personality and the Behavior Disorders,* vol. II, J. McV. Hunt (ed.), The Ronald Press Company, New York, 1944.

19. Page, op. cit., p. 209.

20. *Ibid,* Page, p. 211.

21. Neustatter, W. Lindesay, *The Mind of the Murderer,* p. 124, Christopher Johnson, London, 1957.

22. Nice, Richard W., (Editor) *Crime and In-*

sanity, chap. IX, "In Favor of the Durham Rule," Philosophical Library, New York, 1958.

23. *Ibid.,* "From M'Naghten to Durham and Beyond," Chap. VIII.

24. American Law Institute, Model Penal Code, No. 4, Article 4 Responsibility, Section 4.01, p. 27.

25. *Op. cit.,* (Nice, Editor), "Not Guilty by Reason of Insanity," chapter VI.

26. Weihofen, Henry, *Mental Disorder as a Criminal Defense,* p. 346, Dennis and Co., Inc., Buffalo, New York, 1954.

27. State v. Daley, 54 Ore. 514, 103 Pac. 502, 104 Pac. 1 (1909).

28. See also; Wise v. State, 251 Ala. 660, 38 So. 2d 553, 556 (1948).

29. *Not Guilty by Reason of Insanity,* by Dr. William H. Haines and John Zeidler, paper given at the Medical Correctional Association meeting in Los Angeles in 1956.

30. *Why Psychiatrists Do Not Like to Testify in Court,* Manfred S. Guttmacher, The Practical Lawyer, Volume 1, Number 5, May 1955, p. 53.

31. The American Law Institute, Model Penal Code, Tentative Draft No. 4, section 4.07, para. 4, p. 33.

THE PSYCHOLOGIST IN TODAY'S LEGAL WORLD

DAVID W. LOUISELL,
Professor of Law, University of California

On five occasions during the past several years the writer has had the opportunity of addressing meetings of psychologists on some of the current legal problems of interest to them and their profession.[1] Each meeting was followed by a question period which helped the writer to comprehend the more acute current interests and problems of psychologists, and of lawyers called upon to advise them and their professional groups, which concern the clinical practice of psychology, the conduct of litigation and judicial administration.[2] This article is a response to requests that the writer's remarks and answers to questions be reduced to permanent form. Perhaps most of this article is of primary interest to the clinical or practicing psychologist, whether full-time or part-time, but some of the problems discussed are also of interest to the psychologist in teaching, research, industrial work, or counseling at educational institutions or otherwise. The principal subjects discussed are

(1) The psychologist as an expert witness
(2) The status of statutory regulation of psychological practice in the United States vis-a-vis medical licensure statutes

71

(3) The privilege of confidential communication between the psychologist and his patient or counselee

(4) Miscellaneous potential legal pitfalls to be avoided by the practicing psychologist.

The Psychologist As An Expert Witness:

While there is no dearth of literature on existent and potential psychological devices and techniques for scientific appraisal of witnesses and diagnosis of testimony,[3] as well as on the psychology of legal practice and advocacy [4] including criminal law administration,[5] there seem to be few cases and little recent discussion directly concerned with the psychologist functioning as an expert witness himself.[6] This of course contrasts with the vast literature concerned with the psychiatrist as an expert witness.[7] Yet the great Wigmore tells us:

> Nevertheless, within the limitations of these special judicial rules (pertaining to partisan presentation of evidence in an adversary proceeding), judicial practice is entitled and bound to resort to all *truths of human nature established by science,* and to employ *all methods recognized by scientists* for applying those truths in the analysis of testimonial credit. Already, in long tradition, judicial practice is based on the implicit recognition . . . of a number of principles of testimonial psychology, empirically discovered and accepted. In so far as science from time to time revises them, or adds new ones, the law can and should recognize them. Indeed, it may be asserted that the Courts are ready to learn and to use, whenever the psychologists produce it, any method which the latter themselves are agreed is sound, accurate and practical. If there is any reproach, it does not

belong to the Courts or the law. A legal practice which has admitted the evidential use of the telephone, the phonograph, the dictograph, and the vacuum-ray, within the past decades, cannot be charged with lagging behind science. But where *are* these practical psychological tests, which will detect specifically the memory-failure and the lie on the witness-stand? There must first be proof of general scientific recognition that they are valid and feasible. The vacuum-ray photographic method, for example, was accepted by scientists the world over, within a few months after its promulgation. If there is ever devised a psychological test for the valuation of witnesses, the law will run to meet it. Both law and practice permit the calling of any expert scientist whose method is acknowledged in his science to be a sound and trustworthy one. Whenever the Psychologist is really ready for the Courts, the Courts are ready for him." [8]

While Wigmore in the foregoing paragraph seems primarily concerned with psychological techniques and devices, there, as elsewhere when he considers in detail scientific psychological diagnosis of testimony, he acknowledges that "Psychometrical data so obtained would of course have to be brought in by the expert witness obtaining them. In that respect the psychometrist would stand on the same footing as the expert witness to insanity, called under the traditional practice." [9] But we search in vain for any substantial analysis, in Wigmore or elsewhere in American legal literature, of the psychologist functioning as an expert witness. This may be due at least in part to Wigmore's, and other writers', primary concern that the law utilize as soon as feasible all available psychological techniques, devices and knowledge, and their relative indifference to whether the vehicle of such use be the psychiatric or psychological profession, or both. And the lack of adequate scholarly attention to the specific problem of the psychologist as an expert witness may also be explained by the paucity of published cases in point. In any event, the aggressive claim of the second paragraph below from *Psychiatric and Psychologic Opinions in Court* by Eliasberg,[10] a physician also trained in psychology, insofar as it pertains to the psychologist as an expert witness, seems as yet to find small counter-point in the published American cases:

"Great progress has been achieved in the differential psychology of testimony. The testimony of children, of boys and girls of prepubertal age, of adolescents of primitive state of mind, of morons, of dwellers in rural areas, the influence of special training, skill, social psychological ties, food, alcohol, drugs were experimentally investigated. At the same time psychology was furthered through the findings of the neurologists especially in cases of aphasia and agnosia. Here it was shown that apparently simple mental processes, as the perceptions, consist of components and that each of them may be put out of commission separately.

"Psychology, assimilating all these teachings to its own findings, has finally become a full fledged science. Small wonder, then, that it demanded to be heard and to contribute its insight to the solution of burning problems, not as a hand-maiden that carries the train but, to use the famous comparison of Kant, walks ahead of her mistress and bears the torch for her." [11]

Of course the paucity of published cases involving psychologists as expert witnesses is not a certain indication of the extent to which they presently are functioning as such in the trial courts. It is rather notorious that although no American appellate court has yet approved of the judicial use of the lie detector, it is not infrequently used with consent of the parties in the trial courts.[12] But such use ordinarily produces no published judicial opinion. Several years ago in Minnesota a psychologist appeared as an expert witness for the state in a sensational murder trial [13] of an adolescent who had murdered his foster mother. Because no appeal followed the conviction in that case, there is no published transcript of the testimony nor published judicial opinion on the psychologist as expert witness.[14] One can only speculate on the number of similar instances, which, taking the country as a whole, may be not inconsiderable.

Nevertheless, in view of the development of various branches of psychology, including its rapidly expanding clinical practice, it does seem surprising that more appellate courts have not been called upon to consider the psychologist as an expert witness. Speaking generally, this is not because the psychologist is unready for the courts. If the profession's knowledge and skill are not yet utilized in judicial administration to the full extent presently feasible and desirable, perhaps this is partly because psychologists are not yet sufficiently aggressive in displaying their wares to the courts and to lawyers. It may chiefly be because trial lawyers are not doing the creative or imaginative thinking necessary to adapt psychological developments to testimonial uses.

The psychologists, in common with other professional men, often seem to display an undue hesitancy, amounting almost to fear, to taking the witness stand. Sometimes of course such professional hesitancy is selfishly inspired by realization of the disproportionate expenditure of time in relation to the financial compensation for testifying. This is often an unjustifiable and immoral attitude which engenders public antipathy to professions whose members excessively indulge this attitude. The very definition of a profession implies public service as well as profit, and professional *noblesse oblige* dictates performance as obligations to judicial administration as not the least of the public services. However, the psychologist's hesitancy to take the witness stand more often seems to be inspired by an unreasonable concern over cross examination, a fear of ridicule or harsh treatment typified by the cinema version of trials with its incessant "answer 'Yes' or 'No,'" or a lack of confidence in his ability to communicate adequately in semantics comprehensible by non-psychologists. While such hesitancy is understandable, and such concerns not wholly lacking in foundation, they often proceed from a distorted notion of modern litigation and the true function of the expert witness in it. Therefore it may be profitable briefly to consider the basis for expert testimony in relation to the psychologist's potential contribution to judicial administration.

Bratt v. Western Air Lines [15] represents what may be characterized as the "modern common-sense" approach to the problem of the expert witness and his contribution to judicial fact ascertainment. That was a suit to recover for the death of an airplane passenger who lost his life in a crash which killed the entire crew and all but one of the passengers. The flight crew were highly trained and qualified, and the air was smooth and weather conditions favorable. The crash was apparently caused by a structural failure in flight. However, it was the defendant company's position that the crash was not caused by any mechanical or structural defect of the plane, or any other cause within its control. In an attempt to show that a defective and unsafe right horizontal stabilizer of the plane was the proximate cause of the crash, plaintiff offered the evidence of an aviation mechanic. There was extensive examination and cross examination pertinent to the mechanic's qualifications as an expert. The court of appeals summarized this testimony:

"... He (the mechanic) became interested in aviation in 1927 and since that time has owned three planes of his own; he has flown numerous types of planes including multi-engine and twin-engine aircraft, and has approximately eleven hundred air hours to his credit. The only time he has flown a DC-3 (the type here involved) was after it was taken into the air by a qualified pilot who let him then take the controls. He has never had a commercial pilot's license, but has held a private license and now holds a sudent's license. In 1943 he worked eleven months for Western Airlines as an 'apprentice mechanic' and is now employed as an aviation mechanic by the Thompson Flying Service. His work with the Western Airlines required a general knowledge of aircraft and as a part of his duties he did general maintenance work, including inspection and repairs. He has not been certified by Federal authorities and therefore never signed any Civil Aeronautics Authority forms as an official inspector, but made them out under the supervision of a licensed 'A & E.' He has studied the 'C.A.A.' manuals and read other literature pertaining to the operation, maintenance and construction of DC-3 equipment. He has studied aerodynamics through study courses and classroom work, having attended a class at least once a week for over two years, in addition to manuals and books published for the 'C.A.B.' He stated that he had studied 'load factors and structural aerodynamics'; that he knew metals and had experimented with heat alloy. He also examined the wreckage of the plane at the point of the accident. Over objections of counsel, the court permitted him to describe the purpose of ailerons, stabilizers and rudders, and to discuss the various parts and structures of an airplane with reference to their purpose and function in flight. . . ." [16]

However, the trial court would not permit this witness to answer the following question:

". . . Now taking into consideration your own knowledge and experience and the evidence that I have mentioned—the weather records, the photographs, barograph card—and assuming the testimony of Lt. Gardner (sole survivor of the crash) to be true, I will ask you whether or not you were able to form or express an opinion with a reasonable degree of certainty as to whether the right horizontal stabilizer and the elevator with it was the first part of the first section of this plane to fail in flight?" [17]

To that question the trial court sustained an objection made by defendant's counsel on the ground that the witness was not qualified to render such an opinion. The jury returned a verdict for defendant. This ruling of the trial court was one of the reasons the court of appeals reversed the case and remanded it for a new trial.

In respect of the scope of expert testimony and the qualifications of a witness to speak as an expert, the court of appeals quoted from American Law Institute, Model Code of Evidence: "A witness is an expert witness and is qualified to give expert testimony if the judge finds that to perceive, know or understand the matter concerning which the witness is to testify, requires special knowledge, skill, experience or training and that the witness has the requisite special knowledge, skill, experience or training." [18] The court of appeals then pointed out that the trial court's refusal to let the aviation mechanic give his opinion, was apparently based on its impression that a witness to be competent to give such an opinion "must have either experienced an accident of this kind, or be an 'expert who had figured it out mathematically and had taken into consideration every factor' that goes to the use of the various parts of an airplane." After rejecting as a requirement personal involvement in such an accident "because as we all know, few ever survive to relate their experience," [19] the court of appeals pointed out that a witness may be competent to testify as an expert although his knowledge was acquired through the medium of practical experience rather than scientific study and research. It then stated:

> "The witness had no scholastic standing in the science of aerodynamics, but he was a man of practical experience who said he had made an actual study of the structural stress and strain on the parts of an airplane, and that based upon his examination of the wreckage at the point of the accident and other facts available to him, he had an opinion concerning which of the parts of the plane structurally failed first in flight, and was therefore the proximate cause of the accident. It may be that his testimony was of little value when judged by the substance of direct testimony, or when compared with the testimony of those whose opinions are steeped in the lore of scientific research. But, 'the law does not require the best possible kind of witness' . . . The testimony of a country doctor concerning the sanity of his patient is as readily admissible as the testimony of the most renowned psychiatrist." [20]

The court then enunciated what to this writer is the essence of the "modern common-sense" approach to expert testimony: will such testimony as a practical matter aid the tribunal in finding out the truth?

79

"It must be remembered that the court is not the judge of the quality of the evidence, nor does the witness perform the function of a juror—he can only contribute something to the jury's information and if he can, he should be permitted to do so. Especially is this true, where as here the answer to the crucial question is necessarily left to those claiming special knowledge based upon experience. . . ." [21]

An outstanding authority in his most recent work, McCormick on Evidence,[22] neatly and succinctly puts the rationale of expert evidence:

"An observer is qualified to testify because he has first hand knowledge which the jury does not have of the situation or transaction at issue. The expert has something different to contribute. This is a power to draw inferences from the facts which a jury would not be competent to draw. To warrant the use of expert evidence, then, two elements are required. First, the subject of the inference must be so distinctly related to some science, profession, business or occupation as to be beyond the ken of the average layman, and second, the witness must have such skill, knowledge or experience in that field or calling as to make it appear that his opinion or inference will probably aid the trier in his search for the truth. The knowledge may in some fields be derived from reading alone, in some from practice alone, or as is more commonly the case, from both . . ." [23]

Do not issues often arise in modern litigation as to which the psychologist has "a power to draw inferences from the facts which a jury (or judge, for that matter, sitting without a jury) would not be

80

competent to draw"? The answer is certainly in the affirmative to an extent not indicated by the published cases. In the field of mental abnormality alone—psychoses or insanity, mental incompetence, mental illness, various gradations of mental retardation—to name but one general category of psychology's competence, one would expect to find a substantial number of cases in which a psychologist had appeared as an expert witness. But in contrast to the innumerable cases wherein a psychiatrist has functioned as an expert witness in this field, the published opinions seemingly have little to say about the psychologist in this role.

People v. Hawthorne,[24] however, is a case directly in point. It was a prosecution of defendant for homicide for killing his wife's paramour. The defense was insanity. Defendant's counsel introduced in evidence the testimony of a physician, who testified as an expert, and several lay witnesses, who testified with regard to their opinions of defendant's insanity from observations of his conduct and actions. Defendant's counsel also sought to qualify, as an expert witness on insanity, a professor of psychology from the Michigan State Normal College. This psychologist was a graduate of several educational institutions and held the degree of Bachelor of Arts, Master of Arts, Bachelor of Divinity and Doctor of Philosophy in Psychology. He had done graduate work at the University of California, Columbia University, Boston University, Harvard University Medical School, and the Boston Psychopathic Hospital. He had been a full professor at several universities before becoming affiliated with the Michigan State Normal College, where he had been eleven years up to the time of the trial. He had given courses in normal and abnormal psychology, experimental psychology, educational psychology, mental tests and measurements, psychology and criminology, problems in marriage and family, and problems of child-welfare. One of his texts had been through five editions. He had written articles on the subject of human behavior that appeared in publications throughout the United States. He specialized in the particular field of psychology devoted to motivation and motives of human conduct. He was not of course a practicing physician nor a graduate of a medical college. He had never treated insanity nor was he licensed to practice medicine in any form. However, he had knowledge of the anatomy of the brain, having studied physiological psychology and neurology. He had given insanity and diseases of the brain special study.

The trial court sustained the prosecuting attorney's objection to the competency of this psychologist as an expert on insanity, although it did give the defense an opportunity to recall the psychologist, who had known the defendant as a college student, to testify as to any observations while in contact with the defendant and any conclusions. On appeal to the Supreme Court of Michigan, one of the defendant's principal contentions was that the trial court had erred in holding the psychologist to be incompetent as an expert on insanity. Three justices of the supreme court, who concurred in an opinion which on the other issues in the case is the opinion of the court, thought that the trial court was correct in this holding. On this point, after briefly summarizing the psychologist's qualifications, they said only:

"... Insanity, however, is held to be a disease, ... and, therefore, comes within the realm of medical science, which comprises the study and treatment of disease. Only physicians can qualify to answer hypothetical questions as experts in such science. The court was not in error in excluding the testimony sought to be offered." [25]

The remaining five justices, a majority of the eight constituting Michigan's Supreme Court, held diametrically contrary views on the psychologist's competency as an expert witness. Speaking through Butzel, J. they said in part:

"I concur in affirmance, but I cannot agree with the proposition of my brother McAllister that because insanity is a disease and comes within the realm of medical science that only physicians are competent to answer hypothetical questions on behalf of a defendant in a criminal case. The law does not require a rule so formal, and I do not think we further the cause of justice by insisting that only a medical man may completely advise on the subject of mental condition. . . .[26]

". . . I do not think it can be said that his (the psychologist's) ability to detect insanity is inferior to that of a medical man whose experience along such lines is not so intensive." [27]

". . . No case has been called to my attention where a general medical training has been held to be the *sine qua non* of the competency of a trained specialist to advise on the matter of insanity. . . .[28]

". . . There is no magic in particular titles or degrees and, in our age of intense scientific specialization, we might deny ourselves the use of the best knowledge available by a rule that would immutably fix the educational qualifications to a particular degree." [29]

Nevertheless the five justices who expressed the foregoing views also concurred in the affirmance of the judgment of the trial court because they thought that the prejudicial effect of any error of the trial court was removed when that court gave the defense an opportunity to recall the psychologist to testify as to any observations while in contact with the defendant and any conclusions.[30] To complete the picture of this case, it should also be noted that the five justices, though thoroughly convinced that a qualified psychologist may be a competent expert witness on insanity, nevertheless stated the caveat that "(w)hen a nonmedical is offered as an expert on subjects in the orbit of medical science, the trial court is put on guard and should take greater precaution in the preliminary inquiry to determine the witness's qualifications and the extent of knowledge than might be necessary when a graduate of a medical school is proposed." [31]

Another case from an eminent court, *People v. Rice*,[32] although not directly pertinent in that it did not involve a psychologist, is significant as indicating that the physician, while legally favored as an expert witness on insanity, is not the only specialist capable of being such a witness. That case was also a prosecution of defendant for homicide, with a defense of insanity. The witness called by defendant on the issue of insanity was not a doctor of medicine but a manufacturer of medicines and publisher of medical books. He had studied to some extent medicine and nervous diseases. The trial court held that he was not competent as an expert although he could be examined as a layman. New York's highest court, the Court of Appeals, affirmed the trial court on the ground that the witness had not been sufficiently qualified as an expert. However, the court said:

> "After a careful consideration of the subject we have reached the conclusion that if a man be in reality an expert upon any given subject belonging to the domain of medicine, his opinion may be received by the court, although he has not a license to practice medicine. But such testimony should be received with great caution, and only after the

trial court has become fully satisfied that upon the subject as to which the witness is called for the purpose of giving an opinion, he is fully competent to speak. The witness Fenner was not *prima facie* competent, for he had not been licensed to practice medicine. It was essential, therefore, to prove him to be an expert before the defense acquired the right to have him testify as to the sanity or insanity of the defendant." [33]

Psychology's purported competence in respect of mental status or processes is of course not limited to the mind which deviates from the normal because of psychoses or mental retardation. Often in litigation the status of the normal mind is the pivotal issue, as for example when the intention of a party is legally controlling or significant on the issues involved. *People v. McNichol* [34] was a prosecution for issuing a worthless check. The defense was that defendant on the day involved, without eating any breakfast, had consumed a pint of whiskey and four cans of beer, and that he had no recollection of what his conduct was at the time of the alleged offense. Prior to his trial defendant had been examined by a clinical psychologist who had subjected him to an examination while defendant was under the influence of sodium pentathol, a so-called truth serum. During the trial defendant sought to introduce in evidence a report of statements he had made during this examination, but this testimony was excluded by the trial court. However, the clinical psychologist did testify at the trial, in response to hypothetical questions, that one who had consumed the quantity of liquor defendant had consumed would not be conscious of an intent to do an act to obtain money—that his intent would not be a conscious intent. He also testified that subconscious matter might be brought out by putting the party into a hypnotic state by the administration of sodium pentathol; that he had so treated the defendant and that during the treatment notes had been made of what was said by defendant. But, as stated, the trial court would not permit the psychologist to state the context of those notes. The trial court's judgment of conviction of defendant was affirmed despite defendant's contention that such exclusion of the notes was error. There is no suggestion in the opinion of the appellate court that it was wrong for the trial court to permit the clinical psychologist to testify to the extent indicated above.

There is no reason why psychology's potential contribution to judicial fact ascertainment should be limited to criminal jurisprudence. *United States v. 38 Dozen Bottles* [35] was a seizure action brought under the Federal Food, Drug and Cosmetic Act [36] charging that the drug "Tryptacin" was misbranded by reason of failure of its labeling to bear adequate directions for use. One issue was whether a newspaper advertisement of the drug conveyed the impression that the drug was offered as a cure for ulcers. In holding that it did, the court depended in part on the testimony of experts in the field of advertising and marketing psychology. The court said:

> "In addition to reading and examining the advertisement, I base my finding as to the impression conveyed by the advertisement upon the evidence presented on that point. Libelant's witnesses, Dr. James N. Mosel and Dr. Howard P. Longstaff, experts in the field of advertising and marketing psychology, presented exhaustive analyses of the content of the advertisement and the effect which it was intended to have upon the prospective purchaser of the drug. Such testimony is admissible to determine the meaning of an advertisement. Federal Trade Commission v. National Health Aids, Inc. D.C. Md., 108 F. Supp. 340.

"Moreover, Dr. Mosel introduced evidence relative to two hundred individuals whom he surveyed concerning the impression which they received from the 'Tryptacin' advertisement. A substantial portion of those interviewed indicated that they received the impression from the advertisement that 'Tryptacin' would 'stop,' 'cure' or otherwise bring about some permanent relief of ulcers. The forms filled out by the individuals questioned, interview cards, and tabulations made by Dr. Mosel of the answers received, were placed in evidence by libelant." [37]

Claimant's opposing evidence on the import of the advertisement's language included testimony of two representatives of a firm which handled the drug's advertising. These advertising men testified that in their opinion the advertisement offered the drug as a means of relieving acid pain and not of curing stomach ulcers. They also testified that they had showed the advertisement to a number of their associates in the advertising business, newspaper censorship boards and other persons, and inquired as to the impression the advertisement made; and that not a single person questioned received the impression that the advertisement offered a cure for stomach ulcers. There was similar testimony by doctors, who had discussed the meaning of the advertisement with other doctors, nurses, patients and others. Claimant's evidence obviously did not impress the court as cogently as libelant's did, possibly because claimant's had not been accumulated and presented in accordance with recognized scientific criteria for valid testing procedures. In any event, the court said of claimant's evidence:

". . . The likelihood of error or prejudice developing in the course of such interviews would seem to be great, particularly since none of the witnesses of claimant, including both advertising men and doctors, were qualified by education or experience in the taking of formal public opinion surveys." [38]

Thus the psychologist's training in statistics and scientific techniques necessary to validate testing procedures would seem to give him an advantage in certain kinds of expert testimony not necessarily possessed by the businessman or other professional men.

There is currently pending before Chief Judge Gunnar H. Nordbye in the United States District Court for the District of Minnesota an anti-trust suit [39] for treble damages brought by a theatre owner against a number of movie distributors. One of plaintiff's claims is that it should have a position in the movie distribution scheme, a so-called playing position, better than the typical neighborhood theatre. Plaintiff called a psychologist as an expert witness to establish the range and degree of competition between plaintiff and other theatres and to show the drawing power of plaintiff's theatre. In view of the apparent paucity of published material on the actual functioning of the psychologist as an expert witness, it may be valuable to make available both to the legal and psychological professions the testimony of that psychologist.[40]

There is a group of cases which, superficially viewed, might be construed in derogation of psychology's claims to competence to provide expert witnesses. This superficial view, however, yields to precise analysis which shows that these cases turn upon some refined evidential rule, usually concerned with impeachment or character evidence, and properly have no derogatory connotation respecting the psychologist as an expert witness. Typical is *State v. Driver*,[41] where defendant was convicted of an attempt to commit rape upon a girl twelve years old.

When this girl was offered as a witness for the state defendant objected to her competency on the ground that she was a "moral pervert, and not trustworthy." However, she was allowed by the trial court to testify, and defendant attempted to impeach her testimony by evidence from the chief psychologist of the Ohio Bureau of Juvenile Research to the effect that the girl was "a lying moron and unworthy of belief." The West Virginia Supreme Court affirmed the conviction, holding that the trial court's preclusion of this impeachment was proper, thus limiting impeachment of a witness' truth and veracity to the conventional method of showing poor community reputation for those qualities. Whatever is thought of the court's restriction of impeachment to the orthodox method,[42] the decision clearly is not a rejection of the psychologist *per se* as an expert witness; in fact in the same case a physician's testimony was similarly rejected as improper impeachment. In *People v. Villegas*,[43] where defendant was charged with armed robbery, his defense was that he was coerced into participation by his co-defendant who threatened him and menaced him with a gun. Defendant called a witness whom he attempted to qualify as a psychologist. Defendant offered to prove that the psychologist had known defendant for fourteen years and that by reason of her study of psychology she was in a position to testify that defendant's will power was weak, that his physical condition was bad, and that he therefore was without sufficient force to "resist the impulse of this other boy to take him out on these robberies." [44] In affirming the trial court's preclusion of this testimony, the appellate court said simply:

". . . It was both incompetent and immaterial, and she (the psychologist) was entitled only to testify, as she was permitted under the court's ruling to do, concerning the general reputation of appellant (defendant) in the community in which he lived for the traits involved in the offenses charged." [45]

Thus the court was unwilling, as a matter of evidence law, to permit the defendant in a criminal case to do more, in respect of so-called character evidence, than make the conventional showing that he has a good community reputation for the traits involved in the crime charged.[46] There is in the case no necessary deprecation of a psychologist *per se* as an expert witness.

In the well-known case of *United States v. Hiss* [47] the trial judge who presided at the second trial permitted testimony offered by the defense, in an attempt to impeach the credibility of a principal government witness, which did not fall into the conventional impeachment pattern to which the West Virginia court adhered in *State v. Driver*. In the *Hiss* case both a psychiatrist and a psychologist were permitted to testify over government objection that such witness was in their opinion a psychopathic personality.[48] The psychologist who so testified also had the degree of doctor of medicine, but he was from the Harvard Psychological Clinic, had worked for many years in psychology and testified, "I would call myself a psychologist." [49] The brief opinion of the trial court [50] permitting this method of impeachment, and refusing to follow *State v. Driver*, was written in reference to the testimony of the psychiatrist, but the decision to admit the psychiatrist's testimony apparently also settled the question of admissibility of the psychologist's testimony.

The psychologist is discouraged sometimes by what he interprets to be an unduly slow acceptance by the courts of his claim to an expertise which can be helpful in judicial fact ascertainment. He should remember, however, that the conservatism of the law is at least in part dictated by its preoccupation with vital issues of property, liberty and even human life itself, and not academic debate. A certain amount of cultural lag is perhaps inevitable. Until a new technique or device is accepted as accurate and reliable in its own scientific orbit, it can hardly be expected to play a role in disposing of men's property, liberty or lives. And quite reasonably, the accuracy and dependability of the technique or device must appear to the court's satisfaction. When the scientific validity of a new technique or device is accepted as "capable of immediate and accurate determination by resort to easily accessible sources of indisputable accuracy," [51] the courts reasonably may be expected to take judicial notice of such acceptance and permit judicial use of the technique or device unless there is a valid reason for exclusion despite scientific acceptance.[52] The absence of such scientific acceptance does not necessarily mean that the technique or device is untrustworthy. But such absence does mean that the proponent of the technique or device for judicial use must affirmatively establish by evidence the fact of dependability. Thus, when a party calls a psychologist as an expert witness in a domain as to which psychology's expertise does not yet enjoy such scientific acceptance, the burden is on that party to prove that psychology does have pertinent expertise in the field involved.

This is well put in Frye v. United States.[53]

"Just when a scientific principle or discovery crosses the line between the experimental and demonstrable stages is difficult to define. Somewhere in this twilight zone the evidential force of the principle must be recognized, and while courts will go a long way in admitting expert testimony deducted from a well-recognized prin-

91

ciple or discovery, the thing from which the deduction is made must be sufficiently established to have gained general acceptance in the particular field in which it belongs. . . ."[54]

Often courts are willing or even eager to accept so-called amicus curiae briefs from persons or associations not directly involved in the pending litigation who have nevertheless an interest in its adjudication.[55] Psychologists or their professional associations which have an interest in judicially establishing the competence, reliability and trustworthiness of a particular psychological technique or device may from time to time have the occasion to submit such a brief to a court. Naturally the effectiveness of such a brief is dependent upon the thoroughness, accuracy and scholarly quality of the scientific data it marshals in support of its thesis. Such a brief to be effective requires close collaboration between the lawyers and the scientists whose technique or device is involved.

The history of judicial treatment of various scientific devices should give encouragement to scientists inclined to think judicial steps toward acceptances of their wares too desultory. Not long ago courts were rendering decisions of paternity in illegitimacy proceedings against men whose innocence was scientifically established by the exclusory nature of the blood tests. Now, however, the courts are holding that where it is shown that the testing processes were accurate, exclusory results from blood testing must be deemed conclusive.[56] The "drunkometer" may be on its way to judicial acceptance,[57] and the so-called truth serum is making its claims.[58] While the lie detector, in the absence of stipulation for its use, has not yet been accepted by an American appellate court, the judicial attitude toward it may fairly be said to be a friendly one of "waiting to be shown"; in fact, the courts have gone as far in accepting it as its most prominent proponents would have them.[59]

Perhaps, therefore, there is an attitude among scientific men including psychologists too prone to be critical of the courts for their conservatism respecting scientific data and devices, and judicial treatment of the expert witness. Recently a psychiatrist, in reviewing the much-discussed *Psychiatry and the Law*,[60] made certain observations which, though specifically directed to psychiatrists, are not impertinently applied to other professional experts, including some psychologists. He said:

"The authors (*of Psychiatry and the Law*) disapprove of the current legal definition of insanity. It is true that many psychiatrists object to being pinned down to a *yes* or *no* answer. But I think it is a godsend that there are at least some situations where psychiatrists are forced to give a simple answer to a simple question. Social living, with which the law deals, makes this necessary. Instead of the test of the 'irresistible impulse' the authors suggest 'inability to adhere to the right.' This would describe most people as well as most murderers.[61] There is room for critical discussion of the different legal definitions of insanity. But this book is a good example of the unfortunate tendency to emphasize this point as if it were the main trouble with present-day forensic psychiatric usage. Instead of putting their own house in order, psychiatrists like to claim that most, if not all, that is wrong are the legal definitions. Throughout this book the impression is given that the lawyers are backward and psychiatrists progressive. Many lawyers, judges and district attorneys would like to get psychiatric advice and help, as well as treatment, for defendants. Their main trouble is to get psychiatrists in cases where large fees are not available. They have much less difficulty with other medical specialties." [62]

Generalizations are dangerous, and many lawyers including the writer will react to the above criticism with numerous instances they have observed of psychiatrists grappling with problems as difficult and complex as the human mind must face, with a consummate skill and soul-searching conscientiousness and selflessness that is the ideal for professional service. But all professions, including psychology, may well bear in mind the wholesome admonition of the master psychologist:

"The fault, dear Brutus, is not in our stars,
But in ourselves that we are underlings." [63]

Psychologists have often asked the writer questions on a very practical level as to the appropriate method and demeanor of a psychologist called as an expert witness. The varying conditions of judicial administration from place to place in the United States, including the different philosophies, attitudes, temperaments and capacities of trial judges, make generalizations hazardous. The following observations, however, are confidently ventured. The qualified, careful, scholarly psychologist, who sticks to his own field of competence, has nothing to fear in taking the witness stand. Such an expert has no reason to stand in awe of cross examination. If a question can accurately and simply be answered "Yes" or "No," no witness, not even a scientist, should resent judicial insistence that it be so answered. If it cannot fairly be so answered, no reasonable trial judge is going to insist upon such an answer.

The prudent psychologist will, before taking the stand, carefully explain to the lawyer of the party invoking his services what he can and what he cannot honestly state under oath. He will realize that he is not an advocate but a witness. If called by the court as a neutral witness, he will realize that he is even more removed from the spirit of advocacy than when functioning as a partisan witness.[64] He will be candid in acknowledging the degree of certainty with which he holds his opinions. He will recognize that there is no innate excellence in professional jargon, and will clearly explain in words understandable by the non-psychologist the meaning of technical terms. He knows that carefulness and intellectual honesty are as recognizable, and even more important, inside as outside the courtroom. He will be frank to admit the limitations of his specialty or of his own expertise within it.[65] He will realize that his function, however important, is not to decide the case but to contribute what knowledge he can to those who have the burden of decision. However critical of particular lawyers, judges or juries, he will never be scornful of the judicial process. He will be at once, confident but not cock-sure; proud of his profession but humble in his awareness of human limitations.

The psychologist, indeed the scientist generally, may do well to match to a degree the law's conservatism with his own. Perhaps few things are so shocking to the conscience of a liberty-loving people, and therefore inimical to the progressive application of sound scientific principles in the regulation of society, as the serious curtailment of human liberty by applying "scientific" conclusions unsupported by the underlying data, or by drawing in the name of science moral conclusions unwarranted by the realities.[66]

NOTES

1. These occasions were the fourth annual conference of the Minnesota Psychological Association, Minneapolis, May 23, 1952; two addresses sponsored by the Conference of State Psychological Associations at annual meetings of the American Psychological Association, Cleveland, September 6, 1953, and New York City, September 5, 1954; Conference of Administrators of College and University Counseling Programs, Center for Continuation Study, University of Minnesota, November 20, 1953; meeting of the Illinois Psychological Association, Urbana, April 3, 1954.

2. For a psychologist's appraisal of some currently important legal problems faced by his profession and its practitioners, see Wiener, *Some Legislative and Legal Problems of Psychologists*, 8 The American Psychologist 564 (Oct. 1953). For a detailed report of a psychometric study of the case of a notorious murderer who was prosecuted under the Lindbergh Kidnapping Law, 18 U. S. C. § 1201, for kidnapping and killing a family of five, see Smykal and Thorne, *Etiological Studies of Psychopathic Personality: II. Asocial Type*, 7 Journal of Clinical Psychology 299 (1951). Several psychologists as well as psychiatrists apparently appeared as expert witnesses in the federal case, one of them being the author Smykal. *Id.* at 314.

The federal court sentenced defendant to 300 years imprisonment. Later, defendant was prosecuted for murder by California, urged the defense of insanity, but was convicted and sentenced to death. People v. Cook, 39 Cal. 2d 496, 247 P 2d 567 (1952). The opinion of the California court refers to testimony by "psychiatrists" and "alienists" but not "psychologists."

3. See, e.g., Munsterberg, On the Witness Stand (1908, 1923); 3 Wigmore, Evidence § 875, 934, 934a, 935, 997-999a (3d ed. 1940); Eliasberg, *Forensic Psychology*, 19 So. Cal. L. R. 349 (1946); Frank, *Judicial Fact-Finding and Psychology*, 14 Ohio State L. J. 183 1953); Wigmore, The Science of Judicial Proofs, 310-317 (3d ed. 1937); Wigmore, *Professor Muensterberg and The Psychology of Testimony*, 3 Ill. L. R. 399 (1909) (a satiric critique of the ambitious claims for experimental psychology of Hugo Munsterberg, professor of psychology at Harvard, who wrote early in the century. A bibliography of Munsterberg's articles, some of which were reprinted in On the Witness Stand, *supra*, appears in 3 Wigmore, Evidence, § 175, n. 1, p. 368); Hutchins and Slesinger, *Spontaneous Exclamations*, 28 Co. L. R. 432, 439 (1928); Burtt, Legal Psychology, chs. II-VIII (1931); Britt, *The Rules of Evidence—An Empirical Study in Psychology and Law*, 25 Corn. L. Q. 556 (1940); Terman, *Psychology and the Law*, 4 Kans. City L. Rev. 59 (1936).

4. See, e.g., Robinson, Law and the Lawyers (1935); Frank, Law and the Modern Mind (1930); Kennedy, *Psychologism in the Law*, 29 Geo. L. J. 139 (1940); Riesman, *Some Observations on Law and Psychology*, 19 U. Chi. L. Rev. 30 (1951); Watkins, *Jurisprudence and Contemporary Psychology*, 18 N. D. Lawyer 1 (1942); Summary of a Conference on Law and Psychology, 5 Jour. Legal Ed. (1953); Osborn, The Problem of Proof, ch. VI, (2d ed. 1926); McCarty, *Psychology for the Lawyer, passim* (1929);

Britt, *The Lawyer and the Psychologist* 36, Ill. L. Rev. 621 (1942); Vinson, *The Use and Limitations of Clinical Psychology in Studying Alleged Mental Effects of Head Injury,* 31 Tex. L. Rev. 820 (1953).

5. See, e.g., Burtt, Legal Psychology, chs VIII-XIX (1931); Schmideberg, *Psychological Factors Underlying Criminal Behavior,* 37 J. Crim. L. Criminology 458 (1947); Schmidl, *Psychological and Psychiatric Concepts in Criminology,* 37 J. Crim. L. & Criminology 37 (1946).

6. Articles by Rogers, *An Account of Some Psychological Experiments on the Subject of Trade-Mark Infringement,* 18 Mich. L. Rev. 75, 99 (1919), and Eliasberg, *Psychiatric and Psychologic Opinions in Court,* 39 J. Crim. L. & Criminology 152 (1948), touch on the psychologist as an expert witness. The Oct., 1935 issue of Law and Contemporary Problems was devoted to expert evidence, with discussions on medical and psychiatric testimony, criticisms of the adversary use of experts, and other articles. The introductory article is by Rosenthal, *The Development of the Use of Expert Testimony,* 2 Law & Contemp. Prob. 403 (1935).

7. See, e.g., Gradwohl, Legal Medicine, Ch. 31, Forensic Psychiatry, (by Satterfield), esp. 884-887 (1954); McCormick, Evidence § 99-100 (1954); Guttmacher & Weihofen, Psychiatry and the Law, chs. 9-11 (1952); Zilboorg, The Psychology of the Criminal Act and Punishment, ch. 7 (1954); Davidson, Forensic Psychiatry, chs. 15-23 (1952); Bychowski and Curran, *Current Problems in Medico-Legal Testimony,* 37 J. Crim. L. & Criminology 16 (1946); Criminal Responsibility and Psychiatric Expert Testimony, Committee on Psychiatry and Law of the Group for the Advancement of Psychiatry, Rep. No. 26 (1954); Barnes v. Boatmen's Nat. Bank, 348 Mo. 1032, 156 S.W. 2d 597 (1941), presents an interest-

ing consideration of the psychiatrist functioning as
an expert witness on a contingent-fee basis.

8. 3 Wigmore, Evidence 367-368.

9. *Id.* at 639.

10. 39 J. Crim. L. & Criminology 152 (1948).

11. *Id.* at 153.

12. See 35 Minn. L. Rev. 310, 311 (1951); Note
(1943) Wis. L. Rev. 430, 435; note 59, *infra.*

13. State v. Pett, District Court, Carver County,
8th Judicial District, Chaska, Minnesota (1952).

14. The psychologist who testified at the Pett trial
is Dr. William Schofield of the University of Minnesota. He has kindly permitted the writer to quote
verbatim a portion of his manuscript describing his
experience at the trial:

> "During this same trial the writer was asked
> in direct examination for his opinion concerning
> the state of mind of the defendant. As part of this
> opinion, the writer expressed the judgment that
> the defendant was 'not insane.' At this point the
> defense attorney appropriately objected that the
> witness was not qualified to render an opinion as
> to the sanity of the defendant since such opinions
> could only be given by a physician. The judge
> correctly sustained the objection, remarking gra-
> tuitously that while he was not at all sure what
> a psychologist was or could do, he was fully cog-
> nizant that the law of the state specified that
> opinions as to mental illness were the responsi-
> bility of a physician. He then instructed the jury
> to disregard *that portion* of the writer's previous
> statement in which the opinion 'not insane' was
> given.
>
> "This is a particularly pertinent example of a
> common element of courtroom psychology! The
> writer's opinion in response to the question con-

cerning the defendant's mental condition had been a lengthy statement which included observations that the defendant, in handling the various psychological examinations previously described in detail, had demonstrated that he saw the world about him as most people did and that he was capable of responding to it as most people did, that he could comprehend instructions and carry them out accurately, that he was in full command of a superior general intelligence, and that he revealed no gross abnormalities in his thinking processes or emotional responsiveness. It was at the end of these observations that the writer stated the summarizing opinion that the defendant was not suffering psychosis or insanity. In effect, the judge had (with legal correctness) instructed the jury to disregard the expert witness' interpretation of his findings but not the specific factual observations on which that interpretation was based. This little courtroom procedure is not *prima facie* a logical fallacy, and this particular example bears a kinship to the frequent acceptance of the clinical and other data of scientific investigators whose interpretations of the data may be eschewed."

For a psychiatrist's account of the medical evidence in the Pett case, see Michael, *Were the Medical Witnesses in the Robert Pett Case in Fundamental Disagreement?* 20 Hennepin Lawyer 103 (1952). In Minnesota a lay witness may testify as to the mental capacity of a person he has observed after testifying to the facts which he has observed and upon which his opinion is based. Cannady v. Lynch, 27 Minn. 435, 440 (1881); Geraghty v. Kilroy, 103 Minn. 286, 288, 114 N. W. 838 (1908); Johnson v. Hanson 197 Minn. 496, 499, 267 N. W. 486 (1936); Bird v. Johnson 199 Minn. 252, 253-254, 272 N. W. 168 (1937). In Minnesota even a medical witness, at least a general practitioner, whose expert opinion on mental capacity is based upon his observations of the subject, must fully state such observations. Scott v. Hay, 90 Minn. 304, 312, 97 N. W. 106 (1903). *Quaere,* whether the Minnesota Supreme Court today would hold a certified psychologist, or other psychologist professionally regarded as qualified, to be a competent full-fledged expert witness on the issue of mental capacity, if his competency were challenged by objection. *In re* Restoration to Capacity of Masters, 216 Minn. 553, 13 N. W. 2d 487 (1944) was a proceeding on petition for restoration to capacity of a woman who had been adjudged a feeble-minded person. The probate and district courts denied the petition for restoration, but the Supreme Court reversed because the district court had applied against petitioner too strict a rule as to the *quantum* of proof. One of the witnesses called in opposition to the petition was a psychologist. The transcript shows that no objection was made to the competency of his testimony. Of his testimony the Supreme Court said:

"The psychologist . . . was not a graduate physician or psychiatrist and did not claim to be a specialist on questions of insanity. He held a master's degree from the University of Minnesota, where he had majored in educational psychology. For eight years he had been employed by the state as a psychologist for the Bureau of Psychological Service in the Division of Public Institutions, devoting most of his time to conducting tests to determine the intelligence quotient (I.Q.) of persons committed to state institutions as feeble-minded. His qualifications as an expert in this field cannot be questioned. Even laymen are entitled to express in general terms their opinion as to the condition of another's mind, upon a suitable showing that they have had an opportunity to observe the mental characteristics and habits of such other, so as to form a reasonable conclusion or inference from the facts observed. . . .

"The testimony of the psychologist would have been more satisfactory, however, had he recited more fully his observations of (the woman involved) and given more details as to the character and extent of the tests to which he submitted her. Instead of asking details of the witness, counsel was content to ask merely for the witness's *ipse dixit* that (the woman involved) was a feeble-minded individual. Her mental age (M.A.) he said, was ten years and four months, her intelligence quotient (I.Q.) 64.

"The witness, upon direct examination, admitted that (the woman involved) 'seemed to respond quite well' to the tests, and he admitted further, on cross-examination, that while she was on the witness stand she 'did a creditable job on multiplication tables,' and that she corrected counsel when he made a mistake in questioning her. When asked, 'How many witnesses did you ever hear on the witness stand that made a better witness and answered the questions more intelligently than she did,' (the psychologist) replied, 'That is a question, of course, I cannot answer.' In fact the witness declined to take into consideration, in expressing his conclusions, her testimony from and her demeanor upon the witness stand." (Id. at 559-560).

Minnesota now has a certification statute providing for the certification of certain psychologists. Minn. Stat. §§ 148.79-148.86 (1953). There is further statutory recognition of psychologists in Minnesota in that consultation by the commissioner of public welfare with a psychologist as well as with a physician is a pre-requisite to the performance of certain operations upon institutionalized feeble minded and insane persons. Minn. Stat. §§ 256.07, 256.08 (1953).

15. 155 F. 2d 850 (10 Cir. 1946).

16. *Id.* at 852-853.

17. *Id.* at 852.

18. Rule 402.

19. Bratt v. Western Air Lines, 155 F. 2d 850, 853 (10 Cir. 1946).

20. *Id.* at 853-854. It should of course be noted that the last sentence respecting a country doctor and a psychiatrist refers to admissibility and not probative value or weight.

21. *Id.* at 854.

22. McCormick, Evidence (1954).

23. *Id.* at 28-29; see Davis, Administrative Law 466 (1951).

24. 293 Mich. 15, 291 N. W. 205 (1940). See also *In re* Restoration to Capacity of Masters, 216 Minn. 553, 13 N. W. 2d 487 (1944).

25. 293 Mich. 15, 20, 291 N. W. 205 (1940).

26. *Id.* at 22.

27. *Id.* at 23.

28. *Ibid.*

29. *Id.* at 25.

30. In view of this opportunity afforded the defense by the trial court, it appears that from a realistic viewpoint the defense actually had the chance to use the psychologist as an expert except that it was precluded from use of a technique commonly used to adduce expert evidence, namely, the hypothetical question.

31. 293 Mich. 15, 24-25, 291 N.W. 205 (1940); *cf.* Frederick v. Stewart, 172 S.C. 188, 173 S. E. 623 (1934) where the contention was rejected that before a physician could classify a person as a moron he had to be given certain psychological tests by a psychiatrist or a psychologist. 172 S.C. at 194-195. In United States v. Chandler, 72 F. Supp. 230 (D. Mass.

1947), *aff'd,* 171 F. 2d 921 (1st Cir. 1948), *cert. denied,* 336 U. S. 918 (1949), a prosecution for treason, after defendant's counsel made a motion to inquire into the sanity of the defendant on the ground that he was unable to understand the charges against him, the district court ordered defendant transferred to a government hospital for a mental examination. There he was examined by psychiatrists for the government, and by a psychologist for the defense. The opinion states that all the experts testified at length, but the psychologist's testimony is not detailed. 72 F. Supp. at 237. Stemmer v. Kline, 128 N.J. L. 455, 26 A. 2d 489, 684 (1942), was a suit for malpractice resulting in the ruination of a child in its mother's womb caused by X-ray applications. The majority of the court held there was no legal liability for negligently causing harm to an unborn child. Colie, J. while disagreeing with that holding, concurred in reversal of plaintiff's judgment because one of plaintiff's experts based his opinion in part on hearsay. This expert was "a doctor of philosophy with extensive experience in the field of psychology and connections with many institutions handling mental deficients." *Id.* at 460. The opinion analyzes the hearsay problem without distinguishing between this psychologist and a doctor of medicine.

32. 159 N. Y. 400, 54 N. E. 48 (1899).

33. *Id.* at 410-411. See Fox v. Peninsular White Lead & Color Works, 92 Mich. 243, 249 (1892), where a non-physician was allowed to give his observations as to cutaneous diseases resulting from chemicals.

34. 100 Cal. App. 2d 554, 224 P. 2d 21 (1950).

35. 114 F. Supp. 461 (D. Minn. 1953).

36. 21 U. S. C. § 301 *et seq.* (1952).

37. 114 F. Supp. at 462-463. For a discussion of the hearsay problem involved in the testimonial use of public opinion surveys, see 37 Minn. L. Rev. 385 (1953).

38. 114 F. Supp. at 463.

39. Robbinsdale Amusement Co. v. Warner Bros. Pictures Distributing Corp., Civil No. 4584 (4th Division, Minneapolis).

40. There may be a rich vein, not exhausted by this writer, for further research into the possible previous use of psychologists as expert witnesses, in the records of Federal Trade Commission, trade mark and perhaps patent cases. As early as the dawn of this century it was clearly recognized that the resolution of such issues as confusion between marks in trade mark cases could be facilitated by psychological techniques. See Rogers, *The Unwary Purchaser. A Study in the Psychology of Trade Mark Infringement*, 8 Mich. L. Rev. 613 (1910). It may be that behind the general reference to "expert evidence" in appellate opinions in trade mark cases, there are records wherein the experts were psychologists. See Burtt, Legal Psychology, ch XX, p. 424, Trade-Mark Infringement (1931). In Coca-Cola Co. v. Chero-Cola Co., 273 Fed. 755 (App. D.C. 1921), on the issue of whether marks were so similar as to be likely to cause confusion in the public mind or to deceive a purchaser, the court made only a passing reference to the testimony in the opposition proceedings in the Patent Office on application for registration of "Chero-Cola," saying "Nearly 3,000 pages of testimony were taken, and elaborate briefs have been filed. Many decisions by courts in this country and in England are cited, and, besides, we are invited to listen to the teaching of psychology on the subject." (273 Fed. at 756). But we know from Rogers, *An Account of Some Psychological Experiments on the Subject of Trade-Mark Infringement*, 18 Mich. L. Rev. 75 (1919), that elaborate psychological tests were made by an experimental psychologist and submitted to the trade mark examiner in the form of a report by the psychologist, formal proof of the report having been

waived. The report, although objected to, was received, and commented on at length by the examiner. 18 Mich. L. Rev. at 99-103.

41. 88 W. Va. 479, 107 S. E. 189 (1921).

42. Wigmore insisted that *"No judge should ever let a sex-offense charge go to the jury unless the female complainant's social history and mental makeup have been examined and testified to by a qualified physician."* 3 Wigmore, Evidence 460. Is it a significant indication of his thinking that he refers in this connection only to a "qualified physician"?

43. 29 Cal. App. 2d 658, 85 P. 2d 480 (1938).

44. *Id.* at 663.

45. *Ibid.*

46. *Cf.* People v. Jones, 266 P. 2d 38 (Cal. 1954). In that case defendant was charged with lewd acts upon the person of his young niece. At his trial defendant offered the evidence of a psychiatrist that he had examined defendant twice, once without drugs and once with sodium pentathol, and that defendant was not a sexual deviate. The trial court rejected this offer on the ground that it did not constitute proper character evidence. The California Supreme Court, however, held that this testimony should have been admitted as evidence of good character showing defendant's disinclination to this type of crime. See Falknor and Steffen, *Evidence of Character: From the "Crucible of the Community" to the "Couch of the Psychiatrist,"* 102 U. of Pa. L. Rev. 980 (1954).

47. 185 F. 2d 822 (2d Cir. 1950), *cert. denied,* 340 U. S. 948 (1951), *on motion for a new trial,* 107 F. Supp. 128 (S.D. N.Y. 1952), 201 F. 2d 372 (2d Cir. 1953), *cert. denied,* 345 U.S. 942 (1953).

48. Transcript of Record, United States v. Hiss, pp. 2550, 2812.

49. *Id.* at 2800.

50. 88 F. Supp. 559 (S.D.N.Y. 1950).

51. Uniform Rules of Evidence, National Confer-

ence of Commissioners on Uniform State Laws, Rule 9 (2) (d).

52. This paper is not concerned with exclusion of evidence on constitutional or other policy grounds without regard to scientific validity of the evidence, *e.g.*, U.S. Const. Amend. V's provision that no person "shall be compelled in any criminal case to be a witness against himself" or "be deprived of life, liberty, or property, without due process of law," and analogous state provisions. Illustrative cases are State v. Cram, 176 Ore. 577, 160 P. 2d 283 (1945); Rochin v. California, 342 U.S. 165 (1952); see McCormick, *op. cit. supra* note 22, at 264, 298.

53. 293 Fed. 1013 (App. D. C. 1923).

54. *Id.* at 1014. That the law's conservatism in accepting new psychological data, techniques and devices is not without roots in logic and sound policy, see Kennedy, *Psychologism in the Law,* 29 Geo. L. J. 139 (1940); Terman, *Psychology and the Law:* 4 Kansas City, L. Rev. 59 (1936); cf. Britt, *Blood-Grouping Tests and the Law: The Problem of "Cultural Lag,"* 21 Minn. L. Rev. 671, 695 (1937); Britt, *Blood-Grouping Tests and More "Cultural Lag,"* 22 Minn. L. Rev. 836 (1938).

55. See, *e.g.*, Revised Rules, Supreme Court of the United States, Rule 42, Briefs of an Amicus Curiae (effective July 1, 1954).

56. *Compare* Berry v. Chaplin, 74 Cal. App. 2d 652, 169 P. 2d 442 (1946), *with* Jordan v. Mace, 144 Me. 351, 69 A. 2d 670 (1949) and United States *ex rel.* Lee Kum Hoy v. Shaughnessy, 123 F. Supp. 674 (D.C. N. Y. 1954). See McCormick, *op. cit. supra* note 22, at 378-383; 35 Minn. L. Rev. 515 (1951).

57. See Note, *Drunkometer as a Test for Intoxication,* 24 Rocky Mt. L. Rev. 253 (1952); McCormick, *op. cit. supra* note 22, at 375-377.

58. See Dession, Freedman, Donnelly and Redlich, *Drug-Induced Revelation and Criminal Investigation,*

62 Yale L. J. 315 (1953); McCormick, *op. cit. supra* note 22, at 373-375; Note, 23 A. L. R. 2d 1306, 1310 (1952).

59. All American appellate courts called upon to decide the question have held lie detector test results inadmissible in evidence, in the absence of a stipulation between opposing counsel authorizing admission. Frye v. United States, 293 Fed. 1013 (D.C. Cir. 1923); State v. Bohner, 210 Wis. 651, 246 N. W. 314 (1933), 18 Minn. L. Rev. 76; People v. Forte, 279 N. Y. 204, 18 N. E. 2d 31 (1938); People v. Becker, 300 Mich. 562, 2 N. W. 2d 503 (1942); State v. Cole, 354 Mo. 181, 188 S. W. 2d 43 (1945); State v. Lowry, 163 Kan. 622, 185 P. 2d 147 (1947); Boeche v. State, 151 Neb. 368, 37 N. W. 2d 593 (1949); State v. Pusch, 77 N. D. 869, 46 N. W. 2d 508 (1950); People v. Wochnick, 96 Cal. App. 2d 124, 219 P. 2d 70 (1950); Henderson v. State, 94 Okla. Cr. 45, 230 P. 2d 495 (1951). *But cf.* People v. Kenny, 167 Misc. 51, 3 N. Y. S. 2d 348 (County Ct. 1938); see 35 Minn. L. Rev. 310, n. 3. The cases are discussed in a series of A. L. R. Annotations: 34 A. L. R. 147 (1925); 86 A. L. R. 616 (1933); 119 A. L. R. 1200 (1939); 139 A. L. R. 1174 (1942); 23 A. L. R. 2d 1306 (1952). In one of the recent cases, the Minnesota Supreme Court reversed a conviction for arson because the trial court permitted the state to show that defendant had refused to submit to a lie detector test. State v. Kolander, 236 Minn. 209, 52 N. W. 2d 458 (1952). In a careful opinion for the court, Knutson, J. said: "We have no doubt that the lie detector is valuable in investigative work of law enforcement agencies and may frequently lead to confessions or the discovery of facts which may ultimately lead to the solution of many crimes; but we are in accord with the rule that the lie detector has not yet attained such scientific and psychological accuracy, nor its operators such sureness of interpretation of results shown therefrom, as to justify submission

thereof to a jury as evidence of the guilt or innocence of a person accused of a crime." 236 Minn. at 221-222. *Cf.* Tyler v. United States, 193 F. 2d 24 (D. C. Cir. 1951), *cert. denied,* 343 U. S. 908 (1952). Results of a lie detector test have been admitted pursuant to stipulation, which precludes a claim of inadmissibility on appeal, People v. Houser, 85 Cal. App. 2d 686, 193 P. 2d 937 (1948). *Compare* Le Fevre v. State, 242 Wis. 416, 8 N. W. 2d 288 (1943), which ignored a stipulation in excluding results, *with* State v. Lowry, *supra,* which emphasized that no stipulation was involved; see 35 Minn. L. Rev. 311 (1951); (1943) Wis. L. Rev. 430; 23 A. L. R. 2d 1306, 1311 (1952). The writer in recent years has noticed newspaper reports to the effect that trial courts have used lie detector tests for various purposes. See (1943) Wis. L. Rev. 430, 435; McCormick, *op. cit. supra* note 22, at 370, n. 6. Inbau as recently as 1946 seemed to favor admission in evidence of lie detector test results only pursuant to stipulation. Inbau, *The Lie-Detector,* 26 B.U.L. Rev. 264, 271 (1946); *compare* McCormick, *op. cit. supra* note 22, at 371-373, esp. 372, n. 13.

60. By Guttmacher and Weihofen, (1952). For a laudatory appraisal, see Book Review, Hall and Menninger, 38 Iowa L. Rev. 687 (1953).

61. But see Durham v. United States, 214 F. 2d 862 (D.C. Cir. 1954).

62. Wertham, *A Psychiatrist Looks at Psychiatry and the Law,* 3 Buffalo L. Rev. 41, 48-49 (1953).

63. Shakespeare, Julius Caesar, Act 1, sc. ii. That much of the antipathy of the scientist to the judicial process is rooted in confusion resulting from the differing semantics of the scientist and jurist, is a theme pursued in a later installment of this article.

64. One of the most common criticisms of expert testimony, especially medical and psychiatric testimony, is its partisan source and nature. See, *e.g.,* Weihofen, *An Alternative to the Battle of Experts:*

Hospital Examination of Criminal Defendants Before Trial, 2 Law & Contemp. Prop. 419, 420 (1935); Bychowski and Curran, *Current Problems in Medico-Legal Testimony*, 37 J. Crim. L. & Criminology 16, 31 (1946). The writer is not entirely sympathetic with the prevailing view that the use of the so-called neutral or court-appointed expert is a reform which will substantially solve the evils of expert testimony. This view reaches its extremity in Zilboorg, The Psychology of the Criminal Act and Punishment (1954), where the author, a psychiatrist, stated: "The principle of an expert for each side is a corrupting, immoral principle. . . ." *Id.* at 119. So far as this writer knows, no one has satisfactorily demonstrated why the especial competence of the adversary system as a fact-finding device is so vitiated because the subject of inquiry is a scientific question. Too often it is assumed that there is some magic in the mere shifting of responsibility from private hands to state agencies. Yet it must be acknowledged that profound scholarship is behind the movement toward the court-appointed expert, *e.g.*, Morgan, *Suggested Remedy for Obstructions to Expert Testimony by Rules of Evidence*, 10 U. Chi. L. Rev. 285, 293 (1943); 2 Wigmore, Evidence 644 *et seq.*, although it is to be carefully noted that at least Wigmore would not *replace* but only *supplement* partisan expert testimony. *Id.* at 648. See Fed. R. Crim. P. 28; Uniform Rules of Evidence, National Conference of Commissioners on Uniform State Law, Rule 59, both of which provide for court-appointed experts but reserve to the parties the right to call expert witnesses of their own selection. The real reform in this field, it seems to the writer, as in so many other fields of professional activity, is greater integrity by the professional man. But such a reform is at once too simple, and too difficult!

65. "When testifying as an expert witness, a psychologist should make only such statements as he is

qualified to offer on the basis of his professional training and experience, and which he can substantiate by evidence that would be acceptable to recognized specialists in his same field." Principle 1.22-2, Ethical Standards of Psychologists (proposed), American Psychological Association 14 (1953).

66. Illustrative, to this writer, of such unjustified curtailments of liberty essentially in the name of science are the situations presented by Psychopathic Personality of Dittrich, 215 Minn. 234, 9 N. W. 2d 510 (1943) (law-abiding, capable, hard-working farmer, of good moral character, at least so far as his relations with the community were concerned, condemned to indefinite commitment under the psychopathic personality law because of his ardent sexual nature); *In re* Restoration to Capacity of Masters, 216 Minn. 553, 13 N. W. 2d 487 (1944) (mother of ten apparently normal children, two serving in army, committed as feeble-minded and family broken up, apparently essentially because she was thought a sloppy housekeeper; I.Q. fixed at 64 by psychological testing). See Louisell, Book Review, 79 The Scientific Monthly 332 (Nov. 1954).

Since this article went to press, Watson v. State, 273 S.W. 2d 879 (Tex. Cr. App. 1954) has been published, in which a psychologist testified as an expert on the issue of insanity in a murder case. The writer is also informed that *Hidden v. Mutual Life Ins. Co.* (4th Cir. 1954) involved a psychologist as an expert witness, but the opinion is not yet published and has not been seen by the writer. See The Daily Record, Baltimore, Dec. 25, 1954, p. 5.

V

THE PSYCHIATRIC APPROACH TO CRIME AND CORRECTION **

MANFRED S. GUTTMACHER, M.D.
*Chief Medical Officer, Supreme Bench
of Baltimore, Maryland*

The psychiatrist has a peculiarly tolerant attitude toward criminal behavior, which is born out of his recognition of the welter of antisocial impulses occurring in noncriminal individuals. This has been known to wise men throughout the ages. Goethe said, "There is no crime of which I do not deem myself capable." [1]

The psychoanalytic studies of normal individuals have revealed a quantum of aggression and hostility in everyone. Indeed, most persons have sadistic fantasies and murderous dreams. The fascination that newspaper accounts of crime, crime novels, and crime dramas have, for vast numbers of people, is surely dependent, in large measure, upon the ubiquity of antisocial impulses. The ease with which peaceable men can be transformed into relentless warriors is further evidence of this. People do not stop to consider the fact that evolution is a painfully slow process and that the child born in the modern aseptic delivery room is as savagely amoral as that produced by our neolithic progenitors. Indeed, socialization is, in many respects, as marvelous a phenomenon as physical growth itself.

112

The psychiatrist realizes that a psychological differentiation between the neurotic criminal, who heedlessly and persistently risks his freedom to acquire money illicitly, and the miser, who legitimately amasses a fortune and has a monument erected to his memory, may be a very fine one. The pedophile and the revered leader of the boys' club may be close relatives, indeed. The findings of Professor Kinsey's researches, showing the prevalence of deviant and legally-prohibited sexual behavior among all groups of the population,[2] were largely anticipated by psychiatrists. And Sutherland's studies of white-collar crime[3] and surveys like that of Wallerstein and Wyle[4] demonstrate the high incidence of lawlessness that occurs among individuals never convicted of crime and the general acceptance of such practices by large numbers of people.

Prior to the advent of modern dynamic psychiatry, great stress was laid upon heredity. Vague concepts like neuropathic tainting were given prominence. During the early decades of this century, sterilization laws for the mentally defective and certain groups of the insane, as well as for certain classes of criminals, chiefly major recidivists and sex offenders, were passed in many states.[5] With the development of modern psychiatry, however, the pessimistic fatalism toward insanity resulting from the emphasis on the constitution gave way to an over-zealous optimism in regard to the treatment of mental disorders. With it, there has developed an almost total disregard of heredity, since it does not lend itself to therapeutic efforts. Investigations making use of the twin method, by the psychiatrists Johannes Lange on crime,[6] Rosanoff on juvenile delinquency,[7] and Franz Kallmann on mental disorder and homosexuality,[8] have not received the attention among behavioral scientists that they merit. Freud himself did not belittle the role of heredity. He often spoke

113

of the important, though unfathomable role of the constitution in all types of mental disorder. But his method of intensive exploration of the individual, which has held the center of the stage in recent decades, is not suitable for studying the role of heredity.

These matters lead us to consideration of determinism versus free will and to that of criminal responsibility. It is in this area that psychiatrists generally differ most profoundly from members of the legal and correctional disciplines. Some psychiatrists applaud the pronouncement of Ernest Jones, who said, "By accepting the legal view of free will they (doctors) abandon the only fundamental canon of all science." [9] Certainly, everyone who has worked in psychiatry must have been impressed with the vastly unequal opportunities afforded individuals to develop healthy egos. Furthermore, the degree of mental health that the individual possesses bears a direct relationship to the freedom of choice which he is able to exercise. A daily awareness of these facts gives psychiatrists an unusual tolerance for the vagaries of human behavior, whether it be criminal or noncriminal. In psychiatry, one's orientations must, in large measure, be deterministic.

It is surely scientifically unsound to hold that men must be divided into two distinct categories, the responsible and the irresponsible. There must be degrees of responsibility. Yet, as residents of the world of reality, we have to admit that the vast majority of men must be held responsible for their behavior. Even if certain philosophers conclude that man has no freedom of choice, such a construct must be established for practical living, just as the concept that all men are created equal must become an axiom of democratic societies. Apparently in testing the limits to which Freud would go in upholding determinism, he was asked whether a man should be held responsible for his dreams. The master retorted that if the dreamer was not responsible for his dreams, who should be? [10]

Nevertheless, in certain psychiatric groups, it has become a sign of modernity and scientific maturity to go all out for determinism, to believe that man is a helpless victim of his genes and his environment. To subscribe to this is a symbol that one is not dragging one's scientific heels. The more sage leaders of American psychiatry, however, have accepted the fact that man is not without freedom of choice. Professor John Whitehorn, a leading eclectic psychiatrist, wrote in 1953: [11]

> So far as I can see, there exists a range of freedom of choice between different possibilities in conduct or behavior. The range of freedom of choice appears to me to be much narrower than is implied in most of the exhortations to reform by "willpower," and the range of freedom of choice is particularly restricted in the condition that we characterize professionally as illness, but seldom if ever is the range of freedom reduced to zero, as is implied in a strictly deterministic view.

And Franz Alexander, who has been in the forefront of the psychoanalysts who have studied criminal behavior, recently said of the doctrine of strict determinism.[12]

> The basic error in this whole reasoning is that it treats the conscious and unconscious portions of the personality as two completely isolated systems without any intercommunication, like the left hand is not knowing what the right hand is doing. This assumption is contrary to our knowledge. Slips of the tongue and other parapraxias

are committed via our voluntary muscles, yet under the influence of unconscious motives. In such cases behavior is influenced by fully or partially unconscious motivations which infiltrate by various psychodynamic processes into territory otherwise under the control of the conscious ego. The intercommunication between the two systems, conscious and unconscious, however, is a two way traffic. Not only do unconscious processes influence conscious processes, but also conversely conscious processes influence the unconscious. . . . Punishment of careless drivers, even if their accidents are the result of unconscious motives, will increase almost every driver's sense of responsibility and consequently his vigilance over his movements. To eliminate punishment for accidents from traffic laws would undoubtedly result in an increase in accidents.

Although the whole range of behavior falls within the interest of psychiatry, its particular concern is with that behavior which results from mental disorder. There has been no psychiatric study which gives us a true measure of the incidence of psychiatric morbidity in the criminal population. There have, however, been statistical surveys which bear on this point. Dr. Winfred Overholser, while Commissioner of Mental Hygiene in Massachusetts, recorded the findings in the examinations carried out under the Briggs Law over a fourteen-year period, which showed that fifteen percent of those examined were psychiatrically deviated to a significant extent.[13] Bromberg and Thompson analyzed the findings in ten thousand consecutive cases examined in the Psychiatric Clinic of the Court of General Sessions in New York, and they reported significant psychiatric defects in twenty-two per cent of these defendants.[14]

116

Both studies found 1.5 per cent to be psychotic. But in the material for both studies, factors of selection were operative.

It is interesting that three psychiatrists, with extensive experience in criminal psychiatry and with different scientific orientations, entirely independent of one another, have expressed an identical opinion as to the incidence of psychiatric abnormality in the criminal population. The late Sir Norwood East, the very conservative leader of criminal psychiatry in England,[15] Dr. Gregory Zilboorg,[16] a leading psychoanalyst in this country, and the writer of this paper have all indicated that in their opinions, about eighty percent of criminals are psychiatrically normal.

It is noteworthy that Franz Alexander and Hugo Staub in the first edition of their valuable book, *The Criminal, the Judge and the Public,* stated that the number of "normal criminals," the dysocial individuals who have identified with criminal superegos, was small.[17] They were then writing on the basis of their European experience. In the recent new edition, however, after Dr. Alexander had been exposed to American culture for a quarter of a century—and surely it cannot be gainsaid that Chicago was the ideal place for such exposure—he expresses a different opinion: "The prevalence of the latter (normal criminal) group in the United States is beyond question." [18]

Some psychiatrists are loath to accept the view that a large proportion of criminals are not psychiatrically abnormal, particularly the recidivists. When one argues the point, they say, "But surely, nearly all murderers must be sick individuals." It seems to the writer that in dealing with these questions, consideration should be given to statistics on the racial incidence of crime. For example, in 1957, the homicide rate for Negroes compared to whites in Baltimore was eleven times their incidence in the

117

population.[19] I know of no study, however, indicating a greatly higher psychiatric morbidity rate for Negroes than for whites.

II

Both the treatment and the prevention of disease progress haltingly until its pathology is established. In most instances, the great strides must wait upon the discovery of aetiology. As far as crime is concerned, whether it be normal criminality, which is essentially a social disease, or crime dependent on mental morbidity, its pathology is poorly understood and its aetiology is essentially unknown. We find ourselves in a position similar to that of the systematists of the eighteenth century; we must be satisfied largely with description and classification.

One of the greatest difficulties in psychiatry is its esoteric vocabulary. Its special terminology not only makes communications with other disciplines difficult, but its technical terms have varying connotations and, in some instances, even varying denotations for psychiatrists. In the writer's efforts to understand the criminals that he examines, he has grouped them under several categories. But no classification which he has come upon seems adequate. At present, he would suggest the following:

1. The normal criminal, the dysocial group made up of individuals who have identified with the asocial elements in our society, generally with morally and socially defective parental figures. They compose seventy-five to eighty per cent of criminals.

2. The accidental or occasional criminal, the individual with an essentially healthy superego who has become overwhelmed by a special set of circumstances. This is a very small group. On the basis of claims made by offenders and their families, this group would appear to be much larger than it

118

actually is. Nearly every mother whose youthful son becomes involved in criminal behavior asserts that he is a good boy, but the momentary victim of bad associates. On investigation, one generally learns that he had for years been a serious school behavior problem and a well-known client of the juvenile court. The bank officials whom the writer has met in prison all had pretty shady reputations before their convictions.

3. The organically or constitutionally predisposed criminal, forming a disparate group which constitutes a small portion of the total number of criminals and is comprised of numerous subgroups: the intellectually defective, the postencephalitic, the epileptic, the senile deteriorative, the posttraumatic, etc. Of course, the vast majority of persons with these maladies are noncriminal.

The role of head injury in the genesis of antisocial behavior is unclear. The high incidence of head injury in the criminal population is probably related to their general heedlessness resulting in their being accident-prone, rather than being an important causative factor in their delinquency. Why individuals, presumably exposed to identical injurious agents develop varying resultant behavioral patterns is uncertain. The effect is probably dependent on the basic structure of the premorbid personality to a greater degree than on the exact nature and location of the injury.

4. The psychopathic or sociopathic criminal, the individual who is not psychotic (insane), but who indulges in irrational, antisocial behavior, probably resulting from hidden unconscious neurotic conflicts which constitute the driving dynamic force underlying his criminal conduct. This is a complex group, comprising ten to fifteen per cent of criminals. Among them are to be found some of the most malignant and recidivistic offenders. For purposes of exposition, it is desirable to attempt to isolate discrete subgroups

based primarily on behavioral manifestations. Until there is a deeper understanding of the psychopathology and some knowledge of aetiological factors, no really satisfactory subclassification of this important criminal group can be devised.

There is the sociopathic type, described so fully in Hervey Cleckley's *Mask of Sanity*.[20] They have shown evidences of life-long social maladjustment reaching back into early childhood. Dr. Robert Lindner used the very apt phrase, "rebel without a cause," to describe them.[21] They are in conflict with society in all areas. Benjamin Rush, the first psychiatrist in America and one of the signers of the Declaration of Independence, called the condition "anomia," a term derived from the Greek word for lawlessness.[22] He postulated the existence of a congenital defect of the moral sense in conjunction with normal, or even superior, intellectual powers. English writers have designated these individuals "moral imbeciles" or "moral defectives." [23]

They are often very bright, attractive, and superficially ingratiating. But this amiability is a skillful masking of an overwhelming hostility. They are socially irresponsible. Other persons are merely objects to be manipulated for their own hedonistic purposes. Distant goals are sacrificed for immediate expediency. It has been suggested that they possess a peculiar incapacity to conceptualize, particularly in regard to time. They possess no loyalties and are suspicious of others. Indeed, this incapacity for establishing satisfying and meaningful relationships with other individuals is their nuclear defect. This makes psychiatric treatment so difficult, for psychotherapy—to be effective—requires that the patient establish a significant degree of identification with the therapist.

There is no agreement as to the causative factors involved in the development of such a crippling personality deformity. The most plausible hypothesis is

120

that these individuals were deprived of deep and nurturing parental affection during their earliest years of life and that, as children, they instinctively developed, as a defense against this deprivation, an aggressive, insensitive relationship toward other individuals. This lack of early love objects with whom strong identification could be established became the crucial defect in their personality development. Bender maintains that a very critical break in total family identification during the second, third and fourth years may produce the same personality distortion.[24] The same hypothesis has been advanced to account for the development of certain schizophrenic disorders. Indeed, the two conditions have marked similarities.

Sociopaths seemingly do not learn by experience, since despite admonitions and punishments, they continue their same pattern of objectionable conduct. This is one of the characteristics that suggests that their disorder is essentially neurotic, since the repetitive element is constantly present in disturbances that are neurotic in origin. Many of the check forgers, swindlers, and confidence men are recruited from their ranks. Dr. Cleckley maintains that these individuals are no better able to conform to society's demands than are the frankly psychotic and that, therefore, it would be only just to treat them as irresponsible.

Karpman has published important studies on these character disorders.[25] He divides them into primary and symptomatic psychopaths. He finds the latter to be in great preponderance—these are the neurotic characters who act out their basic conflicts against society. Their unbearable tension and anxiety is temporarily abated by their antisocial acts. The smaller group, the primary psychopaths, he terms anethopaths. They are the completely amoral, conscienceless individuals who have a grossly deficient superego development. They seem incapable of developing anxiety, even in their dreams. Karpman cannot find significant psychogenetic factors in the backgrounds of many of the anethopaths. In his opinion, their malfunction, in all probability, is the result of an organic brain defect.

There are, of course, many other types of psychopathic offenders.[26] Among them are the violently aggressive and sadistic criminals. In most instances, they have been subjected to harsh cruelties during their formative years in the guise of parental discipline. Life is for them not a very precious commodity—neither their own nor that of other persons.

Most of the sexual offenders, too, are neurotic criminals. It is believed that their abnormalities generally stem from subtly distorting emotional relationships with parental figures in early life. Both the abnormally seductive mother and the mother who is forbiddingly punitive and suppressive may cripple her son in his sexual development. It is now well-recognized by criminologists that many crimes that appear to be nonsexual in nature originate in psychosexual pathology. The number of offenses of this type is probably far greater than we realize.

There is a subcategory of offenders whose crimes arise from what are known as personality trait disturbances who also belong in the large, heterogeneous group of neurotic offenders. Chief among them are the passive-aggressive personalities. In this group, one finds the unusually passive, long-suffering, and nonprotesting people who occasionally, under apparently slight provocation, explode with volcanic force.

Franz Alexander, again, has written widely and informatively on the group of offenders, originally described by Freud, who engage in antisocial behavior in order to achieve punishment at the hands of the law.[27] These are individuals who are in constant conflict with themselves because of intense guilt feelings over some deeply-buried early-life experience or emotional attitude which is below the level of consciousness. Punishment by the authorities for an offense, which is frequently symbolically related to the source of their guilt, gives them surcease from their relentless self-condemnation. Their crimes are often marked by a clumsy stupidity which makes their apprehension easy and certain. They enjoy peace of mind while under incarceration, which is lacking when living in the community. Doubtless offenders of this type exist, but in this author's experience, they are relatively rare.

The writer has been impressed by another small group of neurotic offenders who appear to court capture by the authorities. These are immature individuals who feel helpless before their own antisocial impulses and compulsions and have a real fear of them. Like the small child who runs to his parents to fix things, they turn to the authorities, feeling that in some magical way, they can help them gain control. This type of reaction is most likely to occur in sex offenders.

Heedlessness, although fundamentally self-destructive in nature, does not necessarily originate from an inner need for punishment. Great segments of the population display an amazing degree of heedlessness in their daily living, which stems from an inability or unwillingness to face issues realistically. In every city, long queues form on the day that old automobile licenses expire, waiting for hours to buy new ones, despite the fact that at the cost of a few pennies, they could have received them well in advance by mail. And one need only consider the number of persons living precariously beyond their means, who lose the many possessions they are purchasing on the installment plan as soon as they are without a job. In professional gambling, the gambler is more likely to lose than to win. Some people are psychologically motivated in their incessant gambling

123

by a need to punish and destroy themselves. But there is little reason to believe that most excessive gamblers are of this type. A more frequent dynamic pattern in the neurotic gambler is his need to triumph over others and to achieve disproportionate and immediate rewards from what he sees as his small investment.

5. The psychotic criminal, the individual whose antisocial behavior is a symptom of his insanity. He suffers from one of the major mental disorders. These insanities are marked by regressive behavior in which the ego is overwhelmed by primitive aggressive drives. These may be directed against himself or against others. As bizarre and as unintelligible as much of insane behavior appears to be, it has an economic utility for the individual. Were we wise enough, its meaning and significance could in every instance be deciphered.

Only one and a half to two per cent of criminals are definitely psychotic. There is, of course, no sharp dividing line between health and disease. At what point the psychological disorganization of the individual reaches sufficient proportions to be designated a psychosis is a matter of judgment. This problem presents its greatest difficulty in cases of short-lived psychosis. There are cases of temporary insanity. Alcoholic deleria and confusional states associated with epilepsy are widely recognized as such. Combat psychiatrists saw men who succumbed under great stress for brief periods successfully mobilize their psychological defenses and rapidly regain their stability.

III

A diagnosis and classification of offenders along such lines is of real value because of its usefulness in disposition. Psychiatrists are unanimous in the

124

belief that disposition must be individualized and that the focus must be on the offender rather than on the offense. They recognize, however, the dilemma to which such an emphasis inevitably leads.

The writer recently asked the Danish psychiatrist, Dr. George Sturup, the very able director of the institution for recidivistic and psychopathic criminals at Herstedvester, for his views on American penology. He said that its two most serious defects were the inequality of sentences and the huge size of our institutions. He did not see how good morale could be effected in a convict given ten years for robbery, when the man in a neighboring cell, convicted of the same offense, was serving a sentence of two years. Admittedly, this is an almost insuperable obstacle. To accept such a disparity in sentences, the criminal must recognize its rationale and its justice. And how rarely can he be made to see this. Psychiatrists would also agree with Dr. Sturup's strictures on the gargantuan proportions of most of our penal institutions. Two decades ago, it was the vogue in the United States to build huge psychiatric hospitals for the purposes of economy and efficiency. But now, the tide is running in the opposite direction. It is felt that in these great hospitals, patients lost their individuality and their ability to identify with the institution to a large degree. Dr. Sturup feels that three hundred inmates is maximum size for efficiency in both psychiatric and penal institutions.

The barren coldness of our great prisons is a manifestation of the basic philosophy behind our whole system of punishment. Its keynotes are fear and deprivation. It has its roots in moralistic and religious principles. Penitentiaries were intended to produce penitence in the wicked, who were kept in complete isolation in order to facilitate the production of this desired state of mind. Pride and vanity were evils that were antipathetic to reformation; hence, the lock-step and the prison stripes. Gluttony was taken care of with bread and water, slothfulness by useless repetitive activity, venery by isolation from sexual objects. Men were to be intimidated from repeating their antisocial behavior by the fear of the jailer's whip and of having to live again in such an environment. The noncriminal members of the community were deterred from wickedness by the fear of being subjected to it. Much of this has survived. There have been certain humane changes, but the basic philosophy has changed very little. Our reportedly mounting crime rate and our undeniably high rate of recidivism gives us reason to pause. How sound is this philosophy? It is perhaps outmoded, as outmoded as the "hell fire and brimstone" religion of old, with its concentration on fear.

The writer does not suggest that it is possible to do away with penal sanctions. For certain individuals, imprisonment undoubtedly has some curative value. There is every reason to believe that such offenses as income tax evasion and illicit gambling would increase tremendously if there were not the possibility of receiving a prison sentence. But, the writer does believe that there is much more faith in the power of the fear of imprisonment than is merited. Moreover, there is, he believes, far more value given to the long sentence as a deterrent than is justified. Surely long sentences are desirable as a means of incapacitating serious criminals whose behavior is unmodifiable, but their value as deterrents is unproven. Many adults, living for the moment, are almost as incapable as the child in conceptualizing long periods of time, and criminals are generally recruited from their ranks. Persons most likely to be particularly impressed by the threat of prolonged imprisonment are not likely to be involved in criminal behavior.

The sole value of long sentences lies in the isolation of criminals from the community thereby effected.

126

There is a tendency on the part of seriously aggressive criminals to become less dangerous with advancing years. Crimes of aggression are essentially crimes of youth. Whether the beneficial change with the years is attributable to the natural loss of restless energy that marks aging or results from a retarded emotional maturing, which some believe characteristic of delinquents, is uncertain. The improvement in the conduct of the young delinquent after a long prison sentence, however, is probably a natural phenomenon rather than a specific response to his incarceration, which rather tends in many cases primarily to increase his resentment toward society.

If there is any common denominator for the minds of criminals, it is their inability to face reality squarely and their ability to rationalize. The feeling that "in some magical way, I'll get away with it; I won't get caught this time," pervades their thinking. But, perhaps, this is not so unrealistic, after all, when one realizes that only one-fourth of major crimes reported to the police are followed by convictions. Cesare Beccaria's emphasis, two centuries ago, on the deterrent effects of certainty of capture and certainty of conviction,[28] is as sound today as it was then. The deterrent effect of greatly improved law enforcement has been too little appreciated.

One of the main purposes of the law—perhaps its chief one—is to create a sense of security in individuals, to give them peace of mind. In criminal law, this is achieved by the conviction of the offender. Certainly, the need for vengeance still exists. It springs from the reflex response toward retaliation when one is struck and the unconscious realization by the conformist of how he has sacrificed to restrain his own asocial impulses. This is the chief demand made of him by the process of socialization. In order to continue his sacrifices, he demands expiation from violators.

127

There is, however, no justification in the law's pandering to the primitive demands of the mob when it cruelly cries for blood. This weakens rather than strengthens the individual's sense of security.

Psychiatrists would temper and, as far as is practical, replace the negative pattern of fear and repression which has dominated penology with the positive approach of treatment. This would have as its chief goal the production of insight in the convict —that is, an effective knowledge of oneself—an essential to real self-mastery. It would also aim to give him direction and guidance. This would necessitate a radical revision of prison ideology. As Franz Alexander has recently put it.[29]

> One cannot apply successfully all three penological principles at the same time—retaliation, intimidation, and reconstruction—as is done at present in our institutions. . . . One cannot make the prisoner hate his authorities, fear them and at the same time expect the prisoner to trust them and accept from them advice and guidance.

For the first and by far the largest group of offenders in our classification—the normal criminals— chief hope for reformation for those who are incarcerated must lie in the general rehabilitative forces of the institution. Psychiatric institutions make great use of occupational therapy. Constructive work-therapy and industrial training should play a vital role in prisons. Moving coal from one end of the jail yard to the other in wheelbarrows is surely no great improvement over the penitentiary treadmills of the eighteenth century. The commitment of a passive, motiveless, borderline mental defective to a penal institution for six months, because he has failed to work to support his family, and then forcing him to remain idle the whole time is a stupid mockery.

128

Of the special therapies, group psychotherapy for selected normal criminals should prove to be of great value. It was found to be successful in the Army Rehabilitation Centers during the war. In group psychotherapy, ten to twelve individuals meet under a professionally-trained leader, whose role is chiefly that of catalyst, and a great variety of topics are brought upon spontaneously for discussion. Ventilation of gripes and grievances against society and the institution is encouraged. The chief value in this therapy, particularly for delinquents, is the social judgment of one's peers. The offender feels that judges, wardens and other official big-shots do not belong in his world, their condemnations seem hollow. But when fellow prisoners condemn him for his attitudes and his behavior, it carries a powerful impact.

The second group—the occasional or accidental criminals—makes ideal probation material. It is often necessary to enlist the help of community social agencies in his cause.

The third group—the organically or constitutionally predisposed criminals—is disparate, and the treatment of its members must be based primarily on the causative factor involved. The role of intellectual deficiency as a primary crime factor is now given far less importance than formerly. Some investigators maintain that the intellectual level of the criminal population is not below that of the general population. There is, however, a small group of recidivists living in urban centers who are ill-equipped to compete legitimately with normal persons because of their deficiency. They are more likely to have a high nuisance value than to be dangerous. They adjust admirably in a farm-type prison colony. Most of the senile-deteriorative group have been involved in sex offenses with children. This may come as a very early manifestation of their organic deterioration. Even though it may be difficult to prove that they are irresponsible under the *M'Naghten* rules,[30] they belong in a mental hospital, rather than in a penal institution. If they have family members with a sense of social responsibility, it is often possible to keep them at home under strict surveillance.

The fourth group—the psychopathic or sociopathic criminals—presents the most difficult treatment challenge. Many of them are inveterate recidivists, no matter how they have been dealt with during incarceration. Although most of them accept the realities of the prison situation and adjust to it, there is a small nucleus that forms the most difficult disciplinary segment of the prison population. The legal disposition of the psychopath is at present in a state of confusion. There is a growing tendency on the part of the law to isolate them from the general stream of criminals, recognizing that although they are not committable as insane, they are mentally and emotionally abnormal. Half of the states now have sexual psychopath statutes,[31] some of them providing for commitment to a psychiatric hospital. Many hospital administrators, however, are opposed to having psychopathic offenders sent to their institutions. They present a difficult custodial problem and are very recalcitrant to treatment.

They occasion special confusion in the District of Columbia, which employs as the test of criminal responsibility the *Durham* rule,[32] which states that if the defendant has a mental disease and his alleged criminal act is a product of it, he is insane. There is disagreement among psychiatrists, however, as to whether psychopathy should be considered a mental disease or merely a character deformity. The Royal Commission on Capital Punishment and the tentative draft of the Model Penal Code of the American Law Institute, both attempt specifically to exclude psychopathy as a cause of criminal irresponsibility.[33] Yet, under the standard system of classification of the American Psychiatric Association, this is one of the subgroups under "Mental Disorders." [34] The distinction between mental disease and mental disorder offers a real problem for semantic specialists.

Maryland now handles this problem in a rather unique way. Instead of a special sexual psychopath statute, it has enacted a defective delinquent statute, which is broader in scope.[35] It seemed to the writer and other members of the commission which drafted this statute, wise to consider all the emotionally-maladjusted criminals as a unit, rather than to isolate only those guilty of sexual offenses. The statute specifies that the intellectually-defective and the emotionally-unbalanced criminals who have demonstrated a propensity to become involved in criminal behavior which is dangerous to society and who are not insane may, upon conviction and sentencing, be sent to the Patuxent Institution. There, they are carefully studied by psychological and psychiatric techniques to determine whether, in the opinion of the professional staff of the Institution, which is directed by a psychiatrist, they should be diagnosed as defective delinquents. If the decision is affirmative, their counsel may seek independent psychiatric opinion at the expense of the state. The issue of defective delinquency is then tried before the court as a civil issue. If a defendant is found to be a defective delinquent, the original sentence is revoked and he is indeterminately committed to the Patuxent Institution. There, he is given specialized treatment which emphasizes group psychotherapeutic techniques, although individual therapy and other methods of treatment are also employed. If and when the institutional Board of Review feels that he is ready to live outside of the Institution, he is released on a probationary status. During this period, he continues to see a psychiatrist regularly. Whenever possible, he continues treatment under the therapist who worked with him in the Institution.

Maryland's defective delinquent statute gives recognition to several salient realities: there are degrees of responsibility and abnormality, and not just the sane and insane; certain offenders are impelled to carry out antisocial acts because of mental abnormality which does not meet the criteria of psychosis or legal insanity; these individuals can be most effectively treated in a special type of institution which has the salutary features of a hospital and the necessary features of a penal institution; and, above all, the cornerstone of the criminal law is the protection of society.

Of course, some of those committed to such an institution will have to remain incarcerated for a very long period—in some instances, for life. Under the ordinary determinate sentence, one is often forced to release men with malignant characterological defects, who, one knows, will soon again be involved in dangerous crime. Many of the defective delinquents have personality traits which render their treatment very difficult; chief among these are: basic distrust of everyone, an incapacity for establishing meaningful relations with others, and a need for immediate gratification of impulses. Yet, Alexander, who has had wide experience in dealing with these patients and is an outstanding therapist, considers the neurotic character to be closer than the ordinary psychoneurotic patient to the normal individual and favorable material for therapy.[36]

The fifth group—the psychotic criminals—presents no real difficulty as to disposition. They are sent to the criminal division of state psychiatric hospitals for appropriate psychiatric treatment. In passing, however, the writer might observe that invariably this is the most unattractive, ill-equipped, and poorly-staffed division of our state psychiatric hospitals.

132

The method of commitment of these psychotic offenders varies greatly. Because of the general dissatisfaction with the *M'Naghten* rules of responsibility found among psychiatrists as well as among many leaders of the bench and bar, and in order to prevent the injustices these rules may occasion, there is a growing tendency in this country and in England to commit summarily to hospitals even mildly psychotic defendants and never to bring them to criminal trial. Although this is, in many respects, desirable, it is not wholly unobjectionable. This procedure automatically stops the investigative efforts of the police. And although it results in sending a psychotic person to the hospital, there may be no real certainty that he was the perpetrator of the particular crime. A complete trial of the issue involved, therefore, gives the public a greater feeling of security that open-handed justice has been done. Moreover, there are some psychotic offenders, particularly those who are paranoid, who prefer to have their day in open court and are more easily handled during their hospitalization if they have had it. Of course, no one would advocate the mockery of subjecting a grossly insane defendant to a criminal trial.

IV

There are certain principles in regard to the treatment of criminals upon which there would be general agreement among psychiatrists. The value of prevention over treatment of criminality would be emphasized. Criminals rarely come from homes in which there was strong parental affection and kindly, consistent discipline. Loyalty to a cohesive family group, in which there was clearly present the attitude of one for all and all for one, is a powerful force against delinquent behavior. Combatting the great social scourges of poverty, overpopulation, and social and job inequality are necessary steps in crime prevention. A school system with special facilities for diagnosing and efficiently handling children with learning and behavioral difficulties is essential. Adequate recreational facilities in urban areas, so that children can dissipate their energies in constructive rather than destructive activities is of proven value. The role of crime and horror programs, presented through mass media, in the production of juvenile delinquency is, as yet, unknown. That it might be great must be admitted; but this is far from proven. It offers an important subject for carefully controlled research. Whether the down-graded valuation of human life and the insecurity that comes with wars and the concentration on weapons of destruction are responsible for the reported increase in violent crimes committed by youth today is also a significant subject for study.

Juvenile courts should have adequately-staffed psychiatric clinics attached to them for the purposes of diagnosis and the treatment of selected cases. Juvenile court judges should be specialists, trained in the behavioral sciences. Probation officers should have special training and should have case loads sufficiently small to permit them to work intensively with the delinquents and their families. Training schools for delinquents should be small, with large, competent staffs trained in group therapy. All communities should have access to special psychiatric institutions for the care and treatment of children who are severely disturbed emotionally.

Adult criminal courts should have psychiatric clinics attached to them, so that sentencing judges can have the benefit of psychiatric and psychological studies in selected cases before disposition. The focus of such reports must be on the basic character structure of the defendant, with special attention directed toward his treatability and the social threat afforded by his release into the community. Pre-empting judicial functions must be sedulously avoided. The preservation of the "father figure," wisely and justly punishing transgressors, is worthy of preservation by society. The clinic report should not deal with the guilt or innocence, the general deterrent effect on community members of the punishment of the defendant, nor the attention to be paid to the demands of the community for retaliation. As yet, the psychological disciplines have no definitive knowledge to contribute on these issues, and they are best left solely to the discretion of judicial authority.

Probation and parole officers should have special training in social case-work techniques. Several of the larger communities are now offering didactic courses and seminars in psychology and psychiatry for probation officers.

As far as this writer knows, there are, as yet, no psychiatric out-patient departments specifically designed for treating defendants while on probation. Were there such a facility, it would be possible to recommend probation in certain cases in which this is now not practical. As a rule, hospital out-patient departments will treat these patients, but they are, to a certain extent, stigmatized and are not eagerly welcomed. Moreover, attendance in nearly all clinics must take place during the week's working hours, which may seriously interfere with the work adjustment of these individuals, who are already laboring under a handicap. A clinic to treat probationers successfully must operate during evening hours. Moreover, junior residents and the advanced students, who generally form the nucleus of out-patient therapists, are not equipped to minister to such patients. They are difficult to treat and require skilled and experienced therapists for both individual and group psychotherapy. To obtain the maximum number of successes in treatment, it would be necessary to employ spe-

135

cially-equipped probation officers as the clinic staff social workers. Selection of probationers for out-patient psychotherapy would be limited to those cases which the psychiatrist, advising the court on disposition, considered favorable treatment prospects.

In regard to the treatment of individuals incarcerated in penal institutions, psychiatry would emphasize individualization. Attempts over the years to crush the rebellious spirit by lock-step, prison uniforms, prohibition of personal decorations in cells, referring to inmates by number, etc., have apparently failed. The building of huge institutions is in line with this policy. To be sure, they can be more economically run. But, if it be true that their size offers an obstacle to their primary objective—rehabilitation—their economy of operation would prove to be illusory. It is our experience that most criminals have marked feelings of inferiority, and building up their self-image rather than tearing it down further seems the desirable goal in the vast majority of cases.

Needless to say, there is need of intensive psychological and psychiatric study of prisoners after they have entered the prison system, so that they can be assigned to the proper facilities to meet their specific needs. Literacy training and physical rehabilitation are to be taken for granted. Those with aptitudes for acquiring special industrial skills should be given instructions. The success in this area achieved at Walkill Prison in New York is noteworthy.

Certain prisoners should be chosen for special training in group living. This has been highly developed by Dr. George Sturup in the institution for serious offenders at Herstedvester, Denmark. There, the less than two hundred inmates are divided into groups of fifteen to twenty. Each individual group lives in the same dormitory, works in the same shop, and eats together in the small dining room. The group has its own custodial officers. Group therapy sessions are held daily. There develops mutually sustained pressure by members of the group toward social conformity during twenty-four hours of the day. Hedonism gives way gradually to communalism.

Undoubtedly, behavior scientists would advocate the use of indeterminate sentences as far as is practical. No individual can be gifted with divine prescience. The value of the indeterminate sentence is, in large measure, dependent upon an accurate determination by institutional staffs and releasing authorities of the prisoner's adjustment and changes in attitude during his incarceration. That an acceptable degree of excellence by these staff personnel is seldom available must be admitted.

Radical treatment methods of criminals have been tried sporadically. The reports of the few lobotomies performed have not been favorable. Electroshock has also been used, but with no lasting benefits reported. Even on theoretical grounds, improvement could be hoped for only with the use of intensive electroshock therapy, necessitating the use of a great number of treatments given in close succession. This has been used in treating schizophrenia. It produces a temporary regression of the individual to an infantile level with incontinence, almost complete loss of memory, etc. It is not without danger of permanent brain damage. According to its advocates, it breaks up old thought patterns and facilitates the creation of new attitudes. Hypnotherapy has also been used in treating criminals. Its value lies not so much in the creation of new, powerfully suggested modes of behavior, as in uncovering the basic dynamics behind the criminal acts of certain character neurotics.

Tranquilizing drugs are being rather widely tried. They are of great value in the handling of certain tense, restless, and rebellious prisoners. It also often makes them more receptive to group therapy and individual psychotherapy when they are available.

Castration has been employed in Europe for decades in the treatment of sexual offenders.[37] Many of the reports have been very favorable. The general attitude among medical and legal leaders in this country, however, is that it is cruel and inhumane punishment. Furthermore, scientific objection has been registered against it on theoretical grounds. If sex offenses are the response of character neurotics to deep-seated conflicts, removal of the gonads should not cure them, but rather lead to their expression through different channels. One must admit, however, that our knowledge of sexual pathology is as yet very uncertain. But to the writer, it seems unwise to shut our minds completely to the possible good that may result from the use of castration in the rare and very cautiously selected case. Perhaps it is, after all, more humane than permanent incarceration for the dangerous recidivistic sex offender.

NOTES

** Reprinted from a symposium, *Crime and Correction,* by permission, from Law and Contemporary Problems, published by the Duke University School of Law, Durham, North Carolina, Copyright, 1958 by Duke University.

1. See Theodor Reik, The Unknown Murderer 45 (Jones transl. 1945)

2. Alfred C. Kinsey, Wardwell B. Pomeroy, and Clyde E. Martin, Sexual Behavior in the Human Male (1948); Alfred C. Kinsey Et Al., Sexual Behavior in the Human Female (1953).

3. Edwin H. Sutherland, White Collar Crime (1949).

4. Wallerstein & Wyle, Our Law-Abiding Law-Breakers, 25 Probation 107 (1947).

5. Cf. e.g., Buck v. Bell, 274 U. S. 200 (1927); Skinner v. Oklahoma, 316 U. S. 535 (1942).

6. Johannes Lange, Crime and Destiny (1930).

7. A. J. Rosanoff, L. M. Handy, & I. A. Rosanoff, *Criminality and Delinquency in Twins,* 24 J. Crim. L. & Criminology 923 (1934).

8. Kallmann, *Genetics of Psychoses: An Analysis of 1,232 Twin Index Families,* 2 Am. J. Human Genetics 385 (1950) *Twin and Sibship Study of Overt Male Homosexuality,* 4 *id.* at 136 (1952).

9. Quoted in Szass, *Some Observations on the Relationship between Psychiatry and Law,* 175 *Archives Neurology and Psychiatry* 299 (1956).

10. Unpublished lecture of Dr. Gregory Zilboorg.

11. John Whitehorn, in *Psychiatry and the Law*, 1953 Proceedings of the American Psychopathological Association 153 (1955).

12. Franz Alexander & Hugo Staub, The Criminal, The Judge, and the Public 129 (rev. ed. 1956).

13. Overholser, *The Briggs Law of Massachusetts*, 25 J. Crim. L. & Criminology 859 (1935).

14. Bromberg & Thompson, *Relation of Psychosis, Mental Defect and Personality to Crime*, 28 id. at 70 (1937).

15. Norwood East (Ed.), The Roots of Crime 44 (1954).

16. Gregory Zilboorg, The Psychology of the Criminal Act and Punishment 43 (1954).

17. Franz Alexander & Hugo Staub, The Criminal, The Judge, and the Public 209 (1931).

18. Franz Alexander & Hugo Staub, The Criminal, The Judge, and the Public 11 (rev. ed. 1956).

19. Department of Post Mortem Examiners of Maryland, 18th Ann. Rep. 30 (1957).

20. Hervey Cleckley, The Mask of Sanity (3d ed. 1955).

21. See Robert M. Lindner, Rebel Without a Cause (1944).

22. See J. C. Bucknill & D. H. Tuke, A Manual of Psychological Medicine (1858).

23. See J. C. Pritchard, Treatise on Insanity (1835); Curran, *A Psychiatric Approach to the Offender*, In East (Ed.), *op. cit. supra* note 15, at 27, 39.

24. Bender, *Psychopathic Behavior Disorders in Children*, in Robert M. Lindner & Robert V. Seliger (Eds.), Handbook of Correctional Psychology 360, 362 (1947).

25. Karpman, The Myth of the Psychopathic Personality, 104 Am. J. Psychiatry 523.

26. See Guttmacher, *Diagnosis and Etiology of*

140

Psychopathic Personalities as Perceived in Our Time,
in Current Problems in Psychiatric Diagnosis 139
(1953).

27. Franz Alexander, Fundamentals of Psychoanalysis 238 (1948); 4 Sigmund Freud, Collected
Papers 342 (1949).

28. Cesare Bonesana Beccaria, An Essay on Crime
and Punishment 73, 93 (W. C. Little ed. 1872).

29. Franz Alexander & Hugo Staub, The Criminal,
The Judge, and the Public 239 (rev. ed. 1956).

30. See M'Naghten's Case, 10 Clark & F. 200;
8 Eng. Rep. 718 (1843).

31. For more detailed discussion of these statutes,
see Comment, *Use of the Indeterminate Sentence in
Crime Prevention and Rehabilitation.* 7 Duke L. J.
65, 72-80 (1958).

32. See Durham v. United States, 214 F. 2d 862
(D.C. Cir. 1954).

33. Royal Comm'n on Capital Punishment, Report
139 (1953); Model Penal Code 160 (Tent. Draft No.
4, 1955).

34. Am. Psychiatric Ass'n, Diagnostic and Statistical Manual 85 (1952).

35. Md. Ann. Code art. 31 B, §§1 *et seq.* (Supp.
1957). For general discussion of these statutes, see
Comment, *supra* note 32, at 80-85.

36. Franz Alexander & Hugo Staub, The Criminal,
The Judge, and the Public 102 (rev. ed. 1956).

37. See M. S. Guttmacher, Sex Offenses 105
(1951).

VI

JUSTICE AS A PSYCHOLOGICAL PROBLEM

Joost A. M. Meerloo, M.D.

One of my most astonishing experiences as a prisoner of the Nazis during World War II was observing the appeal made by both prisoners *and* jailors to the abstract principle of "justice." The masters of the torture chamber spoke more about their "sacred rights"—justifying their crimes with various mythical theories, than the victims themselves. But a fog of justifications, mixed with fear and anger, kept both persecutors *and* persecuted far from any objective viewing of facts. The same basic human drives and desires were operating in both. The only difference was that one group was in power and the other was not.

This confusing and contrasting appeal to "justice," I believe, is one of the outstanding psychological and psychiatric problems of our times.

The psychologist, and especially the psychotherapist who treats so many feelings of guilt and so many raging complaints about unfairness and *in*justice, looks upon "justice" in a way far different from that of a lawyer. Although most lawyers consider law as being founded on a general sense of justice, few are aware of the subjective and psychological origins of common man's feeling of what justice is. The lawyer's study is devoted to the growing aggregate of the law and to the definition of its rules and limits. The psychologist studies man's subjective and instinctive reactions to law. He inquires into the origin, extent and operation of individual and group attitudes toward justice and injustice, and investigates the ways in which these attitudes influence actions.

Most human beings have very strong feelings about "what's right" and "what's wrong," but the application of such judgments is usually made not to the way man, himself, behaves toward other people, but to the way he feels about the way people behave toward him. He is continually asking himself whether he is being treated justly or unjustly.

As a newborn infant, man is outraged at being suddenly exposed to a cold world where air, warmth and food are necessities to be conquered instead of passively absorbed as they were in the womblike state, and he carries a residue of this outrage throughout his life. From early childhood, he battles nagging feelings of injustice, reacting with horror, outrage, anxiety, shock and resentment to the way the outside world is handling him.

If life has not beaten him too much into submission, he will fight to protect himself against injustice, be it real or imagined. Injustice may invoke in him a spirit of indignation and revolt, and he may envision a theoretical righteous world in which injustice does not exist. Usually, however, the man who complains most about injustice and unfairness has only a vague notion of what justice, in terms of the law, really is.

What is "justice"? Only a legal code of mutual behavior? Only a variation of the Golden Rule: "Don't do unto others what you do not want others to do unto you"? Is it merely a nostalgic yearning for the security of the womb? Or is it a psychological trick of man's conscience turning irritation and hostility about bad treatment into utopian ideal?

The word "justice" has appeared on many banners through the ages, democrat and antidemocrat alike. Every country on earth has used an appeal for "justice" when going to war. Even the criminal sees his criminal acts as being "justified." Nearly everybody strangely enough, believes justice to be on his side.

It is tragic that man's deeply rooted need for moral and legal evaluation at the same time bears in itself the germ of such bitter confusion, contrast and conflict.

THE COMPLEXITY OF THE FEELING OF JUSTICE

How does man's conception of justice develop? It is rooted, first of all, in man's basic biological instincts and needs. Unlike the animals, man—eternal baby and erect-walking animal—is utterly dependent on environmental and parental care. He needs to be fed. He needs warmth; affection. His first awareness of the existence of *in*justice in the world comes from infantile feelings of deprivation; a recognition of all the frustrations inherent in merely being human. His first strivings for law and justice are in the nature of collaborative efforts with others to eliminate some of these deprivations and frustrations. Yet, the child in each of us still expects *automatic justice,* a spontaneous gratification of its feeling of *unfairness.*

Among primitive peoples, the feeling of justice is a typically collective feeling, experienced only as a group. It is usually some threat to the tribe or tribal habits which leads to defensive or corrective action. Even in the animal world there exist strange "penal sanctions" against those not conforming with customary ways of the herd. Chickens, for instance, after an initial fight for power, stick to a rather constant pecking order. In certain flocks, weak animals are not allowed to suck or pick at all but are thrown out in order to die.

So-called "customary law" which Greek philosophers defined as a "universal true law," ingrained in man by nature, has its origin in the primitive concept of inviolable tribal laws. Members of the community are usually expected to live by a set of rigid rules as having been given by a tribal god. At first, convention and custom, mores and traditions have the function of keeping the individual members within the proper bounds. Out of these habits or mores grow primitive morals, consisting of a mixture of practical customs and sacred rules. This is the usual way that in each social formation a kind of consistent code develops which we call customary laws.

Rigid customary law is often a dangerous stumbling block to the development of newer and better rules of mutual accommodation. In this primitive idea of justice, it is not only the individual who sins against the code of the collectivity who is punished. The person who attempts to raise the level of the group and speed up the evolution of collective thinking is also warded off by rules of law. On the whole, man has an instinctive reaction against accepting any novelty which might change his acquired pattern of behavior, and habit and tradition can become the great justifiers of all evil. In the summer of 1957, I made a trip to Far Eastern countries to study discrimination in cultures where age-old prejudice against people was practiced. Most interesting were the various explanations given by the pariahs to justify their own inferior position in the community. Some of these minority groups accepted their menial position without protest, viewing it as a punishment for some ancestral sin in which the transgression of sexual taboos played an important role. Dependent man, in short, grows accustomed to everything, and even slavery may come to be felt as an agreeable condition. At the time when slavery prevailed, the slave himself agreed with its ethical justification as

145

long as no glimmer of a new law or a new outlook on human relations reached him.

Even now, a primitive fear of change prevents people from breaking sacred customs or from violating taboos. Man is afraid that the security of the social formation may be broken; that supernatural protectors may be sinned against. In many primitive societies, those who sin against the archaic traditional feelings of the community are subjected to a sacramental ordeal in which the tribal god is called upon to judge the innocence or guilt of the accused. The ability to walk unharmed through fire or to survive after being thrown hand-tied into a river are considered tests as to whether or not the gods are willing to protect the accused and judge him innocent.

Thus, in the first development of justice, the feeling is determined by various traditions of the group to which a man belongs—family, tribe, class, nation. Individuality is suppressed for the sake of collective security and collective tradition. There are, however, many confusing, ambivalent feelings caused by this necessary choice between self-protecting egocentricity and social responsibility and conformity. We will have a sharper view of these ambivalent feelings in the chapters to come.

Collective security requires that codes come to prevail by which individual drives and desires are curtailed and controlled. This is what the ancient philosophers called the law of *commutative justice,* regulating the relations and exchanges between individuals with the goal of giving man freedom from the risk of interpersonal aggression. When this form of protective law and justice ceases to operate, deep feelings of fear may take hold of people, as happens, for instance, during a revolution or war. I became keenly aware of the common legal needs of people through my experiences in the caps of exiles and dis-

146

placed persons during and after World War II. Most of these people sought immediately to establish a set of rules for everybody to obey, although soon they were involved in the usual legal squabbles about interpretation of these self-made laws. It is through the strict form of law that man tries to make social order a reality and to escape the danger inherent in human arbitrariness.

A system of rules of law, however, strives for more than prosaic relief from inter-human risk and fear. It aspires also to become a growing and expanding institution, a law of so-called "distributive" justice regulating the relationship between the social formation and its individual members with a view toward establishing a consistent harmonious agreement to eliminate future clashes. Soberly speaking, this urge for human harmony and higher justice may again be described psychologically as a mutual agreement to curb the destructiveness and egotism of the individual. It is a kind of barter in which man abstains from vengeance and aggression against his fellows hoping that he will gain affection and appreciation from them in return.

During the period of mental development in which the mind of man liberated itself from its sacred theocratic bonds, still another notion of justice developed. Justice here implies a higher aspiration to social and moral perfection; of man living in a more reasonable society. In this so-called *normative* phase of development, right and justice are seen as absolute values, born out of a rigid structure of the human mind. Justice is no longer viewed as mere protection against mutual fear, or merely serving the establishment of security and peace. Now the idea is created that something of higher value, so-called "sacred rights" are at stake. The Declaration of Independence speaks of the unalienable "rights" with which all men are

147

endowed by their Creator, among which are predominant, "Life, liberty and the pursuit of happiness."

There exists an intermediate phase in which religious sanctification is bestowed upon existing mores and customs. The idea of justice is linked to the command of God or other sanctified parental images as, for instance, in the Ten Commandments. According to the Old Testament, Justice comes from God who taught men to live in peace; righteous deeds come from sinful man who, by striving to serve God, strives to serve his fellows. A more modern expression of the same idea would be: justice is a natural sense dormant in man. He gradually becomes aware of it by the Grace of God.

A peculiar paradox may arise, however, when an ideological delusion of justice takes obsessive possession of man. A distorted paranoiac sense of justice, often merely a tricky defense against inner feelings of injustice makes people act destructively and unjustly. Such delusions of justice make us better understand the malicious actions of inquisitions from the Middle Ages and the murderous crimes of the S.S. men in Nazi Germany.

It thus appears that among the various notions of justice and injustice, the following aspects may be distinguished paralleling the growth of the human mind: a collective or magic aspect; an individualistic or subjective aspect and a normative or so-called objective aspect. We will discuss each of these aspects further in the chapters to come.

The Collective or "Magic" Aspect of Justice

The collective aspect of justice claims guarantees, first of all, for the cohesion and maintenance of the collectivity; the community goal is to maintain customs and to perpetuate the cohesion of the group. The various concepts of mankind's common fate influence such *natural law*, in which law means an approximation of reasonable mutual adjustment. Even now, public opinion and the commonweal are often judged to be the test of the law.

In primitive tribal law, collective responsibility plays an important role. The individual is not seen as a separate unit but as part of the collectivity. Each member of the tribe lives in mutual participation and identification with all of the other members and within such a community, a man is punishable not only for his actions but also for what he dreams and thinks. The "magic" crime is to have the wrong feelings and to think the wrong ideas. The entire tribe may be made responsible and punished for the crime of unholy thoughts of a single one of its members.

It is not so strange then that in the totalitarian state with its return of primitive mutual participation the thought-crime still exists. Anyone who refuses to submit to the rational order of the party in power is considered a traitor. Even moral indignation against the immoral order of absolute power is held as treason. If the monolithic party so decrees, the individual must plead guilty to non committed crimes.

In our time, outbursts of collective hate promote the same archaic idea of collective responsibility. During a war *all* enemy citizens are held responsible and hostages must atone for the deeds of others. Collective sanctions against minority groups exist in our day as they did under the archaic laws in communities that have retained a medieval spirit. Thus in Nazi Germany the whole Jewish community was punished and banned for what was imputed to some of its members.

Although modern law only recognizes the individual, the personality, as responsible for his mistakes

149

and contraventions, the archaic, magic idea of collective responsibility and guilt-by-association remains subconsciously in many people.

THE INDIVIDUALISTIC OR SUBJECTIVE ASPECT OF JUSTICE

The individualistic conception of justice claims guarantees not only for the perpetuation of the collectivity but also for the protection of the individual ego and self-esteem. Here, the code of law acknowledges the uniqueness of the individual and also protects the weak individual against the overwhelming power of the collectivity or a fellow being. In exchange for this protection and acknowledgment, the individual must renounce satisfaction of some of his impulses and drives. Individual aggressive and destructive impulses are transferred to the state, and it is the collectivity rather than the individual which is sometimes allowed to indulge in them as, for instance, happens in war.

Such restrictions and sacrifice of drives, however, create considerable inner conflict in most people. Not many are able to check this inner battle. As shown before, there are maniacs of legality who, while emphatically citing the law, commit great injustice toward others. These people believe they have law and justice on private lease. Insisting upon their "personal rights," they misuse the rules of law in a continuing battle against inner feelings of injustice—feelings which, in themselves, are usually a psychic defense against non-acceptable inner hostility.

We may safely say that every individual, at some time, feels it unjust that family, group, tribe, state, corporation, or institution are looked upon as more important than the individuals comprising them. We may say every individual has an ambivalent relation to these formations. He wants to depend on them but resents his dependency.

150

There is a continuous struggle between individual rights and the prevalence of the "legal order," but there is also a steady reciprocal influence and development in action. In a totalitarian state, the community rights and those of the few in power prevail. In a free democracy, the rights of the individual are more emphasized.

The Normative or Objective Aspect

Man expects from the law some satisfaction of his private ideals and claims toward justice. There also exists in each human being the striving for growth and expansion and maturity. Unbearable customs must eventually be broken. But this intellectual expansion, this attempt to break away from tradition, is usually avenged by the group and treated as "unlawful" unless the customs of the group have become ripe for change through one or another inner crisis.

Usually the fictitious *normative* aspect of law—justice seen as an absolute value—is derived from the ideas of moralists and philosophers, while authoritarian rulers try to imprint as such their legal dictates on man. The Russian language, for instance, has one and the same word for truth and justice: pravda. Russian totalitarians define justice as the moral truth of the class of workers; a truth, according to them which is as objectively determinable as scientific truth. Being "just" means to them: being legal in the service of the party in power.

The English words "just" and "justice" come from the Latin word "Jus"—a law. It means right and fair dealing. The very word "just" has a passive and an active root. There exists the stem "jur" (as in jurisprudence and jury) connoting those who are right; and the stem "jud," (as in judge and adjudicate) connoting those who judge.

The ambivalence and inner contradictions of these

151

early concepts are shown more clearly in the origin of the word "fair." Fair first meant beautiful, and this may be derived from the Gothic, *fagr:* "that which is fit," and is related to *fegen:* "to clean." The same word is later used in the sense of foul play and as fake (*feague: "to polish up."*) Interesting also is the Dutch word for justice: *recht* and *rechtvaardig*, meaning "well-ordered" and "traveling a straight line."

Language is a nearly unexplored source to study the variety of meanings and associations belonging to words and concepts, some of which unconsciously still reverberate in us.

The common man has less pretentious ideals and delusions of justice than the professional philosopher. Whether he calls his rules common law or mores and habits depends on whether a governing authority pays attention to them. The common man usually has higher ethical values than he is able to embody into a law.

Paradoxically, however, the same common man often acts in a much more immoral way than he is himself aware. There are strange rifts and vacillations within man's feelings toward justice; between his ethical norms, the way he thinks things ought to be, and the so-called *positive law*, the way things are done.

In times of war, for instance, sabotage, failure to enlist for service, passive resistance, or boycott may be considered as highly ethical or as highly criminal, depending on the judging parties and with what side of the battle we identify.

The Psychological Importance of the Right to Appeal

Every free human relation must be a two-way road of communication. If only the legislator has the right to speak and dictate, law gradually becomes the tool of a dictatorship. He who is judged must have the right to defend himself. He must have the right to construct counter-arguments and to appeal to a higher judge, judging the judges.

Each code of rules should provide an opportunity for the development of new and better rules. It should remain living and flexible, with an open awareness of its limitations. Law has grown from ancient norms to new values which will again be affected by the creation of a better law. One of the highest achievements which we may expect from normative justice is the right of correction of the law. This implies the right of freedom of thought, freedom of speech, freedom of conscience; the right not to conform, to test the law and disapprove of it. This is why justice implies the right of direct appeal to a higher and, let us hope, wiser judging authority.

International law, unfortunately, has neglected this essential psychological link between the right of appeal and the individual's feeling of unbiased justice.

There is, however, no valid reason that this should remain so in the future. Unfortunately many a sovereign state is more afraid of the free, self-corrective spirit of the individual, than of his "boundless" criminality. The Charter of Human Rights as formulated by the United Nations will only really protect the individual when he is allowed to appeal from the rules established by his own government to a higher authority of justice. This sounds utopian, but no international legal and just community can be formed without satisfying these minimal psycho-legal needs in the individual.

How the Feeling of Justice Works

In the foregoing discussion we have seen that the words "law" and "justice" evoke a variety of emotional reactions in which feelings of unfairness and injustice

153

play a greater role than the intelligent comprehension of law, or code of justice, itself. This can make for a great confusion of emotions. When politicians from the left speak of justice, they mean something entirely different from the conservatives who launch the same slogan. In both views, anger and resentment play a more important role than mythical, subjective and more objective concepts of justice. Because these personal feelings are so vague and undefined, it is easy to manipulate them for propaganda purposes. "Justice" has a deep emotional appeal that goes far beyond any legal or political definition and is related to man's frustrations, his resentments and his hidden feelings of guilt. That is why there exists such a great danger of legal incantation and rhetorical persuasion replacing the idea of justice.

Objective, written, juridical law stands in the minds of many people as almost opposed to the subjective experience of fairness and justice. The so-called written, or positive laws, are mostly a transformed codified version of ancient ponderings and discussions about justice. No matter how carefully thought out this codified law remains fallible human work. It represents a growing embodiment of rules designed to bring about some security against individual passions and the domination by social formations. Codified law is not always rooted in the legal conscience and convictions of the members of a community; rather does this depend on the particular relations of power in the given community. A dictatorship dictates the law.

The codified law must, however, have the power of enforcement. This sanction of enforcement and punishment in the service of legal restriction brings into the world of law and legislation a host of new psychological relations which we are only now beginning to explore.

The need to punish and restrict one's fellow man

154

is often coupled with a disguised or undisguised pleasure in punishing. The collectivity is usually much more swayed by hidden emotions than the individual, so that "pure" justice, free from such hidden affects, is almost unthinkable.

The verdict, the sentence, the "last word" of justice, is spoken, after all, by one man, the judge; or a group of men, the jurors, reflecting the conscience and unconscious collective feelings of their era.

Codified law, however neutral and passive it may seem to be, often realizes its own disguised will for power, its own mistakes and the injustice which it may cause. Therefore, as said before, the opportunity of appeal from a lower to a higher court of justice is created.

Too many rules of law may also be harmful to the attainment of justice. In obedience to scholarly legal codes, the involved moral values may be disregarded. As the old legal aphorism says: "*Summum jus, summa injuria.*" The more law, the more injustice.

However, justice and the laws that try to approximate the feelings of justice could never be established without public opinion and without the public sanction of legal values. Neither can society exist without an authoritative power to enforce the law. Legal sanctions are not required merely for the protection of law itself and of man's feeling of justice, but also for the protection of man against coercion and intrusion by his fellow man. Only a law which has enforcing power develops its prophylactic effect on human wrong-doing.

Legality often serves as a cloak for vengeance. Each individual who contributes to the formation of a new law, unconsciously incorporates into it something of his private vindictiveness, since he must, under the new law, sacrifice some of his own personal drives for the benefit of the collectivity. In primitive criminal law this vindictive character of the law is

155

obvious. The *jus talionis* (right of retaliation), the principle of an eye for an eye, a tooth for a tooth, is the clearest expression of this desire of vengeance and retribution. But in more highly developed law we also find many obvious traces of such ideas of vengeance.

In each collectivity, more or less hidden feelings of hate exist that in turn become responsible for aggressive reactions and collective needs for retributions against individuals and other minorities. The perverted laws by which the Nazis carried out their murderous atrocities against minorities obviously were based on such collective hatred.

The legal sanctions against individuals attacking each other are usually so heavy and the strong arm of the law is feared to such an extent that the citizen today feels rather well protected against the aggression of his fellow citizen. Man's desire for justice, however, needs for its final satisfaction more than legal security. Theoretically and intellectually, justice aims at the realization of ideal rules of law raising the collectivity to a higher moral level. Man's search for fairness requires not merely that minimum of decent behavior enforceable by law but also a maximum of ethical behavior.

The ideal of justice formulates the individual's sacrifice to the community, and logically implies the duty of self limitation.

Unconsciously, however, justice and injustice mean much more than those sophisticated ideals. They contain reminiscences of the infantile complaint about a cruel world that keeps man dependent and doesn't fit in with his infantile megalomania. Whenever the child in us becomes enraged against outside restrictions and feels guilty about this rage, we use the excuse that we are being treated unfairly and unjustly as a subtle defense against the guilt feelings. The just, omnipotent, protective father is a fiction of infantile thinking, a creation to hide infantile fantasies.

The generally accepted ideals of law and justice should not refer only to individuals within a collectivity. The urge to make mutual sacrifice for the sake of a more protective legal order should be expanded also to include relations between collectivities and states. Only in an atmosphere of well-calculated appropriate sacrifice by sovereign nations on behalf of mutual tolerance can the new trend toward a more extensive codification of international law and morality bear fruit.

As the individual must, for the sake of social security and the infantile fiction of justice, curb the free play of his passions, so must the collectivity, the state, with a view to a super-collective international law, gradually learn to restrain its own liberty of actions.

There cannot be international law without mutual sacrifice of liberties and "sacred rights" of self-destination and sovereignty and without the acceptance of duties on an international basis.

THE TRAGEDIES OF JUSTICE

It is the tragedy of law that it is so often emotionally identified with restrictions and limitations starting from the moment man is born, and a rebel will suffer under any law, since any kind of bondage and restriction will oppress him. This is the more true for a collectivity with inbreeding of national pride. The group usually reacts in a more primitive and emotional manner, and its capacity for self-limitation is inferior to that of the individual. It has more difficulty in understanding the concept of rights and justice and tolerance toward other groups. For the more primitive group mind, vengeance goes be-

157

fore the legal pact. It would seem, therefore, that a system of international law is even less possible without legal sanctions.

In the beginning, these international sanctions would have to be applied strictly; the offender dealt with instantly and consistently. Only in this way will it be possible to insure the psychologic and prophylactic effect of mutually accepted codes. Once such international sanctions, however primitive, continued to function, they would improve and refine themselves.

There exists a pressure of public opinion that can have restrictive and preventive action on international crimes, especially if the communicative means are available to assert such opinion against the propagandistic battle cry "It is unfair," launched by the incriminated party. The egocentric arbitrariness of isolated groups can gradually be subjected to the expanding and even more effective law of a new and comprehensive international collectivity. Such basic law has already started with a very simple Charter of Fundamental Human Rights, as tentatively adopted by the United Nations.

There already exist age-old examples that international codification can work. The customary Law of the Sea (Maritime Law) grew out of one of the earliest international codifications of law honored by every country.

Yet the rule of law is only an approximation, a code to be superseded by another code. Always, behind the attempt at codification must lie the principle of justice, rooted in human feelings about norm and value. A universal listening to higher law is only possible when common principles of justice are generally acknowledged and accepted, as for instance, in the Charter of Universal Human Rights.

Law and sanction alone, however, are never sufficient. Punishment breeds new crimes if it is not based on a high level of ethics. Each action causes reaction and even revenge if the moral basis of the sanction is not comprehended. If international sanctions are not rooted in a common acceptance of international arbitration, they lose their value and, by causing deep resentment, may bring about the opposite of what they aimed to achieve.

The same danger is present in punishment for individuals, as, for example, in the death sentence. A masochistic identification with the sentenced may arouse in some persons such inadvertent murderous fantasies that they will, paradoxically, provoke new acts of crime: to finish a new criminal in the electric chair. Such risk of identification is not imaginary. According to British law, those who commit suicide are subject to punishment. The failed suicide stands a chance of being imprisoned. The law here, in an archaic way, seeks to punish the perpetrator of the crime of enforced identification, of "psychic blackmail," by burdening one's contemporaries with remorse and guilt for not having behaved better toward him. Related modern crimes are *menticide* (the killing of the mind under psychic stress) and psychic homicide (the wilful provocation of suicide in others).

International sanctions should parallel those which individual citizens, in wise self-limitation, impose upon themselves. "Take care of us and warn us," they ask of the law, "so that our aggressive and primitive tendencies may not break through." The psychological motivation behind international restrictions might read: "Take care of us and our *national* limitations."

Individuals feel rather secure under a controlling police force which supervises them but, at the same time, hate these supervisors. People like to fool the police, but would not like to be without them. No other authority is met with such ambivalence of

159

feelings. So certainly would be the case with an international police force, e.g. an international occupation force. Such a force would evoke more conflicting feelings than local police, but once this supervising force began to function and proved its worth in preventing conflict, injustice and aggression, people would not want to do without it either. Thus, international hostility and aggression, though not immediately eliminated, would gradually come more and more under legal control. The development of mankind proceeds by trial and error. An international organization under mutually accepted codes is bound to become stronger reality.

No individual can be his own judge, nor can communities or states, though all stick to the "sacred" dogma of sovereignty. There must be some power compelling an offender to appear before a judging body. At this very moment more legal advice could already be asked from the International Court of Justice; not as a power principle but to help to build up international guiding principles of justice. The history of the United Nations shows that the big powers of the world, especially, shun self-limitation and subordination. This is why it is psychologically the more important to have an International Court of Justice which can give guidance to world opinion.

The tragedy of law and justice, and especially of international justice, is that restrictive self-limitation cannot be accepted until people become more aware of the megalomaniacal unconscious forces within themselves which sabotage their conscious wish for mutual tolerance and collaboration. Those hidden forces paradoxically prefer "injustice" to complain about in order to "justify" their unleashed aggressive and destructive instincts. Indeed, in international military strategy, injustice is often provoked in order to justify the planned aggression.

What constitutes the core of the feeling of justice of civilized man? It is most curious to see in what a paradoxical way this feeling takes shape. Various conscious and unconscious motives are instrumental in bringing about legal convictions.

Usually, the querulous attitude and too great an appeal to justice have their roots in a paradoxical desire to dominate. The offending person wants to hide his passiveness and submissiveness behind over-emphasized self-assertiveness. An offended feeling of justice mostly originates from an offense to man's self-esteem, though, of course, an occasional violation of his legal and personal rights may also be responsible.

Many a man who failed in life will try to construct some injustice done to him to justify his failure. Such a person will consider the law only as a means to satisfy his private wishes and personal legal views. Driven by hate and resentment, he claims his full pound of flesh; he claims law for himself, but any compassionate feelings of justice or sympathy with other victims of injustice are strange to him.

It is rather easy to create in other people the feeling of indignation about alleged injustice. Everybody was once a helpless baby who had to submit and sometimes whined about it. Hence accusations, however absurd they may be, can easily be abused as instruments of political dissent. The slogan of injustice and unfairness will always find some quick response, since laws imply restrictions, and everybody, unobtrusively, is also in conflict with the law. Whenever the slogan of injustice and unfairness is being launched, the ancient rebellion against overwhelming giant parents is awakened. The conflict between the burning feelings of injustice on the one hand and the meager approximation of satisfaction by abstract and positive law, on the other, is eternal. That is why law and constitution lend themselves so readily to abuse by political slogans.

Exaggerated sensitivity toward injustice and a rigid attitude toward the law usually originate in those who consider themselves guilty and wicked without being aware of their inner problems. By the very rigidity of "their" private inner rules and frustrations as often expressed in compulsive rituals, they try to make up for their own unconscious feelings of guilt. Often by committing minor offenses, they ask for punishment, thus to atone for more deeply seated unconscious guilt. Crime and punishment are often covering up the drama of unknown unconscious thought crimes.

Frustrated persons always unwittingly ask for some protection against those tensions in themselves. They even demand, though unconsciously, that the impulse they can hardly repress in themselves be curbed in others by severe law.

It is a sign of a rather high culture if the individual personality of the offender with all his inner conflicts and motivations is taken into consideration in judging his crime. It indicates that the community feels itself so sure of its protective rules of law that it dares apply a variable individual measure rather than a rigid generalizing law.

The child, among his companions in school, does not have this secure feeling and, therefore, overcompensates by overstating the importance of "the rule." In general, he has a correct evaluation of just punishment, but he would be more severe than the teacher if he were to handle his classmates and he certainly will blame the teacher if all children are not treated alike.

Every prototype of the feeling of justice and injustice starts in the nursery. It begins with parental justice and later goes on with "unfair" sibling rivalry.

162

Being compelled to share affection is felt as unjust, and so on.

Yet a group of youngsters will overcome anti-social tendencies with comparative ease when special conditions are fulfilled. These are: not too restrictive intervention from without and the acceptance of a chosen leader. The rules of fair play and competition in sports are the prototypes of democratic law, and they are as old as man's games.

In primitive communities and in communities of children, the respect for public opinion is instrumental in bringing about strict observation of customs. It is the evaluation in the minds of one's peers that has a regulating and restrictive action (self-evaluation by proxy). Primitive people even make use of punishment by public contempt or even by excommunication. Even now, Eskimos practice a verbal slander-competition as a kind of legal ordeal. The two opponents in a legal dispute recite all kinds of disgracing incriminations against each other until one of the parties can no longer stand up against the flood of incriminating words.

Our actual system of fines and imprisonment represents a rather primitive form of punishment and revenge, offering little or no opportunity for moral rehabilitation, and provoking the unconscious need for counter-revenge. Moreover, too rigid codification breeds contraventions and repercussions. If something is prohibited, people are all the more tempted to do it. The lure of the forbidden fits into man's moral ambivalence.

LAW AND POWER

Are law and justice nothing but defensive fictions created by the powerless? Are those norms of fairness and justice merely artificial, ideal constructions of the economically and physically weak, invented for the fettering of the strong? "Who is not strong must be shrewd!" says the old proverb. But the stronger one also uses the fiction of justice to assert his rights. While the weak one constructs his ideal of law and justice in a cunning attempt to compensate for his weakness, the strong person enforces his dictates and concepts as a justification of his lust for power. The one builds walls of protective codes and values around his frail body; the other launches deceptive slogans as spearheads of his arrogance and disguised feelings of guilt.

During the German occupation, people in occupied countries were enjoined by the courts of the enemy not to say anything whatsoever against their present "masters." Newspapers were forced to publish lengthy justifications of all German violations of existing international law. The use of the word "enemy" was punishable; the subjected people were forced and bound to give the Nazis the honorable credit of being "protectors." Even jokes about them were held as a punishable offense. Thus, Nazi law was purely an education in hypocrisy. It was built solely upon brutal force, yet was equipped and polished with a whole rigmarole of official courts and judges; all the ritualistic paraphernalia of justice being done. It was as if the oppressor in the battle with his own conscience was frightened of accusations of being unjust both from outside world opinion and from within the occupied country, too.

This rigid fiction of legality is often used to cover up inner guilt. Man does not readily admit his own guilt and unjust actions lest he should have to correct himself.

The so-called right of the strong is, in all its primitivity, a step backward to the animal law of the survival of the fittest. The animal that is victorious in the initial fight thereafter fascinates and leads the herd, until a new victor and leader emerges from another fight. Such leadership is based not on any contracts or agreements, but merely on fear of and submission to the strong.

The pecking order of the chicken coop exists even in a democracy. There are the lobbyists and the "lobbied" ones. Unobtrusive bribing exists everywhere. The problem is how to check and limit it. Every suggestion can be either wholesome or coercive. Let us not forget that the right to shout for the one is the compulsion to listen for the other.

Archaic law conceives of a legal dispute as a battle of arms; the winner in this primitive ordeal is the winner in the law-suit. One encounters a remainder of this archaic view in the juristic verbal duel and rhetorical match between two attorneys.

In law-suits under the native Adat Law of Indonesia, the presentation of each valid argument—according to the judge—is accompanied by the driving into the ground of a small stick; the winning party is indicated by the largest number of sticks.

Originally, all law was based on the supremacy of the strong and mighty—the law of the bludgeon euphemistically called "natural law." Only gradually did the suffering parties construct a different concept of law, based on a majority principle, in order to emancipate themselves from the brutal force of a few giants in power. Even in our own time, the drive for power of a few works to act against the many. A subtle fight for power, influence and importance goes on in every community, openly or secretly as the case may be. Political terror, discrimination, and political upheaval are usually the result of a terrorizing action by a minority that keeps the majority in coercive awe.

Codified law imposes limitations on the continuing struggle for power between majorities and minorities. A dictatorial minority as well as a more passive majority are supposed to feel themselves bound by law. In reality, however, this can only happen when and where the law of justice and the power of might reach a compromise. This compromise is a powerful and just system of law. Yet it is not the power of enforcement that makes the law valid but the common will to submit to the law, that means man's reason and consent.

But law and power cannot do without each other. On the one hand, law opposes the accumulation of power; on the other, law must count upon force to maintain itself. Every moral idea needs not only mutual approval but also physical support. Only then does law become disciplined power or, as Plato called it: a useful and harmonious force. Justice must inspire respect.

Pascal expressed it: "Justice without force is powerless; force without justice is tyrannical. Justice without force is being challenged since there are always wicked people; force without justice is being indicted. It is therefore necessary to couple justice with force and thereby to effect that what is just be strong and what is strong be just."

It becomes easier to harmonize the collaboration between law and power when both are subjected to the judgment and appraisal of man's conscience.

Power should, however, remain the servant of law, since undefended law will not prevent interhuman aggression and lawless power will always cause tyranny, destruction and rebellion. Only legitimate power can maintain and limit itself at the same time. Only a powerful law prevents the mind from getting sentimental and surrendering to the self-pitying tears of hidden hatred and aggression while professing love and caritas. Any other kind of power though apparently strong or even tyrannical will actually be weak in its core, since power over others does not necessarily mean control over one's own drives and inner destructiveness.

Everybody can appreciate the support and protection by strong law. But who is willing to do justice spontaneously without any legal support and compulsion? People usually like to reap the harvest of a moral idea, but not to pay for it.

In everyday practice people usually do not care too much for strict law and morality. Daily, they commit contraventions without being caught by the law and without too many scruples. As a rule the law only interferes in case of serious conflicts or when needed as a political tool against somebody.

The moment the gap between jural law and the correct moral values becomes too wide, law becomes sham and hollow. In a community where law and justice are no longer appreciated and where moral codes are transgressed too frequently, the preventive action of the law ceases to act and injustice and brutality gain the upper hand. Finally, the law has to take into account the tendency of power to become absolute if the law or legal institution does not make rules to check its own failures, foibles and bias. This self-limiting wisdom of power is the beginning of justice.

THE SENSE OF JUSTICE

Even though we can accept psychologically the feeling of injustice as an infantile protest against being restricted and handled in an unfair way; even though we can analyze the intricate, mostly unconscious paradoxes related to this injustice-collecting inner defense, the question remains: is there a positive sense of justice such as philosophers write about? The word "sense" here is used not in its psychological meaning but as representing an inner notion of value.

Justice can be looked at as a guiding moral value only if it can be severed from man's private interests. If man is motivated not merely by his own sufferings;

not merely by his own self-pity, not merely by the wrong inflicted upon himself, but more by the suffering and pains of others—weaker ones and minorities, etc.—then indeed we could speak of justice as a guiding value. To do justice to others in this noble sense one must learn, however, to identify oneself without bias with the victim of injustice and to experience the sufferings of others as one's own.

This capacity for empathy and sympathy is a late acquisition in human history. It is this capacity for empathy and compassion that can lift the law of the mighty out of the vicious circle of cynical self-defense and wicked self-justification. Only when the desire for vengeance, retaliation, and prestige starts to fade away; only when people attempt to look into the psyche and motivations of their opponents, will justice begin to thrive on the basis of acknowledgment of mutual desires and needs. It is at this point that the egocentric desire for private law and justice will gradually grow into an understanding of the relativity of all written law and the high moral duty expressed in the word justice.

The wisdom of mutual adjustment and tolerance is not only to fight for justice but also to learn to tolerate injustice against oneself until the moment for better mutual understanding and adjustment comes. This, man's inner strength and capacity to tolerate, is deeply involved in conquering the feeling of unfairness.

If justice is to be done to others, the judgment is, in the first place, an individual one, depending on the character and strength of the person. His ego strength, his freedom of action, his self-confidence, his tolerance to bear tension and his personality, determine whether he can do to others what seems fair to them and to him. Society, with its greater emotional unstableness and quest for conformity, will generally be much more unjust than the individual is. There is always a strange ambiguity of choice. What shall man do? Apply the law or do justice? Apply his highest values coming from the individual or follow the collective legal code? Be moral or be legal?

The concept of justice itself is a balance of contrasting forces and is beautifully symbolized in Justitia, the woman with the veiled eyes who keeps the scales in her hand, weighing the pros and cons with unbiased view. Balance implies vacillation of powers between those who are equal before the law. Thus, justice expresses not the equality of slaves under the law of power, but the peaceful mutual toleration of those who judge and are being judged. Justitia symbolizes the balance that tries to temper the risk of mutual violation by mutual resignation and relinquence from power. Yet this always implies the psychological conflict between self-assertion and the resignation from dominance in the service of mutual tolerance.

In everyday life there is a continuous conflict between the awareness of codified restrictions and man's battle with his own defaults and with human inertia. Every attempt to protest against some form of injustice meets, after initial emotional approval, dull resistance, hypocrisy, corruption and indolence. Each truth can, by ruse, be turned into a lie. For the sake of their own convenience, many people still give their allegiance to brutal power and force of darkness.

Law, like man's consciousness, is an exacting master. It requires continuous spiritual alertness and incessant inquiry into the hidden motives of the transgressor.

People usually respect the law when there is conformity with their private interests. They want, for instance, the legislation to pass protective laws, e.g. traffic laws. Yet when the law catches up with them, certain ones try to fix the ticket, or to withdraw from its consequences. We find such behavior even more emphasized in human behavior toward prohibition—and vice laws.

People so easily like to forget that toward every right there is a duty. Only the infant has the one-sided right to claim attention and care and protection. But here too the rule of mutuality will soon intrude. The child has to learn to love his parents and siblings in return for their care.

JUSTICE EXPRESSES A SATISFIED PERSONAL RELATIONSHIP BETWEEN THE INDIVIDUAL AND THE CODIFIED LEGAL NORM

The concept of unbiased law stands or falls with the right to speak and argue; the right to test the law. Primitive people sometimes have a better understanding of this than many a modern state. The palaver, the meeting of the tribesmen for the purpose of passing judgment upon actions of members of the tribe, belongs among the most important rites in many a primitive society. The defendant at the palaver enjoys freedom of speech, and judgment will not be passed as long as he is able to bring forth refutations of the indictment. The procedure ends up either in a confession or an exculpation of the defendant. His free opinion may sometimes change a long-existing taboo and revolutionize rigid habits.

International law has so far paid little attention to the *personal* and psychological relation which must exist between the law and the *individual* "holder of rights": the citizen of the world. Again, the process of legal communication must be a reversible one: not only from the judge downward toward the accused, but also from a victimized person upward toward the judge. When the individual has no personal right of appeal to a court of justice, the law does, in fact, not exist for him.

For an international system of justice, such a psychological improvement in legal relations could perhaps be gradually established if an international legal authority could have a token representative body in each nation so that every individual could, within his own national community, appeal to a higher law, covered by and obedient to an Inter-national Charter of Human Rights.

Such an institution, of course, could attract all sorts of querulous complaints against one's own government, but this risk is inherent in every law, and a new judicial authority must be trusted to sift and handle such situations with tact and psychological insight. Important for us, however, is the principle of two-way communication. Again, without *individuals* having the chance of personal legal appeal, no international community based on justice is possible.

JUSTICE AND CONSCIENCE

Moral values have their source in human conscience. Conscience—man's superego—in its turn is rooted in the interaction of fear and power in society. Conscience is also conditioned by the rules of law in the parental home and the influence upon the growing child of values and sanctions prevailing in his environment. We believe, however, that man's conscience has deeper roots in man being a peculiar biological exception, a continually dependent being who never reaches complete maturity. First, a process of mere imitation of and identification with parental values takes place; later on, out of love for his parents, the child genuinely and more consciously adopts and internalizes his parents' values. In man's conscience there develops a selective faculty for either approving or disapproving the rules and restrictions from outside. In this phase of development it is no longer the fear of punishment or of deprivation which determines the inner directives of the child; rather does

171

he adopt social values out of empathy and love for his educators.

The ardent claim for law and justice that is a common symptom of growth in puberty may provoke more egotism when there is no inner acceptance of the existing moral laws. Such immature adolescents no longer ask for law and justice because they are afraid to suffer more restraints themselves. They prefer the private, rather threatening laws and rules of the gang to the moral law of society. This is often the case when the moral rules of the home and the smaller social formation failed to make an impact on the child.

In some people, an instinctive obedience and compliance to the law develops as an almost pathological compulsive legalism; others react with an instinctive rebellion against the law. Whether the individual chooses one or the other mode of reaction is usually dependent on the type of first education received.

The psychological mechanisms of transference and identification count among the most important for the formation of collective norms of law and justice in the individual. Man and law adapt themselves to the variable psychological climate of society. Our epoch accepts manifold pressure groups on "how to influence people." They somehow take part in collective persuasion and coercion, and direct human values.

Only gradually have people become aware of the importance of the mediums of communication in establishing justice among men. Unjust, illegal behavior is often encouraged by a very subtle means of communication. According to actual law, it is criminal to "aid, abet, counsel, command or procure" a fellow man to commit a crime, but there exist many unobtrusive forms of criminal suggestion of which psychology has only become aware during the last decenniae and which are not covered by law. Think, for instance, of the inadvertent seduction to crime

172

caused by movies, television and comic books. In several criminal cases the outburst of illegal behavior could be related to such suggestive influences.

Although, according to church doctrine, sin is not a crime, and to common law heretics, is not treason, these acts will be interpreted in a different way dependent on the "zeitgeist." Such subtle transitions between legal and illegal, just and unjust, are found even oftener in political spheres where unobtrusive crimes (e.g. the crime of neglect) occur repeatedly.

For those in charge of political power it is very difficult to find the middle way between self-corruption by prudence and the masochistic need to expose oneself too much. All these norms and values undergo subtle differences, dependent on the change in public opinion.

From a psychological standpoint, justice is an ambivalent concept, expressing a complicated relationship between men. Whoever appeals to justice must apply the law with regard to restricting himself as well as with regard to restricting others. Only an individual who is obedient to the law (though he may not agree) is entitled to claim law and justice.

Man's inner conscience, originating in fear and dependency and in his battle against his unconscious drives, is a severe inner judge. It administers punishment in a way different from that of the official judge and may even punish where a crime has not yet been committed. It often punishes the bad intention and anticipation: the *dolus*. It also punishes man's megalomaniac fantasies of greatness, his hidden magic death wishes and his unconscious sexual fantasies. Conscience, the unconsciously judging agency, realizes that the criminal intention is often more important for the individual than his actual deed.

The conscience of many a man works like an archaic tribunal, judging and punishing himself in accordance with the old *jus talionis:* "an eye for an

173

eye, a tooth for a tooth." Many neurotic symptoms originate in this unconscious self-judging. Vindictiveness and malicious hate may be transformed into neurotic self-punishment which in turn may cause a psychosomatic deterioration of the functioning of various organs. The passive joy in suffering injustice, the continual feeling of having been wronged as is often observed in depressed patients, may be accompanied by these psychosomatic conversions. Many neurotic heart diseases are the result of imagined injustice suffered or imagined cruelty committed.

Man's confusion between legality and morality is partly brought about by the lawgivers themselves. When psychiatrists are asked to give an opinion, for instance, on whether or not a criminal is mentally ill (legally insane), the answer can be interpreted either according to the concept of the law or according to medical-psychological evaluation. For lawyers, right and wrong are determined only by the letter of the law; for the psychiatrist they mean a combination of various ambiguities of feeling, acting and thinking.

What confusion and ambiguity in identification! When the psychiatrist declares the accused legally insane, the judge usually identifies with the poor mentally-sick man who could not help committing a crime. When the psychiatrist declares him mentally responsible in the choice between right and wrong, identification is transposed to the poor victim of the crime who must now be revenged via the usual penal sanctions.

The conflict between legal codes and the moral values for which man has fought so eagerly has existed as long as mankind. As the old saying goes: "legality is no morality and morality is no legality." Usually the law codifies only a minimum of ethical behavior. Yet this often leads to subtle conflicts in individuals as shown in the following case.

Arthur Miller, the well-known playwright, was

convicted in Federal Court for contempt of Congress. He had refused on moral grounds to disclose to the House Committee on Un-American Activities the names of those he knew to have attended a Communist meeting in 1947. Though he could have protected himself behind the right to be silent on the basis of possible self-incrimination, as granted by the Fifth Amendment, Mr. Miller chose not to do that. He told the Court that he never was a communist or under Communistic rule. His argument against disclosure was that the Committee questions were not pertinent to the pending legislative inquiry.

Judge McLaughlin, in his final judgment, included a statement of great psychological interest, because it shows some of the subtle moral contradictions in those who have to interpret the law, and the intentions of the law-makers. "*However commendable* Mr. Miller's action may have been," wrote Judge McLaughlin, "in refusing to divulge the identity of his associates, he was in contempt for refusing to answer the questions under previous rulings of a Federal Appellate Court." (*Herald Tribune*, June 1, 1957).

This opinion throws light on an intricate psychological and high moral question: the individual's right *not* to betray his former allegiances and associates. In this case no illegal act was committed. The author had visited, out of interest or curiosity, a meeting of a political party that was at that moment not outlawed or even accused of conspiracy. He was asked to divulge names so that those he would mention would later be forced, under legal duress, to betray other names.

At this point, the inner psychological contradiction begins. While the whole investigation is intended to throw light on eventual treason and conspiracy against the United States, the individual is forced to become a traitor toward his own conscience and feelings of honesty and privacy. Here the lawgiver forgets that any betrayal of the community is rooted in initial self-betrayal, forsaking one's own beliefs and moral principles. The law exists not only to protect the community but also to protect the individual against coercion by the community. The paradox is that by forcing a man to betray his inner feelings of moral value, we actually make it easier for him to betray the larger community at some future date. Moral evaluation starts with the *individual*—the strength of his ego; the use of his privacy and reserve—and not with the state. If the law forces people to betray their inner moral feelings of personal loyalty to those who were at that moment legal in their actions, then that very law undermines the integrity of the person, and unobtrusively a form of mental coercion has begun. One of the functions of the law is to protect the individual against the violation of personal moral standards; otherwise human conscience will lose in the battle between individual conscience and coercive legal power.

The judge who so laudably brought this subtle inner contrast between legality and morality to the foreground by calling the defendant's behavior "commendable" could, however, also have expended his judgment about human intentions toward the prosecution. There is danger that official investigations and legislative inquiry may unobtrusively coerce personal moral standards and go beyond the original task of gathering information.

It is for the Supreme Court to give a final judgment in such a case, though the contrast between individual moral values and collective legal values will not be solved by this.

In another judgment, Supreme Court Justices Douglas and Black in their dissenting opinion about the constitutionality of the Immunity Act of 1954, emphasize the purely psychological principle of safeguarding of personal conscience and personal dignity. This indicates that psychology will gradually play a greater role in the solution of these intricate problems.

THE DELUSION OF JUSTICE

The feeling of justice easily becomes morbid, and many people never develop beyond the stage of continuous self-justification. To these people, justice equals that which helps them; never that which restricts them. True, out of passivity, they live obediently in accordance with society's fixed rules and laws. In fact many people value the letter of the law more highly than the spirit and do not go beyond strict legal requirements, thus disregarding higher ethical values. There still exists the myth of abstract justice purely directed at the public weal and denying the psychological fact that everyone contributes his own private loyalties and dependencies to the law, feelings of which only part are conscious.

Morality and legality are too often considered as identical. As has been pointed out, they are actually two different concepts. The law only restrains immorality; it does not cultivate moral action. So-called moralists who indulge too much in legalism, especially with regard to catching others in the maze of legal terms, may unconsciously be driven by their feelings of vengeance and resentment. The best example of such a delusion of justice (and guilt) is what happened in totalitarian countries where victims of brainwashing were forced to plead guilty to non-committed crimes. In these countries all those who do not submit themselves to the order of the party are automatically considered guilty. So are those who show moral indignation against the immoral order of absolute power. "Guilty" and "in conflict with the law" are terms which apply to anyone

177

who does not adjust to the totalitarian system. There is no interest in individual feelings of justice, in pangs of guilt or in actual proofs of innocence.

Some people foster the naive belief that only law and justice are able to maintain peace among men. To be sure, law can curb and restrain mutual hostility, but a constructive peace springs from different sources; from another psychic area.

It is erroneous to think that international law alone will be sufficient to bring peace into the world. Sacrificing one's personal rights and temporarily tolerating injustice in the service of mutual tolerance are more conducive to peace than rigid assertion of claims founded on old verbal codes and legal pacts; psychologically speaking, this means overcoming one's unconscious injustice-collecting defenses. (Bergler)

Any country that goes to war can find a number of legal pretexts to justify the step. Like many a criminal who convinces himself he is acting out of noble motives, the citizens of a warring nation often feel it is their righteous duty to fight, and believe themselves entitled to violate pacts and treaties. This is the common delusion that justice serves private purposes.

The concepts of law and justice will only be operative effectively when individual nations recognize a higher powerful organization on the basis of combined and integrated legality and morality. In other words, only those who are willing to subject themselves to a higher organization of justice can maintain the laws and rules to which they claim to adhere.

JUSTICE AND QUERULOUSNESS

Properly understood, querulousness is the opposite of the quest for justice. It is the delusional concept of law as an instrument for private use, not subject to any control from outside. Thus, querulousness is the freakish hybrid of lust for power and self-justification. The petulant man who cannot conform is continuously hurt in his pride and vanity. He steadily intensifies the quest for his personal rights, and justice thus overstrained naturally becomes injustice. Many depressed people are very sensitive to injustice and commit small violations of justice supposedly to correct it. One of my patients always stole from the A & P when the quality of the food seemed too bad.

It is a psychological fact that people who are blamed for unjust actions usually react by adding new wrongs to their old ones. This is a vicious circle, and is one of the reasons why fines do not always succeed as a prevention of traffic violations. The fine absolves the violator and unobtrusively invites revenge and repetition. A spoken warning would exert a much more desirable psychological reaction.

Querulous people may, in mutual cooperation, establish an authoritarian reign of terror with a common view of eclipsing justice for the sake of their own hurt pride. They may maintain a sham legal community for a time, but since law and justice are for them merely catch-words for mass propaganda, such a community is not likely to last. After a short period of cooperation, the querulous ones usually begin to attack each other.

JUDGE AND JUSTICE

The judge is, and should be, obliged to interpret and apply codified law as much as possible, since he might otherwise, though unintentionally, be biased by intruding private motives. He would often do injustice if he were directed by his subjective feeling of justice. Only if the code does not provide a solution for the question to be decided, may he, accord-

179

ing to some legislation, act as if he himself were the lawgiver of new law. But even then he must observe carefully that body of rules which has, without codification but through traditions and custom, become accepted as "common law."

In his official capacity, the judge should be above the world of human passions. As a token of the magic character of his function, he is clad in the judge's gown, the toga. This symbolizes the idea that law derives from a superior power which is temporarily vested in the judge. The oath of the judge and the right to pardon—as mostly exercised by the heads of states—are likewise symbols of that magic power which is supposed to be operative in the administration of justice. It should be noted that perjury was originally thought of as being automatically punished by the gods themselves. Some primitive people still die out of fear when they realize they have transgressed taboos and sacred rules. The verdict of the tribe brings them into a lethal shock.

It stands to reason, however, that law and legality can never become entirely detached from the subjective human being with his conscious and unconscious motivations. Behind all legal codes lie living people: fallible men—no matter how shadowy they may appear—who create and represent the law. Even the dead letter of the law will always be subject to different interpretations by different men.

The Paradox of Punishment

The act of punishment was originally related to magic feelings of revenge and retribution. Eventually it must be cleared from this primitive concept of the talio, especially since we know that the infantile magic talio usually provokes the repetition of a new act of violence out of a renewed need for punishment. During his years of isolation, a prisoner may have deeply buried his feelings of revenge and wrath, but hidden resentment usually still exists and automatically prepares him to repeat the same crime. Our legal system is not yet enough aware of the fact that many a crime is committed in a quest for punishment for some deeper seated unknown guilt.

In addition to protecting the social order, punishment must give the offender the opportunity of reconciliation and expiation; undoing his unconscious inner guilt. What is even more important, punishment should be looked at as a preventive psychological treatment, attempting to undo the unobtrusive repetition compulsion of committing a crime in order to temporarily expiate more deeply hidden unconscious thought-crimes. If possible, the unconscious crime underneath should be discovered and worked through. This is what happens in many a psychoanalytic treatment of neurosis.

The psychoanalytic core of the therapeutic problem is finding a way to reach the unconscious crime-behind-the-crime, especially where deep-seated psychoanalytic treatment of the offender is not possible. Usually, punishment and expiation act paradoxically as a stimulator of repetition and even the death penalty unwittingly stimulates murderous ideas in many suicidal people who identify with the hanged.

In the future, some better solution of the treatment of criminals could perhaps be found in reaching in a mechanical way the unconscious inner court of primordial justice. Two of my kleptomaniac patients, who used their undiscovered stealing compulsion not only to punish society for their deep-seated feelings of deprivation but also as a defense against much deeper-seated murderous feelings, were, by coincidence, treated by another colleague with electroshock therapy for their general feelings of depression. When I saw them later, back in psychotherapy, I discovered that in both cases the kleptomania was gone, although the depression itself was not cured. The electro-shock had been unconsciously experienced by the patients as such tremendous punishment and as such intensive inner sense of dying and revival that part of their deep-seated guilt about murderous intentions had been expiated.

As far as I know, shock treatment for criminals and subsequent psychotherapy, has not been tried as yet. Such treatment could perhaps become one of the means to reach deep-seated unconscious masochistic wishes, which are paradoxically acted out in destructive sadistic behavior. Electro-shock sounds at least more humane than the electric chair.

Most of our actual handling and punishment do not fit the psychodynamics of the crime and so do not prevent crime. Another important element in understanding the paradox of punishment is the provoking action created by every restrictive law. One example which might be cited is the outbreak of criminal behavior set into motion by "prohibition." Another example of this paradoxical promotion of a "crime" is seen in homosexuality. Where homosexuality became a crime and punishable by law, the infantile polymorph sexuality and feelings of deprivation have been fortified by the official persecution. Self-pity and feelings of injustice push the deprived ones even more into sexual regression and obsessive acting out. I have seen boys pushed into homosexuality by a continual anxiety of being caught and being abnormal. On the other hand, in cultures where not much attention is paid to this infantile acting out, the mature sexual wish usually breaks through.

In every criminal case we must be aware of the fact that a late and delayed trial, plus inappropriate punishment, often provokes the anticipation of further crime. Many a criminal begs unconsciously for sentence but for an adequate one that expiates his guilt.

182

If society doesn't provide such treatment, society is responsible for recidivism and relapse into crime.

In this general survey it is not the place to handle the involved problem of prevention and treatment of criminality. I only want to assert the general psychiatric opinion that in most cases treatment is possible. According to psychological experience, only punishment directly after the crime is able to decondition, though in a superficial way, the criminality pattern. In many simple cases of criminal offense, a form of corporal punishment or an appropriate fine *immediately after* the crime would have done more than years of isolation combined with a most ethical prison treatment. For many people isolation can be more cruel than torture; psychologically, it weakens the ego and so prepares for renewed outbursts of unsocial behavior.

What usually is overlooked in our present system of treating offenders are sufficient psychological premiums for good behavior. This lack of positive education is part of man's general appreciative inertia. People are more ready to criticize than to approve of other people's actions.

The brainwashing enemy in China had quite a system of premiums to seduce prisoners of war into collaboration. Yet, we could learn from some of those inquisitors how to decondition the criminal's mind.

THE PROTECTION AGAINST THE FALLIBILITY OF THE LAW

Codified law attempts to dispense a maximum of justice and a minimum of injustice. It attempts to protect the individual against too hastily established regulations or retroactive rule of law. *Nulla poena sine praevia lege!*—No punishment without a previous law.

Codified law, however, gradually becomes petri-

183

fied, leaving many rifts to develop between the lawyer's concept of legal justice and the layman's idea of natural justice. The layman reacts with uneasiness to the mysterious word-magic of juridical semantics which seem to serve a certain show of verbal power. Indeed, the juristic abracadabra often hurts the average person's feeling for justice. It is as if he were getting words instead of justice by law; stones instead of bread. He feels that the ritualistic machinery of the law is too big and too cumbersome, and sees human feeling become submerged in hairsplitting and formalism. We witnessed this perverse use of legal ritual during recent years in several medical malpractice and insurance suits in which "specialized" lawyers blackmailed the lack of legal knowledge of doctors and jurors to enrich their clients and their own pockets. At this very moment, 20 per cent of the doctors in Los Angeles are victims of a malpractice suit. Such oversophisticated legal atmosphere may well breed a kind of frenzy and turn "parties" into querulous enemies.

Life never can be imprisoned in codified rules. Even the best legal administration has to allow a certain amount of laxity and evasion of the law; even of injustice to be suffered. Man's spirit of opposition makes the desire to be "different"; his ambition and aggressiveness all too often are responsible for people joining anti-legal and subversive activities. Since there is, however, an instinctive leaning in man toward order and away from disorder, even such illegal organizations in turn give origin to special sub-rules of "law" that must be followed by members of the "clan," or the "gang," or the "front." Such petulant cliques built upon rancor and resentment are, however, a continuous danger for the administration of justice.

The legal authority, therefore, tries to take the wind out of the rebel's sails, and tries not to indulge in the armchair work of lawgiving only. Crime can be traced and studied and eventually rules can be detected to prevent crime. Justice must at least put its finger upon sore spots of both society and the criminally-inclined individuals. Attention should not be centered on the meting out of justice and punishment only, but a due share should be given to the prevention of overwhelming feelings of injustice leading to self-righteous criminal actions.

From a psychological point of view, this is an even more important task than codifying the law. The danger of injustice forcing its way through the cracks of the codified rules, of even raising itself to the dignity of customary law, should not be underrated. It is the cultivation of the feeling of injustice and unfairness that breeds crime. That may occur in early childhood in the family or later in the society. Later it is often the clumsy system of punishment that breeds the crime instead of correcting it.

ARBITRATION

One of the main problems in common conflicts between individuals, and between individuals and nations, is the question as to whether a peaceful mutual agreement and adjustment is possible without the interference of a third judging party. Provided there is agreement on the basic issues, a peaceful solution will not be difficult and an understanding easily reached. If, however, interests and characters differ on basic approaches, an appeal to a superior judging authority will become imperative. A world without conflicts among men is beyond our imagination. That is why there cannot be a world without arbitrators—supervising higher authorities making the final decision. Even games of sport must have an umpire.

Arbitration, however, can only be resorted to by

those who adhere to common rules and are reciprocally under the protection of the law. He who has withdrawn from the protection of the law by committing a crime cannot thereafter resort to voluntary arbitration but must first face the severity of legal sanctions. Robbers or smugglers who have been caught have no right to arbitration. They first must humbly submit to their verdict and punishment. Only through suffering punishment and through expiation will they return under the common protection of the law.

This principle of excluding appeal to law and justice by those who put themselves outside the law has confusing psychological reactions. Those who act against law and order cannot always be checked by legal means. Only when they are caught and made harmless can law and justice begin to work in the service of their punishment and expiation.

There exists an over-legalistic thinking that cannot imagine that some people's only aim is to be against the existing laws. Such people who terrorize the law (and their fellow citizens) need effective treatment by some form of counter-terror in order to let the law work again. In pre-Hitler Germany, the over-legalistic-thinking democratic socialists believed they could counteract the street terror of Hitler's SS men with purely legalistic means. They forgot that law and justice are only active when crime and terror—always exerted by a minority—have not their coercive and paralyzing appeal on the masses.

The difficulty of a democracy is that while it needs police, it must also check itself continually not to become a police state. A policing organization has to countervene terror and horror without becoming a terrorizing force itself.

A comparable strategy could be applied to international conflicts. Only after the law-breaking collectivity—always led by a ruling minority in charge —has been convicted and punished, can it again be placed under the protection of international rules.

Man will be much more willing to make up for wrongs he's committed if he feels he is under the protection of the law. He will be much more ready to make personal sacrifices with a view to his greater security if this awareness grows in him. Collectivities, too, can gradually be made to correct their transgressions and to withdraw their aspirations for power if they realize that they are under the protection of a superimposed international legal order. Effective protection, however, can only be based on sufficient power. International arbitration will not be possible without legal international power and a strong international executive backed by strong international forces. The general insecurity in the world is still so prevalent that man's protesting attitude can be easily suppressed if the offending and "unjust" neighbor happens to be more powerful and could take revenge for such a protest.

However emotionally loaded the concept will be, man will stand up against injustice if society will allow him unlimited freedom of speech and argument and free access to arbitration.

The idea of justice as a balance of protective rules against man's arbitrariness will remain alive as long as there is the personal right of opposition. To achieve this goal, the majority of men must abide by the rules of the law, provided a social framework is created in which people need not feel more guilty than their own dependency-need causes them to be.

Only under the protection of powerful national and *no-less powerful* international laws will there ensue a proper development of the concept of justice, and will individual man gradually drop his infantile resentments about being treated unjustly and unfairly.

SUMMARY

The concept of justice is treated as a purely psychological problem of human interrelations, omitting as much as possible the legal implications. The author describes justice as a complex emotion in which the negative quality of unfairness plays a more important role than the positive aspects of the norm of justice. His approach is clinically descriptive as opposed to the way the lawyer tries to conceive the ideal norm of justice. The author propounds the way the everyday layman experiences what justice is done to him.

This approach brings the concept of justice into the field of semantics and focuses upon the confusion around words like *Justice,* and *sacred rights.* Attention is asked for a historical development of concepts that has moved and still moves minds born and molded in different cultures and under different ideologies.

The psychotherapist especially has ample opportunity to detect the manifold subjective aspects of this concept of justice. From the very onset of life the child is subjected to treatment he may or may not experience as outrageous, unfair, or gratifying. The child's appeal to "justice" is a far cry from any legal interpretation of the concept.

The chapter on the complexity of the feeling of justice investigates the collective penal sanctions directed towards those people who don't conform to tribal habits. Here is seen the very beginning of customary law. Psychologically spoken, there exists not only a question of an outwardly imposed customary law rigidly adhered to but also of an inner masochistic submission to power and taboo. Man's innate dependency-need forces him to accept what a powerful majority (or tyranny) prescribes as right. On a higher ego level, however, a code of strictly regulated human relations is accepted in order to

188

escape mutual hostility and confusion of behavior. Even the criminal gang has a strict inner legal code.

The author postulates a phase in the development of the ego—the so-called normative phase—where in the service of individual thinking, values of the outside world are subjected to critical evaluation. This clinical deduction leads the author to accept:

I. *A Collective or Magic Aspect of Justice,* in which mutual participation and collective responsibility for acts done or omitted play an important role.

II. *An Individualistic or Subjective Aspect of Justice,* in which individual ego and self-esteem co-determine the acceptance of norms and values in the society. The ego criticizes the legal order.

III. *The Normative or Objective Aspect of Justice* in which values beyond individual gratification and limitation are searched for. This is what many legal scientists call the search for positive law. Of psychological importance is the fact that in this process identification with a paternal figure or deity has taken place.

Having made the tentative division, the author investigates the system of communication between judge and judged, especially the psychological importance and greater feeling of security when man is allowed to appeal to a higher instance of judgment—to a higher court. Yet, this leads us immediately to unconscious implications of the concept of justice, as the need to punish and revenge one's fellow man may take hold of both the judge and the judged. Even codified law hides disguised will for power. Public opinion inadvertently may force law and lawgivers to acquire a retaliatory avenging aspect, as seen, for instance, in the primitive *jus talionis.* Especially in the mutual relations between collectivities these primitive aspects come more easily to the fore.

Man's unawareness of the limitations of every wise

189

legal system asking for restrictions of his *own* arbitrariness is seen as an intrinsic tragedy of justice. Unconsciously, man asks of the law: "Take care of us and warn us so that our aggressive and primitive tendencies may not break through." No man can be his own judge, yet, especially in international relations restrictive self-limitations, however much needed, are as a rule not accepted.

Attitudes towards fairness and injustice start in the nursery. In the next chapters the author investigates this subjective attitude toward the law of the family and the law of the nation.

It is rather easy to create feelings of indignation and alleged injustice, since everybody has to learn to suppress instinctual wishes. Every slogan of unfairness awakens long-forgotten feelings of frustration. We see this clinically in neurotics with compulsive rituals disguising their infantile rage. Examples are given to show how harshly children judge each other, just because they have to fight so intensely their hostility towards their parents. Their "convict" usually is a scapegoat for deep-seated feelings of injustice.

It is important to investigate the relation between law and power. Arriving at a powerful social position is for everybody a dangerous moment full of inner crisis since from now on he may forsake his former belief in just action. Examples are given of the ancient *Ordeal* and the Adat Law and of our own rudimentary primitive feeling that might makes right.

In the search for a better definition of the *Sense of Justice* we are now sure that this sense has to be severed from primitive magic thinking and from private interest. It implies a universal capacity for empathy and sympathy and inner conquest of the iron law of vengeance and retaliation: An eye for an eye and a tooth for a tooth. On an ideal level the sense of justice may be seen as a balance of contrasting feelings in man, so well symbolized in *Justitia* with her scales. Balance always implies a vacillation of contrasting forces exerted by those who are equal before the law. It may also be expressed as the balance between rights and duties, the balance between freedom and its necessary limitations for the sake of human welfare.

It is clinically important that the development of man's conscience (superego) is needed for the acceptance of the legal order based on human frailties and injustices. Much depends on the positive transferrence between leaders and the members of the community.

Psychologically spoken, justice is an ambivalent concept that not only speaks of legal and ethical values but also of man's tolerance capacity, that means his ability to temporarily tolerate injustice.

There exists much confusion between legality as a mere mechanically existing code and morality as a superimposed ideal of ethical behavior. Clinical psychiatrists have to deal in two ways with this confusion: with neurotics, who punish themselves too severely and who have, paradoxically speaking, to learn to accept their feelings of guilt, and with the judge, who usually also punishes rather heavily, not realizing: "that man can do the wrong thing for the right reason and the right things for the wrong reasons." (Elliot) In each case the mode of action and/or therapy has to be different.

In the next chapter the author investigates how the concept of justice can be misused for propagandistic reasons or to soothe people into feelings of self-justification. Clinically this is especially observed in argumentative querulants. Under the disguise of doing justice they may develop a horrible terror towards others.

The judge through his conscious and unconscious motivations plays an important role in the legal machine, since he influences and co-determines the final

191

decision of guilt and punishment. Unconquered hidden hostilities make a harsh judge out of everyone. Here lies the cause of all prejudice and discrimination. Even the act of punishment influences our legal thinking since the final punitive aim determines our initial logic. Do we believe in curbing criminals? Do we want public revenge or betterment? All this depends on deeper knowledge of the ambivalence of human motivations. There is often a greater desire to help the one who is wrong than to help the wronged. What is the crime behind the crime? What punishment is unwittingly and paradoxically asked for by the criminal himself? What do we really know about the psychology of guilt? It is often a psychological coincidence who the judge is or who the criminal. Our study of gang-crime brought this once more to the fore.

A few examples are given of petty criminality cured by psychiatric therapy. Consequently the question is posed whether or not some form of shock therapy and catharsis could satisfy the deep-seated punishment-need of many a criminal.

In the last chapter, the author shows how in the entire concept of law and justice people ask for safeguards against human fallibility. They demand safeguards against the wrong their fellow men may do to them. They also ask for safeguards against their own coercions and encroachments upon their neighbors without being aware of it. All these laws are made by men so that finally the golden rule may reign: do not unto others what you don't want others to do unto you.

BIBLIOGRAPHY

Bergler, Edmund, *The Superego*. New York: Grune and Stratton, 1952.

Cahn, Edmund N., *The Sense of Injustice*. New York: New York University Press, 1949.

Frank, Jerome, *Courts on Trial*. Princeton University Press, 1949.

Goitein, H., *Primitive Ordeal and Modern Law*. London: Allen and Unwin, 1923.

Meerloo, J. A. M., *The Crime of Menticide*. Am. J. Psychiatry, Vol. 107, 1951.

Meerloo, J. A. M., *The Rape of the Mind*. New York, World Publishers, 1956.

Meerloo, J. A. M., *Suicide, Menticide and Psychic Homicide*. A. M. A. Archives Neur. and Psychiatr. Vol. 81, 1959.

Seagle, William, *The History of Law*. New York: Tudor Publishing Co., 1956.

Van Wynen Thomas, Ann, *The Semantics of International Law*. New York: Southern Methodist University Press, 1953.

VII

THE DEFINITION OF MENTAL ILLNESS

HENRY WEIHOFEN *

I

Mental illness is a medical concept, and so it would seem self-evident that its definition should come from the medical profession and not from either legislators or judges.

But mental illness is a phenomenon that the law does recognize and that may have various legal effects. It may render a person irresponsible for his criminal act; it may justify a court order for his involuntary hospitalization; it may render him incompetent to make a will or a binding contract; it may constitute grounds for divorce. However, mental illness in and of itself does not have any of these legal effects. There must be mental illness; but there is always a second requirement, that the illness be of such form or degree as to meet some legal criterion. In a will contest, where the question is whether the testator was "sane" when he made his will, the question is not merely whether he then had a medically recognized form of mental illness. If not, then of course he was not "insane" in any sense. But even if medical experts agree he was mentally ill, the law asks a further question, which is, broadly, did his mental illness deprive him of sufficient mind to know what he was doing? Did he know it was a will he was

194

executing; did he understand the nature and extent of his property and his obligations toward those persons who are related to him or who have some moral or legal claim upon him? In a commitment proceeding, the question is somewhat different, namely, is his mental condition such that for his own safety or the safety of others he should be confined in a mental institution? In a criminal case, the "test" is still different. Just what the criminal law test should be has been the subject of a vast amount of debate. But everyone agrees that some criterion over and above the mere existence of mental illness is called for.

In short, in each legal situation, the insanity issue really has two parts:

(1) Was the person mentally ill?

(2) If so, was the illness such as to satisfy the legal criterion or test?

Much confusion has been caused by the failure to keep this rather elementary analysis clear. The confusion is aggravated by use of the ambiguous terms "insane" and "insanity." Sometimes these terms are used to refer to mental illness per se, sometimes to the legal consequences of such illness. For example, in criminal cases where the defendant had prior to the criminal act been judicially committed to a mental institution, it is sometimes argued that such proof of prior existing "insanity" should be presumed to continue and so the defendant should be presumed to have been "insane" at the time of the act. This argument is valid enough if by "insanity" is meant merely mental illness per se (and assuming the commitment was for a form of mental illness that can actually be presumed to continue and that the commitment was not too far in the past). But sometimes the word "insanity" is given a shifting meaning, so as to imply that proof that the person was so mentally ill as to need hospital care and treatment some time in the past leads to the presumption that at the later date he was so mentally ill as not to know the nature and quality of the criminal act he was committing or that it was wrong (or whatever the "test" of criminal responsibility may be in that jurisdiction).[1] Another illustration is afforded by cases holding that a person who has been committed to a mental institution is incompetent to make a contract or a will, on the reasoning that he has been adjudicated "insane."[2] The adjudication of course was merely that because of mental illness he needed hospital care and treatment; that is not the equivalent of an adjudication that his illness was such as to render him incompetent to make a contract.[3] An adjudication of the need for hospitalization is not res judicata on the question of contractual competence. Medically, it is not true that all patients in mental hospitals lack the understanding necessary to make any kind of contract, no matter how simple.

Where the elementary distinction we are discussing is made, it is sometimes expressed by speaking of the first issue as "medical insanity" and the second as "legal insanity." But this is unfortunate phrasing, because instead of making clear that *both* questions are always involved in any "legal" issue of insanity, it may give the implication that the medical and legal professions disagree in the definition of mental illness.

The first of our two questions, the existence or non-existence of mental illness per se, is not often a real issue. It is around the second that most of the legal cases revolve. In few of the criminal insanity cases is the issue whether the defendant was truly disordered at all or merely malingering. The only situations where such malingering is likely to be successful is where the jury is looking for an excuse to acquit anyway; the man who shoots his wife or her lover caught in *flagrante delicto,* and then pleads "temporary insanity" and is acquitted, probably did not fool the jury into thinking he was actually insane;

the acquittal is merely the jury's way of applying the "unwritten law." A dubious claim of self-defense might have been just as effective. In the great majority of cases, there is fairly convincing evidence, and often no serious denial, that the defendant was mentally abnormal to some extent. The crucial question is whether the abnormality was such as to come within the legal test of irresponsibility—not whether he was or was not schizophrenic or paranoid, but whether, by reason of such illness, he was incapable of knowing right from wrong. The same generalization may be ventured concerning non-criminal cases.

But this absorption in the legal consequences of mental illness tends to divert attention from the fact that the question of mental illness itself *is* an issue, and in some cases may be important.

II

We have said that the existence of mental illness, like physical illness, is a medical question. This implies that just as in cases where the issue is the existence or non-existence of tuberculosis or a bone fracture, the law should look to factual evidence, and especially, where the fact is not easily apparent, to expert evidence. On its face, it would seem as absurd for the law to attempt its own definitions of mental illness as it would to define for itself what constitutes a physical ailment. Of course, experts on mental disorder may and do disagree, although anyone familiar with personal injury cases knows that disagreements among doctors concerning the nature, extent and effects of physical injuries are hardly any less prevalent. But this is a matter of proof. That the facts may be difficult to establish does not make them any less medical facts.

Unfortunately, the matter is not that simple. Turning to the medical profession to define "mental illness" for us, we find no clear answer. A century ago, "mental disease" was a fairly clear concept; all such disease was thought to be the product of lesions in the brain. Today, psychiatrists recognize that many mental disorders seem to be wholly functional; a postmortem examination shows no organic pathology of any kind. So long as organic pathology was assumed to be involved, it was possible to regard the mentally ill as clearly distinct from those who were "sane." But since the recognition of functional disorders, and especially since Freud, the view that there is a clear, qualitative division between the sane and the mentally ill has largely been abandoned in favor of the quantitative view, that there is no such clear line between the two; there is rather an unbroken continuum from normal to abnormal. But if there is no longer merely black and white, but a continuous shading from one to the other, it becomes apparent that asking the medical expert where he draws the line between two shades of gray is not quite like asking him whether a bone is or is not fractured.

Drawing the line between mental illness and mental health is difficult for another reason. The concept of physical illness deals with the body as a physical object. Psychiatry, it is commonly said, deals with illnesses of the "mind." But the "mind" does not exist as a physical object. Determining whether the "mind" is ill is thereby a materially different task from that of determining whether the body is ill. Dr. Arthur P. Noyes, a leading psychiatrist, has well stated the difference:

> While other branches of medicine deal with parts of the organism, psychiatry or psychobiology studies the individual as a whole, as a biologic unit living in an environment that is essentially social in nature, and deals with the biopsychic life, the total integrated behavior of the human or-

ganism. It deals with data from the biologic, social and psychologic sciences.[4]

But determining whether "the total integrated behavior of the human organism" is healthy or not is obviously not easy. In this context, the concept of "health" is itself ambiguous. Behavior that might be socially well integrated in one culture may be considered "crazy" in another.[5]

The groups most difficult to classify are the so-called psychopaths and severe character neurotics. Psychiatrists are not agreed whether any of these should be included within the term "mentally ill." Most English psychiatrists seem to say no; but in this country psychopathy is recognized as a subgroup under "Mental Disorder" in the standard classification system of the American Psychiatric Association.[6] The training, orientation and philosophy of the particular psychiatrist is likely to be more of a factor in his diagnosis of such cases than any factual questions that can be settled by observation and examination.

At one time, the staff of St. Elizabeth's Hospital in Washington, D. C. took the position that "sociopathic personality disturbance" (the current term to replace "psychopathic personality") should not be regarded as mental disease within the meaning of the test for criminal irresponsibility. They therefore testified that persons so diagnosed did not have a mental disease or defect. Not long afterward, the hospital changed its view and decided that a sociopathic personality disturbance should be considered a mental illness. Thereafter when called to testify in court concerning the mental condition of persons so diagnosed the hospital doctors testified that they were "mentally ill," or "suffering from a mental disease." [7]

This incident points up the fact that the existence or nonexistence of mental illness is not solely a factual question to be determined by objective observation or examination. It is also a question calling for a policy or philosophical judgment concerning what kinds of abnormality should be included in the term "mental illness." It is so much a matter of policy that the question has been raised whether the psychiatrist on the witness stand should even be permitted to say whether in his opinion the person was suffering from mental illness, or from a mental disease or defect. It has been argued that this would be asking him for his opinion as to what is or is not within the legal concept of insanity,[8] a question which it is solely for the jury to decide and so outside the doctor's province.[9]

Another view is that this is a matter of legal policy to be determined neither by the medical experts or by the jury, but by the law [10] itself. The Model Penal Code being drafted by the American Law Institute, after setting forth its test of mental disease or defect excluding responsibility, adds a provision that: "The terms 'mental disease or defect' do not include an abnormality manifested only by repeated criminal or otherwise anti-social conduct." (Sec. 4.01) The purpose is to exclude the so-called psychopathic personality. The reasoning seems to be that (1) the law must act on the assumption that most members of society are susceptible to being influenced by the threat of criminal sanctions; (2) the only exceptions that should be recognized are persons who (a) are socially recognized as being different from ourselves; (b) whose differentness is socially recognized as sickness; and (c) upon the identification of whose condition the experts are most likely to agree among themselves and also with laymen.[11]

Our question in this paper is not whether that conclusion is sound, but the somewhat different, though related, question whether it is wise at this stage of psychiatric development to freeze such a conclusion into a written code. I suggest that it is not. The very concept (and even the name) of psychopathic personality disturbance is a vague and changing one. Research into the nature and etiology of the various conditions that have been lumped together under this label is only beginning. It is entirely possible that we shall see an important breakthrough in the next few years, which may show that these conditions, or some of them, are properly classifiable as mental illnesses, perhaps even organic illness (some experiments have reported finding among psychopaths certain characteristic brain wave patterns similar to those found in epileptics). It therefore seems premature for the law by its own fiat to say that psychiatry will not, at least in the near future, be able to show that these persons are mentally ill, and that they shall therefore be subjected to punitive and not therapeutic treatment. One outstanding characteristic of these persons is that they are not deterred by the threat of punishment or even its actual infliction.[12] The punitive approach is therefore the defeatist one, that there is nothing we can do about such cases except to take them out of circulation for a few years. To take this position concerning a group who are probably responsible for the major part of our violent crimes,[13] just when psychiatry is beginning to have some hopes for finding causes and cures, seems an unduly pessimistic one to freeze into law.

The Model Penal Code provision to exclude psychopaths from the definition of mental disease or defect does not undertake a general definition of mental disease or defect. There seem to be few instances in which law-makers have ventured to formulate a general definition.

A few commitment laws undertake to define "mental illness" or a "mentally ill person" for the purposes of such laws, and these usually do so in terms of need for care and treatment.[14] The Draft Act Governing Hospitalization of the Mentally Ill has a broader definition; it defines "Mentally Ill Individual" as one "having a psychiatric or other disease which substantially impairs his mental health." [15] But since mental illness is merely the opposite of mental health, it is not very helpful to define mental illness as an illness that impairs mental health. Perhaps the word "substantially" adds something, though it is not clear what. The Wisconsin Mental Health Act simply says "Mental illness is synonymous with insanity." [16] It seems that any definition that is not too restrictive is likely to be too general to be very meaningful.

Experience in Pennsylvania shows that the definition of "mental illness" in that state's Mental Health law is vague enough to allow the courts to intrude the M'Naghten Rule in situations where that rule does not properly apply (e.g., where the question is mental competency to stand trial, or, after trial, to be punished).[17]

> Although it was carefully drafted in accordance with psychiatric and administrative principles far more acceptable than M'Naghten, its attempt to define "mental illness" in one paragraph, for application to such varying situations as voluntary admission to institutions, transfer between institutions, commitment of those not charged with crime, those charged with crime and those convicted of crime and sentenced, could not but result in such vagueness of description as to leave much to the discretion of its administrators, interpreters and, we may add misinterpreters.[18]

There seems to be little in the record to lead us to believe that any useful purpose would be served by departing from the policy that the law has, with very few exceptions, followed in the past, of leaving it to psychiatry to wrestle with the question of what does and does not come within the concept of "mental illness," instead of attempting to lay down a legal definition.[19]

III

The second issue in any "insanity" case, the issue whether the mental illness was of such nature or scope as to meet the legal criterion for the particular legal consequence sought, is a question of a quite different kind from the one which we have just discussed, the question of the existence or non-existence of mental illness as such.

To illustrate from the law governing commitment to a mental hospital by court order: as a basis for an order of commitment, the court must of course find that the person is mentally ill. But that is not enough. The law everywhere requires some further finding. What further finding should be required? That if allowed to remain at liberty he is likely to injure other persons? Suppose he is likely only to injure himself (e.g., a depressed patient who is likely to commit suicide)? Suppose he is not dangerous to anyone, but hospital care and treatment would be beneficial to him? Suppose he is not dangerous but hospital care would be beneficial, and he is too disordered to make an intelligent evaluation of his condition and needs?

Whatever legal rule is laid down will reflect a judgment on the basic policy question of the extent to which the state should interfere with the liberty of the individual in the interest of all. The extreme libertarian will perhaps be willing to deprive a person of his liberty only when that liberty endangers others. As for the individual who is sane enough most of the time to understand that in his depressed phases

203

he may commit suicide and who prefers to run that risk rather than go to the hospital, the libertarian extremist might want to allow that choice. At the other extreme are those who would allow the state to act for the person's own good, even when he does not want it. In between, there is room for several other lines of demarcation for those who would weigh individual liberty against social welfare. The Draft Act Governing Hospitalization of the Mentally Ill faced this problem expressly, and chose to permit compulsory hospitalization not only of persons who were dangerous to others, but also to themselves, and also those who are not dangerous but who need hospital care and treatment but who because of the nature or stage of their illness have lost the power to make an intelligent choice or have become so confused as no longer to be able to make a decision having any relation to the factors bearing on the question of hospitalization. Those who need hospitalization but retain the capacity for choice cannot be compelled to enter a hospital unless dangerous.

This is a policy decision. Some doctors, lawyers and social scientists may disagree with it.[20] When a psychiatrist is asked for an opinion whether a given person should be committed, it is therefore important to see clearly just what the import of the question is. If the legal criteria for commitment are not made clear in the question, the doctor may be asked to apply his own political philosophy, determine the fundamental policy issue by his own lights, and give us his policy decision. None of us truly believe that this is purely a medical question to be decided by medical experts. Yet this may be close to what we actually allow under statutes which provide for examination and report by a panel of physicians appointed by the court. When the court, under the belief that the modern and enlightened way to handle commitment cases is to rely on expert scientific examination, gets into the habit of accepting more or less automatically the recommendations of the panel or commission, we may have the medical experts exercising their judgment not only on the medical issue of the existence or non-existence of mental illness, but also on the policy question of what the state ought to do about any given case of illness.[21]

The same point applies in other situations. In contract law, there is the same need for a policy choice. Granting that the person is intellectually weak or unstable; that he is suggestible, gullible, and easily confused or misled; that the psychiatrists agree that he is mentally deficient or even psychotic, whether he should on this ground be allowed to repudiate a contract or transaction depends upon other considerations besides the existence or non-existence of mental illness.

It is a serious matter to deprive a person of his civil capacities or to relieve him of his civil responsibilities. Even though we no longer favor quite as rugged a form of individualism as we did half a century ago, we are still reluctant to exercise too much paternalistic restraint on what we regard as both the right and obligation of the individual to live his own life and abide by the consequences. We do not believe that society should ordinarily interfere to protect fools against their own folly. Infants and psychotic persons we do so protect, but the latter must be "insane" to the extent that they cannot be expected to take care of themselves, and not merely to the extent that therapy is indicated. Moreover, in determining the kind and degree of protection the law should give such persons, it is necessary to strike a balance between their interests and the legitimate interests of businessmen and others dealing with them.[22]

205

This balancing of interests may require taking into account whether the other party acted innocently, whether the contract seems to be a fair one, and whether the parties can be put back in *status quo ante* or whether because the money has been spent or the goods used up this is impossible.[23] The expert judgment of an economist or businessman on the effect of a policy countenancing repudiation of contracts is as relevant to this policy issue as the judgment of a psychiatrist.

During the past twenty years, the public has been much concerned about sex offenders. In some states, laws have been enacted to commit to mental institutions persons suffering from such emotional instability or impulsiveness of behavior or failure to appreciate the consequences of their acts as to render them irresponsible for their sexual acts and thus dangerous to themselves and to others. No conviction of any crime is required under some of these statutes. This of course reflects a valid desideratum: it is socially desirable to apprehend and commit the potential sex offender before he commits an offense. On the other hand, it certainly sacrifices personal liberty, and on unsure ground. It is a serious matter to lock up a person who has not actually committed any offense, on a prediction that he is likely to do so, based on vague constructs such as "emotional instability or impulsiveness of behavior, or lack of customary standards of good judgment." More recent statutes therefore permit such commitment only upon conviction of a sex crime.[24] Again, the choice is a matter of public policy. Psychiatric information about the magnitude of the public danger presented by "sex offenders" and the possibility of identifying potential offenders before the fact are certainly relevant, but the ultimate choice must be based primarily on one's philosophy of government, one's evaluation of the need for social control versus the importance of individual freedom.[25]

206

In criminal law, it has been pointed out that the "test" of insanity is not a clumsy effort by the legal profession to define a psychosis. It is an attempt to answer the policy question: granting that the defendant is more or less mentally abnormal, what should we do with him? Should he be dealt with by the state's penal-correctional program, or by the medical-therapeutic? The answer depends upon our concept of "justice" and the purpose of punishment, our penal policy, the institutional facilities we have available or that the taxpayers are willing to provide, and other considerations. The law, speaking for the community, has to consider the patient, his health and his rights and responsibilities as a free man, the interest of society in the health and safety of its members generally, and also various other, perhaps competing interests. "If total community policy is to be served, a rather complex arbitration may be involved."[26]

It is true that where the legal rule concerns mentally disordered persons, any answer should accord with current psychiatric knowledge.

> It is therefore proper and necessary to enquire from time to time whether the doctrine of criminal responsibility, as laid down by the common law and applied by the courts, takes due account of contemporary moral standards and of modern advance in medical knowledge about the effects of mental abnormality on personality and behavior.[27]

But the ultimate decision is not merely a psychiatric one. It is a major policy decision. This is the legal rationale of the point frequently made by psychiatrists, that they ought not to be asked for their opinions on this policy issue, but should testify only on the medical issue, the existence or non-existence of mental illness. One of the main criticisms that psychiatrists have leveled against the legal test of insanity in criminal cases is that the medical expert, instead of being allowed to restrict himself to giving his medical diagnosis and the basis for it, is asked to give an opinion on whether the accused knew the nature and quality of his act and that it was wrong— questions that are legal, ethical, quasi-religious, but not scientific.

That the psychiatrist should refuse to answer such questions was the position taken in at least one Pennsylvania case. Defense counsel asked his expert to describe the defendant's condition and to give his diagnosis in medical terms, but he refused to ask him whether defendant was "insane" or knew right from wrong, saying that these were legal issues. Dr. Philip Q. Roche of Philadelphia refers to the case in his book, *The Criminal Mind,* and supports the position taken.[28]

Dr. Winfred Overholser, superintendent of St. Elizabeth's Hospital in Washington, D. C., has similarly said,

So long as medical men are compelled to answer questions on such non-medical topics as "malice," "right and wrong," and "criminal intent," so long will the expert be placed in a false light and full justice at times fail to be done the accused.[29]

At least one law professor, Sheldon Glueck of Harvard, has expressed agreement with this view:

The most fruitful source of error and confusion in this field of law is traceable to the requirement that the expert say categorically whether or not the hypothetical person (whom everyone knows to be the defendant on trial) did or did not know right from wrong. This question is purely within the province of the jury, who must answer it as they must any other matter of questionable fact;

208

all the expert should be asked to do, and all his training qualifies him to do, is pass judgment, not upon the ethicolegal question of right and wrong, but upon the *medical question* of whether or not the defendant was mentally unsound, a question that his peculiar training and experience, and his study of the offender's case, entitles him to answer.[30]

So far as I am aware, no one has ever seriously attempted to answer this contention. It deserves attention.

Let us grant that the primary function of the psychiatric witness should be to give us his diagnosis—to tell us (1) the basis for it, i.e., the examination, tests, observation or other data on which he bases his conclusion; (2) what his conclusion is, i.e., whether the person is mentally ill, and if so, what illness he has; (3) the nature and characteristics of this illness; (4) its origin, development and probable future course. But as we have said, the law is never interested in mental illness *as such*. Law is not a panacea for personal problems; it is a form of social control, and it comes into play only where social control seems called for. But while the question of whether control is called for in a given situation is thus a legal question (and as we have said, one that involves important policy judgments), this does not mean that it is improper for the law to obtain expert psychiatric data on which to base a legal judgment. On an application for compulsory commitment to a mental institution, why should we not ask the psychiatrists not only whether he is likely to injure others if allowed to remain at liberty, or whether he would be benefitted by hospitalization? These are "legal" issues, as we have said, but they are issues on which psychiatric opinion would certainly be helpful. There is no reason apparent why we should not ask for such an opinion or why a psychiatrist should refuse to give it.

It is to be noted that most of the demands that psychiatrists not be asked for opinions beyond a medical diagnosis focus on criminal cases and on the traditional right-and-wrong test of criminal responsibility. It is questions such as whether the accused knew that he was doing wrong that psychiatrists object to answering. The objection is so widespread and so bitter that we of the law cannot shrug it off as unreasonable. I believe it has a valid basis. But I do not think that the basis suggested in the statements quoted above is the valid one. As I understand these statements, they assume that the medical function is limited to that of diagnosis, to determining, on the basis of competent examination, whether any pathology exists, and if so, to pigeon-holing that condition in one of the medically accepted classifications. But is that the extent of the doctor's function? What about prognosis? What about prescription? Certainly to us laymen these are the heart of the doctor's work. More important to us than knowing the medical name for what ails us are the questions: Will I die? Can you heal me? What must I do to get well? Should a doctor refuse to answer these questions on the ground that they are not "medical" questions? He may not be *able* to answer, because medical science (or, at least, he) does not know the answer. There are still unknown areas in every field. But that is very different from saying that it is a matter outside his jurisdiction. A lawyer may not know the answer to a legal problem, because the question has never been authoritatively decided (so far as he is aware) but that would not justify his refusing to answer it on the ground that it is not a legal question.

In a criminal case, should a doctor refuse to say whether the accused knew right from wrong on the ground that this is a legal and not a medical question? I suggest not. There is no such dichotomy be-

210

tween legal and medical questions. There are many "legal" issues on which psychiatrists may and properly do express expert opinions—whether a person would be dangerous if allowed at liberty, whether a testator understood what he was doing when he made his will, whether a party to a contract understood the nature of the transaction. Whether the accused knew at the time that his act was wrong is, in theory, no more legal or less medical than these others. To the extent that psychiatrists can say whether a defendant is corrigible or incorrigible, deterrable or non-deterrable, and so enable the sanctioning authorities to foresee the probable consequences of various sanctioning alternatives, they can make an important contribution to the growth of sound legal doctrine and administration.

The real reason why psychiatrists object to testifying concerning knowledge of right and wrong, I suggest, is not that such questions are legal and not medical, but that they are badly conceived and worded. Unlike the legal criteria employed in other situations, the right and wrong test of criminal responsibility seems to most psychiatrists to employ concepts so alien to the conceptology of modern psychiatry that they cannot work with it. Secondly, they find the test is based upon or intertwined with ethical and philosophical attitudes and assumptions that are out of harmony with their own. Indeed, some of these attitudes and assumptions of the law may seem to the psychiatrist to be fundamentally and dangerously wrong: our belief that people have free choice to do or refrain from doing an act, and that they are therefore justly held responsible for their acts; our faith in threats of *punishment* to deter people from committing crime; our reliance on fear and on retributive justice; our assumption that long imprisonments will teach criminals to behave themselves. He cannot help carrying this attitude with him into the court room. There he finds the legal issues as drawn irrelevant or at least inadequate to what he deems to be the basic problem. He becomes emotionally involved. Yet because he appears in the capacity of a scientific expert, he does not want to be emotionally involved. He resents the position in which he finds himself.

But there is a big difference between objecting to all this and wanting to withdraw from it, between saying that the traditional test rests on unsound psychiatry and saying that it has nothing to do with psychiatry. It is one thing to argue that this test rests on such unsound or outmoded assumptions, or uses such unscientific terms, that no meaningful answers are possible. It is another thing to say that the test of criminal irresponsibility is a legal concept and that therefore a psychiatrist should refuse to concern himself with whether a given individual meets the test or not. The first objection could presumably be met by changing the test; the second could not be met at all. If the psychiatric assumptions that the law rests upon are unsound, there is the more need for psychiatrists to continue trying to set us straight, and not abandon us to our ignorance.

IV

CONCLUSIONS

In every situation in which the law allows mental illness to have some legal effect, the issue actually has two parts:

a. Was the person at the time in question mentally ill?

b. If so, was his mental illness of such degree or scope as to satisfy the legal criterion for that kind of situation?

Although both of these are "legal" issues in the sense that both are essential to the deciding of the case, the first is almost always left by the law to be decided as a matter of psychiatric fact or theory. And while the psychiatrists' answer to this question is sometimes not as clear-cut or as unanimous as laymen may like, it is probably unsound for the law to try to clear up the difficulty by legal fiat. It is reported that one legislature once undertook to enact that the value of *pi* should henceforth be 3.1416. But scientific or other problems that are inherently difficult and uncertain are not rendered clear and easy by legislative knot-cutting.

The second of the two issues, that of the proper degree or "test" of mental illness that shall be required for any given legal consequence to follow, is a legal question in the stricter sense that its solution depends not solely upon scientific or other factual data, but upon a policy judgment as to the extent to which mental illness should be given the particular legal effect.

Such policy decision, however, like most policy decisions, should not be made in a vacuum. Experts in various relevant fields of learning, including psychiatrists, may well be able to contribute helpful data that will throw light on what the proper rule should be. Even more, they can provide the data necessary for intelligent application of the rule.

But one should not lose sight of the distinction between this factual background and the ultimate policy decision.

The generalization above, that experts can supply data that will be helpful in deciding the legal policy issue, applies in the particular issue of mental irresponsibility for crime as it does elsewhere. Suggestions that psychiatrists should refuse to testify to opinions on whether a defendant satisfies the requirements of the "test" of criminal responsibility rest more soundly on objection to the specific test that the law employs (particularly the right and wrong test) rather than on the ostensible argument that this is a "legal" matter on which it is improper for psychiatrists to give an opinion.

NOTES

* Professor of Law, University of New Mexico. Reprinted with permission of the Ohio State Law Journal

1. For cases, see Weihofen, Mental Disorder as a Criminal Defense 228-29, 234 (1954). In some of the cases where the courts refused to hold that proof of prior commitment required a conclusive presumption that defendant was criminally irresponsible at the time of the act, the result was based on the fact that the time interval between the commitment and the criminal act was so long that he might have recovered his sanity. But in at least one case, this way out was closed to the court. In People v. Willard, 150 Cal. 543, 89 Pac. 124 (1907), as the judge at the conclusion of a commitment hearing was signing the commitment order, the patient drew a pistol and shot the complaining witness dead. Being thus forced to face the issue, the court properly held that the fact that the person had just been found so mentally ill as to require hospital care did not raise a conclusive presumption that he was so mentally ill as not to know the nature of his act or that it was wrong.

2. Cubbison v. Cubbison, 45 Ariz. 14, 40 P.2d 86 (1935); Sanders v. Omohundro, 204 Ark. 1040, 166 S.W.2d 657 (1942); Rohrer v. Darrow, 66 Colo. 463, 182 Pac. 13 (1919); Walker v. Graves, 174 Tenn. 336. 125 S.W.2d 154 (1939).

215

Under Ohio Law, no person in a mental hospital (except a "sane epileptic," a voluntary patient, or a person temporarily in the hospital for observation) is deemed competent to execute a contract or deed unless approved by the committing court. Ohio Rev. Code § 5123.57 (1954). The opposite provision, such as found in the Draft Act Governing Hospitalization of the Mentally Ill, seems sounder: that every patient in a mental hospital retains his civil rights, including the right to contract, unless he has been adjudicated incompetent.

3. The better view is, therefore, that evidence of prior hospitalization is admissible and entitled to some weight to prove incompetency to contract, but it is not conclusive. Ross, "Commitment of the Mentally Ill; Problems of Law and Policy," 57 Mich. L. Rev. 945, 988 (1959).

4. Noyes, Modern Clinical Psychiatry 66 (4th ed. 1953).

5. Szasz, "Psychiatry, Ethics and the Criminal Law," 58 Col. L. Rev. 183 (1958).

6. American Psychiatric Ass'n. Diagnostic and Statistical Manual 85 (1952).

7. Blocker v. United States,—F.2d—(1959).

8. Defense counsel so argued in Blocker v. United States, *supra* note 7.

9. Judge Bazelon of the Court of Appeals for the District of Columbia said of the decision of the St. Elizabeth's Hospital staff that sociopathic or psychopathic personality should not be regarded as mental disease within the meaning of the Durham rule, Durham v. United States, 214 F. 2d 862 (1953), "This inevitably encroaches upon the jury function." Briseol v. United States, 248 F.2d 640, 644n (1957).

10. Whether, if "the law" should determine this matter, it should be laid down by the legislature or by judicial decision is a question not discussed in this article.

11. The official comments to this provision do not spell out the reasoning. However, it is found in Swartz, "The Definition of Mental Disease," Tests of Criminal Responsibility (1955). Professor Swartz, assistant to the Reporter, submitted this memorandum to the Advisory Committee on October 8, 1955.

12. Brancale, "Psychiatric and Psychological Services," in Tappan, Contemporary Correction 195 (1951).

13. Dr. E. Glover testifying before the British Royal Commission on Capital Punishment, said: "The true psychopath . . . can be the most dangerous, and in the absence of proper treatment, intractable criminal." And again, "Most crimes of violence are pathological, perhaps 70%." Royal Commission on Capital Punishment, "Minutes of Evidence," 492, 512.

14. N.Y. Mental Hygiene Law § 2 (1951); Pa. Stat. Ann tit. 50, § 1072 (1954).

15. "A Draft Act Governing Hospitalization Of The Mentally Ill," U.S. Pub. Health Service Publication No. 51 (rev. ed. 1952).

16. Wis Stat. § 50.001 (1957).

17. See Commonwealth v. Patskin, 375 Pa. 368, 100 A.2d 472 (1953); Commonwealth v. Moon, 383 Pa. 18, 117 A.2d 96 (1955) and other cases discussed in Carroll & Leopold, "The Current Influence of Psychiatric Concepts in Determining Criminal Responsibility in Pennsylvania," 31 Temp. L.Q. 254 (1958).

18. Carroll and Leopold, *supra* note 17, at 257. See also Polsky, "Present Insanity—From the Common Law to the Mental Health Act and Back," 2 Vill. L. Rev. 504 (1957).

19. The recent report of the British Royal Commission on the Law Relating to Mental Illness and Mental Deficiency recommended: "In our opinion it would do more harm than good to try to include in the law a definition of psychopathic personality on the analogy of the present legal definition of mental

defectiveness. It is far preferable that, in referring to various forms of mental disorder, the law should use general terms which will convey a sufficiently clear meaning to the medical profession without trying to describe medical conditions in detail in semi-medical language. . . . It would in any case be particularly difficult to find a suitable detailed description of psychopathic personality. Such a description would probably have to mention the particular aspects of the personality which may be affected, and possibly also try to give some guide as to the cause of the disorder. But there are too many different types of psychopathic personality, and too little is at present known about their essential nature and causes, for a description of this kind to be easily agreed; and even if one were agreed now, increasing knowledge might soon make it out of date. Lack of knowledge about the nature and causes of particular forms of disorder does not mean that they cannot be recognized and successfully treated in individual patients." Royal Commission on the Law Relating to Mental Illness and Mental Deficiency (1954-1957). Report. Comnd. 169. H.M.S.O., (1957). Quoted in Morris, Comment, 21 Modern L. Rev. 63.

20. See Whitmore, "Comments on a Draft Act for the Hospitalization of the Mentally Ill," 19 Geo. Wash. L. Rev. 512, 522 (1951).

21. Ross, "Commitment of the Mentally Ill; Problems of Law and Policy," 57 Mich. L. Rev. 945, 960-64 (1959).

22. Guttmacher & Weihofen, Psychiatry and the Law, 324 (1952).

23. See Comment, "Mental Illness and Contracts," 57 Mich. L. Rev. 1021 (1959).

24. For a summary of the statutes in various states, see Weihofen, Mental Disorder As A Criminal Defense 195-206 (1954).

25. For discussions of these considerations, see

Fahr, "Iowa's New Sexual Psychopath Law—An Experiment Noble in Purpose?" 41 Iowa L. Rev. 523 (1956); Guttmacher & Weihofen, "Sex Offenses," 43 J. Crim. L., C. & P. S. 153 (1952).

26. Dession, "Deviation and Community Sanctions," Psychiatry and the Law 1, 11 (Hoch & Zubin ed. 1955).

27. Report, Royal Commission on Capital Punishment, para. 281 (1949-53).

28. Roche, The Criminal Mind 142 (1958).

29. Overholser, "The Place of Psychiatry in the Criminal Law," 16 B.U.L. Rev. 322, 329 (1936). See also Zilboorg, The Psychology of the Criminal Act and Punishment, 112-13 (1954).

30. Glueck, Mental Disorder And The Criminal Law 309n (1925).

VIII

TREATMENT FOR THE CRIMINAL

MERRILL T. EATON, JR., M.D.

What can psychotherapy do to help society cope with the problem of crime? To what extent can these techniques benefit society by reducing the incidence of crime and recidivism? To what extent can they benefit the individual criminal by helping him become a happier and better adjusted citizen, freed of the impulses toward criminal activity which may place his freedom or even his life in jeopardy? The answers to these questions are important, not only to therapists engaged in the treatment of criminals, but also to those whose opinions and decisions may have something to do with whether criminals obtain treatment. In the courtroom the expert witness will testify as to responsibility and will rarely be asked about prognosis and treatment. However, as a consultant to the attorneys and the Court, he must be prepared to discuss the problem. Attorneys and judges consider what to do *about* the offender in addition to determining his guilt and responsibility.

The number of therapists engaged in the treatment of criminals is not limited to those employed by courts, prisons, and institutions for the so-called criminally insane. For purposes of this discussion a criminal may be defined as one who has committed one or more serious offenses or even one whose behavior patterns are *likely* to lead to such offenses. Many therapists in private practice will see offenders who are referred for treatment rather than tried; offenders who are on parole or suspended sentence; others who have completed sentences, but seek help on their own initiative or at the recommendation of prison authorities; and, less frequently, patients who have been found not guilty by reason of insanity.

While the therapist is obviously interested in problems of technique, the attorney or judge is also interested in treatment problems to the extent, at least, of wanting to know what can and will be done if a criminal is referred to a therapist for out-patient treatment, is sent to a state hospital, or is sent to prison.

THE CRIMINALS WHO MAY BE HELPED BY THERAPY

Criminals who may be candidates for therapy include: (1) The neurotic and psychotic; (2) the psychopath or sociopath; (3) the recidivist or potential recidivist.

The first group, those criminals having clear-cut neuroses and psychoses, present treatment problems related to their particular disorders rather than specifically related to the crime. In determining responsibility one, of course, considers whether the crime is the product of the illness, simply an intercurrent event, or even whether the illness is the result of the crime and the stresses associated with trial and confinement. No attempt will be made here to discuss all of the possible treatment situations presented by this group. One example will suffice. Let us suppose that a woman suffering from a psychotic depressive reaction attempts to drown her children feeling that, in doing so, she protects them from the suffering which she feels is an inevitable part of life. Such a woman is quite likely to be found, correctly, not guilty by reason of insanity since her crime is the product of illness and, even if the M'Naghten Rules are applied, she cannot be said to understand fully the nature and consequences of her act. Treatment is obviously needed and is likely to be effective.

Though in individual cases, psychotherapy or drug therapies may be used in severe depressions, the usual treatment is electric shock therapy and this would be indicated in the case described just as if her symptoms had not included the crime. The only possible difference in the management of her case would be that, because of the severity of the symptoms, a prolonged follow-up period to detect possible recurrence in advance of serious symptoms might be necessary.

The second group, the psychopaths or sociopaths, includes those criminals with weak or distorted superego. The lack of superego values, including a lack of moral standards, coupled with the impulsivity associated with the relative inability of the sociopath to tolerate frustration or defer pleasure, frequently leads to antisocial acts. While psychopathy is a relative matter and almost anyone may show some minor aberrations of the superego, a degree of this disorder sufficient to merit diagnosis and permitting of objective confirmation by examination findings and psychological testing probably exists in 10 to 25 per cent of criminals.

The writer has previously advanced the hypothesis that, in addition to the first two groups described, many recidivists and potential recidivists are sick and that recidivism is a repetitive pattern or characteristic pattern of living, emotionally determined, and creating a painful maladaptation and failure in the life of the recidivist. [1,2] Repetitive crime represents a specific syndrome closely related to the obsessional neuroses. The obsessive character of kleptomania, arson, and certain sex offenses is generally recognized, but this is less frequently recognized in other types of recurring crime. Since more than half of federal prisoners, for example, are recidivists, any treatment which could reduce the incidence of recidivism would have great practical value. This fact, incidentally, should also make it apparent that punishment alone and/or punishment combined with presently available techniques of rehabilitation fails to cure recidivism and, accordingly, fails both to protect society and to spare the criminal the discomforts of repeated incarceration.

ATTITUDES TOWARD TREATMENT

An objective discussion of treatment for the criminal is often made difficult by unrealistic partisan attitudes. These unrealistic attitudes are encountered, both in those opposed to treatment and those favoring it. On the superficial level, those opposed do not generally limit themselves to doubts as to the *practicality* or *efficacy* of therapy, arguments which would lend themselves to objective reply through pilot studies and statistical research. More often objections center around the belief that the psychologist, psychiatrist, and social worker side with the criminal and are eager to help him avoid imprisonment or if he is imprisoned, to make his confinement brief and pleasant.

This is far from the truth. The therapist does not want a dangerous patient at large; nor does he want a treated patient released prematurely. His reasons for being conservative include his responsibility for the protection of society of which he himself is a member and his responsibility to the patient whose future well being is jeopardized if he is *allowed* to commit another crime. In his responsibility to the patient the therapist does not want the patient to be in a situation where he will encounter additional punishment or even about which he will have guilt feelings which may undo some of the benefits of therapy. On a less objective and altruistic level, the therapist's own narcissism would lead him to do everything possible to avoid having his clinical failures forcibly demonstrated to himself and the public. He does not want to open the newspaper with a prayer nor to hear a broadcast about a shocking crime with the sinking fear that a patient of his might be involved.

Underlying factors in the resistance to the idea of treatment for the criminal include projection of guilts and hostilities and in some instances a defensiveness related to fear of losing authority. The latter is a factor in some of the objections made by lawyers, law enforcement officials, and prison officers.

The attitude of some proponents of therapy for criminals may also create problems. Psychotherapy is a long and difficult process. Unduly optimistic expectations of what will be accomplished by adding one or two psychologists to a prison staff or securing a consulting psychiatrist can lead only to disillusionment. The optimistic advocate of treatment may far over-estimate the number of patients who can be helped by a therapist and may under-estimate the time required by each patient. In fact, as one receives referrals from the Courts, one gets the feeling that there are a few attorneys and judges who believe that some magic will take place for even the most chronic case if a therapist will only agree to *see* him. This is an attitude which leads to one of our most vicious social hypocrisies.

It is only too easy to refer a patient to a *school* for the mentally defective or a *hospital* for the mentally ill, assuming as it were, that the word provides the teaching or treatment. Unfortunately, some of these *schools* are without teachers or if, indeed, they have trained and licensed teachers, the teachers are not engaged in actual teaching, but instead hold administrative or other positions. Likewise, some state *hospitals* are virtually without qualified therapists and such professional personnel as may be available are occupied with routine tasks which preclude intensive treatment of the patients. The idea that a patient found, for example, not guilty by reason of insanity and sent to an institution for the criminally insane will actually receive a treatment program in any way comparable to that obtainable in an accredited private psychiatric hospital or on the psychiatric ward of an accredited general hospital would be quite unrealistic in some of our states. A transfer from prison to mental hospital may be nothing more than a movement from one custodial facility to another.

Both opposition and over-optimism about therapy are mentioned because the therapist must expect to encounter them and must prepare to deal with them on a basis of an understanding of their dynamic significance and of the realities involved. Likewise, the therapist must keep these attitudes in mind as he meets the public in speaking to various groups or through his contacts with the press.

Treatment Methods

It is our purpose here to discuss real rather than nominal treatment. In discussing treatment no attempt will be made to outline a *specific* therapeutic technique. A variety of techniques may be used effectively and the choice in a particular case will depend upon the training and personality of the therapist and the problems and personality structure of the patient. In discussing several points about the treatment of the criminal, problems associated with the setting in which treatment takes place will first be considered and then suggestions will be offered concerning the management of the two major groups which might be benefited by treatment—the sociopaths and the compulsive recidivists.

THE SETTING IN WHICH TREATMENT TAKES PLACE

The therapist who treats the criminal as an outpatient is usually treating a patient who comes under duress. The patient may be ordered by the Court to obtain therapy. His liberty may be at stake. He may be coming as an alternative to facing prosecution. The problem is more than one of poor motivation. The feeling of being compelled to seek therapy will be displaced to the therapist who will be blamed unrealistically for making him come for appointments. The patient is bound to begin therapy with hostile and negativistic feelings which he may or may not conceal. It is essential to bring these into the open and to acknowledge them. One cannot expect to eliminate them and should not try. Efforts to reduce or eliminate the patient's hostility and negativism may lead the therapist to "take sides" with the patient to the point of committing himself to actions on the patient's behalf which may later prove to be impractical or unwise.

Rather than trying to win the patient over to the idea of therapy, it is better to face the fact that the patient would rather be elsewhere doing something else as perhaps, indeed, would the therapist. Agreeing to this, patient and therapist may reach a reasonably mature decision to make the best of the time anyway. If the patient's negativism and hostility is not acknowledged and dealt with, a prolonged but unproductive therapy may result in which the patient chooses topics for discussion remote from his central problems and feels only that he is going through a required ritual and if he gains anything at all, it will be only a shade of ego support from the feeling that he has fooled the therapist.

Another problem in out-patient treatment concerns those patients referred by Courts, prosecuting attorneys, and parole officers. The therapist accepting such a referral is wise to make very sure that he understands what his subsequent relationship to the source of referral will be. If treatment is recommended, is the patient compelled to accept it? If so, for how long? Who pays for it? What steps are to be taken if the patient misses appointments? Is the therapist expected to notify someone? If so, what will be done? If there is a lack of progress, to whom should this be reported? To what extent is the therapist expected to report what goes on in therapy and to what extent may he promise that material will be kept confidential? Generally speaking, laws governing privileged communication prohibit the therapist from discussing anything told him by the patient in connection with his illness. Since crime is part of the illness for which such a patient is referred, anything connected with crime is a privileged communication. However, in a referred case the therapist may well find himself the agent of the source of referral and this privilege may be explicitly or implicitly waived. These are things that must be understood by both therapist and patient if effective communication is to take place between them. The foregoing may seem only too obvious. Experience has shown, however, that this is not as simple as it sounds. Oftentimes the referring agency has not thought beyond "getting rid" of a problem.

The problem of confidentiality is also a difficult one in cases of self-referred criminals, particularly those whose crimes have not been discovered. Since law and precedent differ from state to state, the therapist finding himself involved in such a case should consult his own attorney before proceeding.

Because conflicts are acted out both by the sociopathic offender and by the compulsive offender, a problem arises when the "symptom" or form of antisocial behavior is dangerous to others or places the patient in danger of arrest. Like all acting out tendencies, these increase under stress. Psychotherapy is in itself stressful in that it leads to insights through which the patient may at times learn things about himself which are disturbing and/or which are not egosyntonic. Also, as he attempts to implement insight by acquiring new behavior patterns, he has the stress of new adjustments. Stresses also occur in the transference relationship. In dealing with the neurotic patient, we expect transitory *increases* in symptoms in the course of therapy even though the general progress of the therapy is favorable. When the symptom is acted out and when its acting out endangers the patient or others, extreme caution is necessary. This is quite analogous to the problems in out-patient treatment of the alcoholic or addict. Few therapists will attempt to treat a seriously ill alcoholic as an outpatient at the start, even if he comes for therapy "dry." With the alcoholic, getting the therapy on a firm basis while he is an in-patient is almost essential or at least was almost essential before the introduction of Antabuse and Temposil.

When beginning work on an in-patient basis is impractical, the therapist must avoid those stresses which are likely to increase acting out tendencies. With the out-patient he is scarcely in a position to *prevent* acting out tendencies and if he tries to forbid them, his "or else" is likely to be disruptive to therapy. Quick interpretation as an alternate method of handling acting out tendencies is often impossible. His only recourse is to build the patient's ego strength

228

and to approach stressful areas with extreme gentleness.

If a patient is found not guilty by reason of insanity and is committed, like any other patient, to a state hospital so that dismissal from the hospital may take place according to usual hospital policies when the patient recovers and so that no additional restrictions need be placed upon the patient than would be placed upon any other patient, in-patient treatment presents few special problems.

However, if the patient is sent because he is unable to stand trial (that is, because his mental illness is such that he cannot understand the nature of the charges against him and/or is unable to cooperate in his own defense) and presumably has to face trial after recovery; if he is sent to a state hospital in lieu of sentence, awaiting further order of the Court, or until restoration by the Court; or if he is transferred during his sentence from a penitentiary, new difficulties arise in formulating a meaningful treatment program.

Paradoxically, the hospital often becomes more restrictive than the prison. The well adjusted prisoner in most penitentiaries can acquire a degree of personal liberty; he is allowed minimum security custody; he accumulates good time and is considered for parole as soon as eligible.

The patient in the state hospital often does not have these advantages. Sometimes this is because the law does not allow them. At other times it is because professional people involved are ignorant of the proper procedures. It then becomes the duty of the psychiatrist and psychologist in such a setting to learn what procedures may be used in behalf of the patients. A certain skepticism about curbstone opinions on the subject is warranted. Information can be sought from the attorney general of the state or from the director of institutions.

A problem in public relations exists when the hospitalized criminal leaves the hospital without permission. Often this creates far more adverse publicity than the escape of an inmate from a penitentiary. Good press relations and care in how the press is informed of these events is important. With the tendency of the modern and progressive mental hospital to be largely open ward, any requirement for custody creates a strain upon the hospital. It requires, in effect, that a prison ward be created in the hospital and, if indeed, such a special facility is necessary, it could equally well be created as a hospital ward within the prison.

The patient who must stand trial after recovery or who must return to a prison to serve a sentence has an obvious problem in motivation in therapy and experiences special stresses as improvement takes place. There is no easy way to handle these. Like the negativism of the unwilling out-patient, open and candid discussion with the patient is necessary.

Treatment of prisoners within the prison itself is nearly always limited by a shortage of qualified personnel. This leads to difficulties in the choice of patients. Where personnel qualified to treat prisoners is quite limited, treatment is likely to be restricted to those patients with serious intercurrent illness. While this is worthwhile and necessary just as the treatment of any other intercurrent illness is necessary, it does little to aid in reducing criminal activity.

The next group of prisoners most likely to receive treatment are those who create custodial problems, for example, certain aggressive sociopaths. Another group fairly likely to receive treatment are prisoners who are incapable of adjusting in the general prison population even though they may not show a recognizable psychiatric disease. Borderline cases of inadequate personality, emotionally unstable personality, and other personality pattern and trait disturbances together with some passive homosexuals form this group. They find their way to the prison hospital for their own protection and to simplify the smooth running of prison industry and other routine activities. That the groups of patients just mentioned may not be those most likely to benefit from definitive psychiatric treatment is apparent.

Only too often the choice of additional patients for treatment by prison psychiatrists and psychologists is made at random and by whim rather than systematically. Sometimes patients are chosen because they are "interesting" or, by the younger therapists, to provide experience. Though this is not desirable, it would be much less undesirable if any therapist undertaking the treatment of even a few prisoners, would keep adequate records, maintain well matched controls, and make some plan for follow-up study. It can only be through case reports and small pilot studies that we can learn enough about the potential value of treatment of the criminal to justify large scale studies and it is only through the latter that we can reasonably expect to make long range plans and to provide data necessary to convince the authorities and the public of the need to provide and train sufficient personnel to treat an appreciable number of criminals.

Group therapy not only conserves personnel, but has certain other advantages in the treatment of some criminals. The problem of motivation exists in the group as it does in individual therapy. One finds many patients who are not aware of a need for therapy or possible benefit from it. Likewise, one finds patients with ulterior motivation who wish only assistance in mitigating punishment or manipulating environment. The therapist is an official or at least an employee of the prison and is so viewed by the patients. His actual role as an official leads to a certain reserve in discussing problems with him. In addition to this, feelings, realistic or otherwise, about other officials are displaced to the therapist. While these may be brought into the open and worked through in individual therapy, often they can be handled more rapidly and effectively in the group.

Not all members of the group will distort reality in the same way at the same time. When one member calls attention to another's projection or displacement, it may be more acceptable than if the therapist made the interpretation since the fellow inmate making it does not share the therapist's official role.

The social role of being a patient while in prison creates difficulties both in individual and in group therapy. While being a psychiatric patient is relatively fashionable in the upper social and economic classes, it carries a stigma among the lower social classes which comprise the majority of the prison population. Usually the prisoner in psychotherapy will be viewed with contempt or suspicion. There are some exceptions to this in group therapy programs where those selected may be envied especially if there are certain secondary benefits related to group membership. While it is rarely done, the psychiatric patient outside of a prison can keep the fact that he is in therapy from being known by his friends and associates. Prison grapevine and the fact that receptionists, secretaries, and other adjunctive personnel are frequently fellow prisoners makes this secrecy impossible in the prison. The patients in therapy may be grouped together in separate areas though this may not be practical in all prison settings.

An alternative to creating a special role for the prisoner in therapy is to have a majority of prisoners involved in some form of group therapy. At first thought this might seem impractical for a small staff. However, groups may vary in size and selected patients may be in groups of six or eight for investigative dynamically oriented therapy, whereas others, including controls, may be in larger groups, utilizing didactic or inspirational methods, projects, and other less intensive and specific therapeutic techniques.

In stressing the merits of the *large* group therapy program in prisons and other institutions, an analogy may be offered. Suppose there is one music teacher in a fairly large school. He can regard his situation as hopeless and confine himself to leading occasional group singing or playing records for the pupils. If he tries in some such manner to reach everyone, his work will be superficial. On the other hand, he may try to give private instruction or semi-private instruction to only a few very talented pupils. The rest get nothing. His most effective way of coping with the situation would be to have a combined program with a few students receiving special instructions, others with sufficient aptitude organized into orchestras, bands, and glee clubs, and the remainder given an opportunity to participate and to enjoy themselves in periods of music appreciation and in activities at the level of the rhythm band. Of course, that is really just about the way it is done. We can learn something from it.

Another problem in treating prisoners is the class difference between therapist and patient. It has been established that there is some tendency of therapists to elect to treat people of their own social class.[3] There are some who even believe that the therapist cannot empathize with, and treat effectively, patients of a markedly different background than his own. While this may apply to some techniques of therapy, it does not apply to relatively passive investigative therapies if the therapist is aware of the difference between himself and the patient. He must know that his solutions to the problems of living and the behavior patterns which are successful in his own society will not work for his patient. His difference from the patient offers the same advantage that the foreign

233

therapist frequently has. This lies in the ability to ask questions that the person of similar background could not ask and expect to have answered.

Failures in adjusting to and dealing effectively with one's society stem in part from failure to understand it. In order for the patient to understand his maladjustments he must become aware of his ignorance, misunderstanding, and faulty perception of his social environment. The therapist assists in this with questions that help the patient clarify and revise his ideas and recognize his need for observation of the successful adaptations of others.

When the therapist and patient are from similar backgrounds each takes a great deal for granted about the other's experiences and perceptions. Should the therapist ask about usual life experiences, mores, or folkways, the patient is likely to dismiss the question as trivial or as something the therapist should know. His alternative is to suspect a trap or to feel that he is being given subtle criticism or advice.

Though he may resent probing by an outsider, once a working relationship is formed he can accept the need of a therapist from a different background to ask questions.

THE SOCIOPATH AND THE RECIDIVIST

Having considered the problems created by the various settings in which one may treat the criminal, let us consider the treatment problems of the two main groups, the sociopaths and the compulsive recidivists.

For the sociopath somatic treatments are of little value. Lobotomy was at one time recommended. However, though it might be expected to relieve tension that some of these patients show, one would logically expect frontal cortical damage to add to some of the other symptoms. Many lobotomized patients show an

234

increase rather than a decrease of antisocial and, if not immoral, at least unmoral behavior. Impulsivity is also exaggerated by frontal lobe damage.

None of the pharmacological agents recently introduced have been shown conclusively to help the sociopath. In fact, since many of these preparations act as sedatives or stimulants, the possibilities of addiction and of hedonistic misuse are high. Occasionally a reduction in tension and, accordingly, some reduction in acting out tendencies may be accomplished through the use of subcortical depressants. Basically the treatment is psychotherapy. The patient's need is for superego values and these can best be acquired through identification. Therefore, the early phases of psychotherapy of the sociopath are devoted more to forming a good working relationship than to dynamic investigation. To permit the identification necessary for subsequent investigative therapy, certain qualities are almost essential in the personality of the therapist. The therapist himself must have a successful and happy adaptation to living. Otherwise, the patient has little reason to elect to model himself after his therapist. The therapist's own attitudes must be socially acceptable. He must not be exercising a tenuous restraint upon antisocial impulses nor can he envy consciously or unconsciously the freedom of the sociopath from conventionality. On the other hand, his attitudes must be sufficiently flexible that identification is possible. The patient could scarcely identify with someone completely opposite to him. The therapist should be free from hypocrisy.

The sociopath, having few superego values, suspects their authenticity in others. Sometimes parental hypocrisy may be an etiological factor in sociopathy. If the patient's disbelief in the sincerity of his therapist's expressed attitudes finds confirmation, an effective relationship is impossible.

The therapist must not allow the sociopath to ex-

ploit him or to use him to manipulate the environment, unless this is allowed with the intent to bring
it to the patient's immediate attention, non-critically,
for purposes of analysis and study.

Once an adequate identification with the therapist
has occurred, the therapy of the sociopath is similar
to that of the patient with an anxiety reaction, save
that investigative and interpretive activity must be
carried on with greater caution than in the average
psychoneurotic patient since there is less ego strength
and, accordingly, less ability to tolerate the stresses
intrinsic in investigative therapy.

As yet there are no somatic treatments which are
helpful to the compulsive recidivist. As with almost
any compulsive symptom, the patient's antisocial behavior pattern is more likely to occur in situations of
stress and anxiety or in the face of feelings of depression. Accordingly, when the patient experiences
tension, subcortical depressants may be useful and
mild stimulants may be helpful when there are depressive elements.

Like all compulsive patients, these are difficult to
treat. They are slow to form working relationships.
Compulsive patients generally tend to resist external
compulsion or anything that is perceived as external
compulsion. They are parsimonious and hold things
within themselves; and there are strong hostile components in their personalities. All of these factors influence therapeutic technique. The patient resents any
probing as a form of external compulsion; he hesi-
tates to *give* accounts of his experience or to *give*
any display of emotion. He is hostile toward the therapist, not only because of the authoritarian role in
which he casts him, but also because the therapist is
a convenient object for the diffuse hostility within
him.

The therapist must be patient, must not insist on
the patient *giving* much, must avoid compulsion and

authoritarianism, and must be able to accept hostility comfortably and discuss it objectively with the patient without replying in kind or becoming defensive. As in treating any compulsion, the therapist must focus on the total personality and not upon the symptom.

The symptom is secondary to underlying social maladjustments, intrapsychic conflicts, and anxieties. When these are resolved the need for the symptom is eliminated. The symptom itself may symbolize a conflict or have some other dynamic significance, but this is often hard to discover, and if discovered may not be useful. Some discussion and therapeutic investigation of the symptom itself is quite appropriate, but work with the symptom should not be disproportionate.

If group therapy is to be used with these patients, it is desirable to match the group, not only according to background, education, and age, but also as to type of criminal pattern. If the groups do not consist of all one type of criminal pattern, there should at least not be any isolated case in the group. That is, if there is to be one embezzler included, another must be found to join him in the group. If this is not done, the patient will isolate himself from the group and its problems.

CONCLUSION

It has been the purpose of this chapter to make some general suggestions concerning the treatment of the criminal. There must be many techniques which will help prevent crime and reduce the incidence of recidivism. These include steps to provide a better environment for youth. Education, job training, and all of the other aspects of rehabilitation are important. Adequate law enforcement itself is a factor. We must retain perspective and avoid feeling that psychotherapeutic techniques in themselves offer a complete answer to this complex problem. However, even a moderate reduction in recidivism would benefit not only the successfully treated patients, but also those who might have been their victims and the taxpayers who must support the prisons.

The question of treatment is of coming importance in forensic psychology. The classical question of forensic psychiatry was, "Is he responsible?" The relevant question of today is, "Can he be cured?"

NOTES

1. Eaton, Merrill T., Jr. A psychiatrist views rehabilitation of the criminal who is mentally ill. Symposium on criminal responsibility, *Kans. L. Review*, Vol. 4, 3:356-360, March 1956.

2. Eaton, Merrill T., Jr. Chapter 10, "Functions of the psychiatrist in the court and prison," *Crime and Insanity*. New York: Philosophical Library, 1957. pp. 165-186. Richard W. Nice, editor.

3. Hollingshead, August de Belmont and Redlich, Frederick C. *Social Class and Mental Illness; a Community Study*. New York: Wiley, 1958.

IX

TREATMENT OF OFFENDERS: THE FAMILY INFLUENCE

ROBERT E. STEPHENS
Psychiatric Social Worker,
New Jersey State Reformatory
for Men, Bordentown, N. J.

For many years, penal institutions, law enforcement agencies, corrective organizations and rehabilitative instrumentalities have experienced an increasing number in the referrals of social offenders. It is common knowledge that probation departments and crime prevention organizations for both youths and adults are taxed almost beyond capacity in trying to cope with constantly climbing case-loads; reformatory, corrective and penal institutions at all levels, from local to federal and from coast-to-coast, are dangerously over-populated; and, parole systems, along with privately endowed associations which offer rehabilitative assistance to offenders who are embarked on the difficult journey toward restored social acceptance, are hard pressed to keep up with the demands made upon them, to say nothing of extending their services. These few comments can serve to illustrate the breadth, depth and magnitude of one of today's biggest social problems.

Many diversified scientific specialties have devoted their thinking and understanding toward the goal of finding a solution to the problem of a rising crime rate and those skills which focus upon the therapy and treatment of aberrant social behavior have collaborated in the use of their abilities to re-orient, re-educate and rehabilitate offenders in a variety of ways and a diversity of settings. In using the words "therapy" and "treatment" with reference to the relationship with offenders, there is an intent to distinguish between the requirements of certain classes of offenders, for them to change from asocial behavior patterns to socially acceptable ones; and to differentiate between the specialized skills employed by the professional person in his dealing with offenders.

"Therapy" is a highly specialized word, from the field of medicine, that refers to doing something of a unique nature to cure or alleviate a disease. "Treatment," however, is a distinctive word meaning the handling or processing of a thing or person with the objective of making it or him better. There is no desire or intent here to show partisanship in, revive, add fuel to, or resolve an intense controversy between professional colleagues about their respective roles in helping people. I merely wish to clarify a social work view of the issue and set up a frame of reference for a better understanding of effecting "a change for the better" in those people in trouble designated "offenders."

With respect to the settings in which we can work to treat, or offer our specialized help to offenders, there are three generalized areas. These are all of significance to many people and in many ways. Each is of equal difficulty in which to work and all are of major importance.

Chronologically, the first area is that with the class of offenders who have not established asocial patterns of behavior. These are usually people who have committed an act, for the first time, of such a nature that a Court takes cognizance of them and their act. Dependent on the impact of this particular act on the community conscience, the Court may fine the offender, place him on probation, or commit him to an institution. In effect, society tells the offender, through the Court, that he must refrain from further asocial behavior for a designated period of time, during which he is to be responsible for reporting his activities to a representative of society, his probation officer.

When called upon to function in this situation and with this class of offender, the professional helping person plays a vital role and has multiple obligations. The significance of his role stems from the manner in which each aspect of obligation is met. One of the prime duties is to identify and isolate those persons in this class who will potentially repeat their asocial behavior and tend to become chronic offenders. At this point of contact with the offender, collaboration among the various helping professions with the law enforcing agencies and the judiciary is of greatest value. It is here that the specialized contributions of such services as psychiatry, psychology and social casework can begin to combat the social problem of crime and delinquency in its incipient stage.

Through its diagnostic processes, psychiatry can screen out those persons whose unacceptable behavior emerges from an acute, chronic, or incipient mental disease. Where positive findings are discovered, the next obligation of this particular helping profession is to advise the police authorities and the courts of the nature of the person with whom they are dealing, then recommend and make available the therapeutic services needed by the offender. It is at this phase of beginning to understand and treat the offender that the influence of the family becomes significant, both as a causative factor in the person being an of- the annals, journals and text books of this professional fender and as a medium in effecting his change. Since discipline have recorded in detail its efficacy in the diagnosis and treatment of offenders that come under its purview, no attempt will be made to expand on this here.

By means of measuring devices and testing techniques psychology contributes a great deal to our comprehension of the potentiality and capabilities of the offenders we seek to treat. It is of signal importance for every therapist and treatment person to have some knowledge of the capacities and abilities of the person to whom his services are tendered so that the goals and objectives of the helping relationship can be geared toward realistic aims. Extensive research in the area of treatment failures seems to indicate that one of the factors involved is the attempt on the part of either the subject or the helping person to attain a level of performance beyond that which the subject is able or ready, at a given point in time, to reach. It has also been demonstrated that a pattern of inadequacy in interpersonal relationships is contributory to a person engaging in attention-gaining devices to acquire status and acceptance by others. The offender has simply resorted to socially unacceptable modes of behavior to satisfy this basic human need. To be most effective his therapeutic or treatment experience must be different from his prior feelings of failure and provide him with a sense of accomplishment and fulfillment.

Here again the influences of his family emerge, since the primary and significant experiences in interpersonal relationships of every person are with his family. Regardless of the impact that the family has had in the formation of his personality patterns, despite the methods of behavior he has adopted to acquire a sense of individuality, attain a feeling of social acceptance and satisfy his basic human need of personal realization, or self-effectuation, no person can exceed the potentiality he possesses at a given time. Although he may move on to increased depth, greater breadth and finer integration of his personality through the growth process which is inherent to the therapeutic and treatment relationships, the process must be limited to the developing capacity and motivation of the offender as he experiences his exposure to and use of the helping services offered him.

It is my conviction, as a member of one profession engaged in the rehabilitation of offenders, that our psychology colleagues make their greatest contribution, at this phase in the process of effecting "a change for the better" in offenders, through the use of their measuring and testing skills to define and clarify the potentials and limitations of the subjects with whom we have to work. This is not to deny or minimize the treatment skills that psychologists have to offer in designated situations. This kind of knowledge about an individual's "weaknesses and strengths" is of major importance to law enforcement agencies, so they can know how to handle the offender they have apprehended; of vital value to the courts so they can select between a fine, probation or commitment, intelligently; and essential to whatever on-going service is indicated, whether it is therapy, treatment, or institutionalization.

Because the role and contribution of psychology in the treatment and rehabilitation of offenders is more detailed elsewhere in this volume and thoroughly explored in the archives, those sources are recommended as a medium of information.

Through education, experience and emphasis the profession of social work is best equipped to deal with the social realities that impinge upon its clients and the principal efforts of this discipline are focused on those significant social realities which are contributory to the client's feelings and actions that make him a social and community problem. For the class of offender in the area being considered, the services of trained social workers can be of signal value in both direct and indirect help. Beginning with the offender, through the use of the unique knowledge, skills and understanding of his profession, the social worker can enable those offenders who come within the area of his special competence to mobilize and utilize their strengths to change from destructive activity to productive modes of behavior. This treatment to effect "a change for the better" directly benefits the person who is able to accept the service offered. With respect to the law enforcement agency, every individual who is influenced in his incipiency to give up his proclivity for breaking the law results in less demands upon it and a decrease in the crime rate. The court calendar is less burdened by each person who is redirected from asocial toward more acceptable behavior in his community relationships. In addition to these examples of direct benefits, indirect values accrue to the community at large by the growth in the number of contributing members and a reduction in the per capita cost of personal and property protection. The relatives and friends of this class of offender are also benefited by not having to pay those intangible costs with which they are taxed by the knowledge that a loved one is a community menace.

The foregoing is not any claim that any one of, or combination of, the helping professions referred to is a panacea, or has the final answer to the major social problem of crime. It is only to say that, if adequately provided and properly used with identified and isolated persons in this phase of the development of the problem, the growth of the problem can be deterred and the effects of it mitigated.

As the focus of social work is on social realities, the most effective use of this profession can be made by engaging its skills with one of the most important social realities that everyone, including offenders, has. This is the family. From the time that he begins to gain awareness of anything apart from himself, a person's first and most significant social reality is his family, as a unit and as individuals. The manner in which he relates to, interacts with and separates from this unit and those individuals who are his family forms the basis upon which and from out of which he emerges as a distinctive personality.

Numerous organizations and individuals have investigated and reported on the contributions made by the family to the biological, psychological and emotional growth and maturation of the individual. Because no summarization could do justice to this wealth of material, convey the significance of its meaning, or estimate its worth to the growing fund of scientific understanding of the individual and society, a simplified condensation is deliberately being avoided: suffice it to say that the field of social work and those who are engaged in the professional education and training for social work constantly extract, analyze and utilize the discoveries and contributions of all sciences and arts to augment its comprehension and functioning within the sphere of special competence to which it has limited itself.

These generalized comments about the therapy and treatment of the professional services mentioned up to this point are not intended as a complete and definitive statement of their role, differences and limits; but rather to indicate some of the specialized contributions each can make to the prime problem of dealing with the social offender in unique ways so that "a change for the better" might be effected.

Proceeding to the next area and class of social offenders with which the helping services deal in offering their specialized skills, we come to those persons who, by reason of repeated violations, or more outrageous invasion of the personal and property rights of others, are committed to reformatory, or penal, institutions. It is vitally important for the professional practitioner, in this situation, to remember that his patient, or subject, is confined for punishment because he had not kept to social expectancies and limits in his behavior.

Because of the nature of this kind of setting, the penal aspects are of equal and, in the case of some inmates, greater importance than the therapy and treatment aspects. One necessary requirement of the professional who is functioning under these auspices, is that he accept fully and support wholeheartedly the punitive features of the total process in which the inmate is involved.

The inmate is in the institution out of his own choice and responsibility so, to derive the most from it, physically, emotionally and intellectually, he must experience the fullest impact and the most profound significance of his institutionalization.

Unlike his functioning in private practice, where the motivation, objectives and responsibilities are personal to his patient-client relationship and his professional self, when he is operating in the institutional setting, the professional is part of a collaborative team with the motivation, objectives and responsibilities imposed by the society that creates and maintains the institution and to whom the institution, in all of its aspects, is accountable. Every institution that comes within the general category of the type being considered has a three-fold purpose which the professional, regardless of his specialty, has to become identified with, integrate into his functioning and support with all of his professional integrity.

One part of the over-all purpose just indicated is custody. The intent of custody is partially punitive and partially protective. The punitive feature consists of depriving the subject of his freedom for a designated period of time as a forfeit for his failure to conduct himself within the limits of social expectancy. In our culture this is considered exaction of a person's most valuable and precious possession. The protective aspect is embodied in the fact that, while he is in custody, society, which includes his own family, is secure from the havoc to person and possessions he has demonstrated an ability to render. Since it is such an essential to the *raison d'etre* of this type of institution and basic to the significance of the experience to the inmate, the necessity and value of custody cannot be over-emphasized.

The next segment of institution purpose is discipline. As all existence is predicated upon some form of discipline, as used here its meaning is distinctive. The importance of the concept of discipline to the inmate of an institution is his exposure and requirement to adapt himself to disciplinary structures and limits in his day-to-day living and contact with inmate peers and institutional personnel. In the ideal situation, every inmate should be given an orientation course on his arrival at the institution, so that he knows, understands and has all questions clarified about what is expected of him and what he can expect of the experience he is about to have. This is not to say that detailed specifics can be fully explored and clarified at this point, but the broad outline of expectations and limitations which structure the life process within the specialized institutional society can be identified for behavior for every one involved. It is this foundation upon which the offender's interpersonal relationships in this setting and for the time he is a part of it is based.

It has been a conclusion of many studies that the element of discipline, in either a positive or negative way, has been contributory to an offender embarking on a pattern of asocial actions in his intercourse with other people. The role of his family in the initiation, development and maturation of the phenomenon has been the subject of numerous scientific investigations, the basis of innumerable creative writings of all na-

248

tions and societies and a vital essential feature of biography, or autobiography, which has made any contribution to our understanding of the human race.

A third part of the over-all purpose of institutions to be considered is the handling and/or processing of the offender in such a manner by all individuals, who constitute the organization's official family, toward the goal of effectuating in the offender "a change for the better." Depending upon a number of factors, this handling or processing is called various things. The first factor to be considered is the nature of the problem that the offender has and from this flows his needs. It is in this phase that the diagnostic, evaluative and metric knowledge, skills, techniques and understanding of the professional services are of signal importance and significance. This is not to deny, or minimize, the value and importance of the contributions that non-professional and lay personnel can make to the totality of what is needed to be of maximum benefit to the offender. It is at this point of beginning his experience that the collaboration, cooperation and integration of all areas of special competence that the institution has to offer must be consolidated for the ultimate benefit of the offender.

Having made at this point a tentative determination of the nature of the problem with which we have to deal and a provisional decision about the needs that have to be met, we can then institute those procedures which seem most applicable to the situation. I do not advocate that any one technique is better than the others, will not attempt to show any line of demarcation where one process begins and another ends, or infer that there is a superiority of effectiveness among the various helping processes that can be made available. I do say that, provided an authentic diagnosis examination is done, an accurate measurement of potential is made and, a thorough evaluation of the realities completed, an effective and efficient assignment of the proper helping service can be made.

Let us assume the situation in which a particular offender has been thoroughly "worked-up" by every available professional service that the institution utilizes. If each one can give complete, appreciative consideration and value to the contributions of the others, this collaborative effort would result in the best possible benefit to the subject. This requires, of course, that each professional discipline is clearly cognizant of and takes full responsibility for the limitations of its areas of special competence. In the classical clinical treatment team there is no question that the psychiatrist carries ultimate medico-legal responsibility for the final decisions and recommendations emanating from the treatment process. This is not to say that a medical degree, with specialization in mental diseases and emotional disorders, makes the psychiatrist omniscient.

There are instances in which the psychiatrist must and should accept being the advisee, instead of the advisor, within the collaborative team effort. In short, during both the preliminary diagnostic phase and the on-going treatment process there are times when the unique knowledge, understanding, skills and techniques of another professional discipline are the most accurate, knowledgeable, scientific and beneficial for the best ultimate beneficence to the subject. Let us consider some simplified and brief illustrations to demonstrate how one collaborating profession may become the advisor and "expert" for the others, because a question or problem within its area of special competence needs clarification for the process of bringing about "a change for the better" to proceed.

During the diagnostic procedures on an institutional offender it was shown by recent past and longitudinal history that there were no indicia of chronic mental disease. All of his sociological factors regarding his familial relationships, attitudes and interests were established as being positive. There was a general agreement that all signs seemed to indicate that this individual could derive benefits from becoming involved in a re-educative and rehabilitative process. Because he had a persistent pattern of failing to sustain his efforts toward an attained goal, the Classification Committee was reluctant to assign him to a program in which he would experience another failure. In order to make the most meaningful and profitable assignment for this person it was essential to know what potential capacity he possessed, what limitations restricted him at this time and how much motivation and interest he had to aspire toward achievement.

The only member of the clinical team who has the background, tools, techniques and understanding to evaluate and recommend what is needed in this instance is the psychologist. In this specific area and on this particular aspect of total handling of the individual involved, the psychologist's findings and opinions are paramount and should take precedence in making the recommendation. His contribution can certainly be utilized by the colleagues on the team in carrying out their distinctive and unique functions. In this situation there has been no usurpation of the psychiatrist's province of mental illness, no infringement of the social worker's specialty of social realities, yet a major contribution is made to the understanding of both cooperating professions for a more effective fulfillment of their specific functions. The ability to be aware of and accept one's own professional limits, while valuing and utilizing the role and fund of knowledge made available by others is a recurring lesson for every practitioner who aspires to the pinnacle of professional discipline.

In another situation the social realities, or factual factors, may be the paramount and precedent issue upon which the team decision is founded. There are numerous examples that would illuminate this point and I am sure that everyone who has had occasion to collaborate with another professional discipline can recall instances in which he needed the superior specialized knowledge of a colleague. In spite of the assault upon our narcissism, accepting, valuing and utilizing the contribution of others is the essence of the team approach which seeks to attain a fruitful goal.

The finest prototype of collaboration is in the musical art form of the orchestra. Here one can see and experience the basic theme being carried by different choirs of the ensemble at various times, while each has to play ancillary, supportive and subsidiary roles as required for the interpretation and execution of the joint process in which all are engaged to have vitality and meaning. It is elementary that this mutual enterprise must have leadership and direction, so the orchestra has its conductor. In a like manner the institutional handling of offenders needs guidance and this is predicated upon the ability of each segment of the institution's totality to integrate the institutional objectives with its own specialized functioning.

It is of minimum significance whether or not the handling of the offender is based upon the existence of a mental disease, emerges from an arrested development, is predicated upon some reality factors, grows out of limited learning or is founded upon a lack of motivation; the therapy, or treatment indicated, should be the prime responsibility of that member of the team in whose province of special competence the problem properly belongs. However, in the ongoing process, the unique knowledge and skills of collaborative services will possibly be necessary for eventuation of the ultimate goal. Reverting to our earlier example, here again the thematic material may move from the soprano, diapason or bass clefs, but each is of equal importance, value and necessity for the fullest expression and interpretation of the complete composition.

Beyond the pre-institutional and intra-mural dealings with the offender, the third setting and area in which the handling of him is indicated is on his release from confinement and resumption of community living. The generic term for this, when the offender's continuing to be a part of the larger community is contingent on his refraining from committing any asocial or illegal acts, is "parole." When he holds this status, the offender possesses most of the rights, privileges and licenses of any other citizen; he is expected to carry, in a responsible way, the duties, liabilities and obligations of every other citizen; but he is under supervision and the surveillance of an officially designated representative of the institution, the court and society, his parole officer.

When the offender has served a definite sentence, as penalty for his illegal act, he is not paroled, but completely discharged and could, if he so desired, begin an entirely new life, free from any supervision, surveillance, or any other kind of relationship to the social authorities, as long as he does not become involved again in any type of asocial offense. For various reasons, which no attempt will be made to explore at this time, the discharged offender is not offered any therapeutic or treatment services, nor is he usually encouraged to seek this kind of help. For those who do have the insight and motivation to utilize helping services the initiative for discovering their availability is primarily based on personal desire.

From my personal experience with some professional helping people in a few reformatory and corrective institutions, when terminating the intra-mural process of offenders who are about to return to community living, a referral to a private or public community resource is sometimes made. Unfortunately, the vast majority of confined offenders do not have the benefit of much exposure to a help-taking relationship and, of those that do, only a few are willing to accept and follow through with availing themselves of those resources that can be utilized. I do not wish to place the whole onus upon the offenders, because the fact is that in many locales therapeutic and treatment facilities simply do not exist and, where they do, in many instances the lack of adequate personnel and/or long pending lists result in the service not being actually available to the person at the time when it is most vitally needed.

Resuming with those offenders who leave the institution on parole status, the fact of treatment for them during this vitally important period of re-orientation, when the transition from life within the walls, with close supervision and strict discipline, to social living, with self-imposed limitations for acceptable behavior and controls, is more mythical than real. There are very few, if any, parole departments which require the specialized training, supervised experience and developed skills upon which professional treatment is based. This fact was dramatically brought out during the 1960 National Conference on Social Welfare in one panel discussion. A representative of one of the Eastern Seaboard States, which has a reputation for providing progressive, enlightened and pioneering services to its offenders, said, among other things, that there was not one professionally trained person in the entire parole system of his State.

If this is a condition that can be found in one of the better areas, how intense can the situation be and how difficult is the problem of effectively treating offenders in those places where services are less available? This is not intended as a criticism of the particular State referred to or a condemnation of general parole systems. I merely wish to emphasize the woefully thin line of resources that man the barricades in an effort to meet, cope with and, hopefully, stem the rising tide of crime, delinquency and asocial deviant behavior that constitutes one of the largest social problems of our times.

Even in those locales where trained and experienced personnel are being recruited and integrated into parole systems, overwhelming case-loads, lack of clearly-defined jurisdictional limits, confusion about functional differences and hazy concepts about the objectives sought tend to vitiate the efforts of well-intentioned and dedicated practitioners. For one example of the professional quandary regarding roles, functions, limits and objectives, the remarks of one speaker at the meeting of the Essex County Society of Psychologists in Private Practice, held April 23, 1960 in Irvington, N. J., are penetrating and perspicacious. Because the full import and significance of what was said would be lost in a resume of this speech, and the impact lessened through taking extracts from it, I recommend highly the full text as reported in the July 1960 issue of *The Welfare Reporter,* the official publication of the New Jersey State Department of Institutions and Agencies. This particular article, "The Semantics of Delinquency," is one of several which are contributory to a better understanding of the generic problem of tendering a helpful service to offenders.

This generalized, panoramic view of the broad areas into which the professional services can insinuate themselves in the therapy and treatment of offenders is neither exhaustive nor definitive. We can only focus the penetrating light of inquiry upon the unfinished canvas and expose the bare spots and gaps of knowledge which require completion through fuller research, more experimentation, better knowledge and greater experience. To augment our present fund of information, intensify our operations in those areas extant and push back the frontiers of functioning in our efforts to deal with offenders of every degree and at every stage of development, requires the same kind of imagination, fortitude and pioneering spirit that characterized the early explorers and is the significant feature of modern adventurers and investigators of celestial and interstellar mysteries.

We can borrow from many sources to stimulate our conceptualizations of the realms possible, provide incentives to become engaged in application of our skills, examine and evaluate our practices and permanently record our findings, as a further contribution to the store of knowledge and basis for continued investigation and discovery. It was ancient mythology, in the story of Icarus, that predicted man's ultimate solution of the mystery of flight. This fantastic imagining was an integral part of human literature long before the science of aerodynamics matured, long before any dream of an efficient machine emerged and long before the idea that a controlled power supply was available had germinated. It is, also, creative fiction that fantasized about the "self" and "personality" long before the social sciences amassed, tested, evaluated and interpreted the meaning of individual behavior and the effects of interpersonal interaction. In addition to creative and fictional accounts of living, biographical and auto-biographical memoirs have recorded what, where, when and how things happened with people, without any attempt to explain or interpret why the particular events occurred. This aspect of why specific things did occur, in terms of the conscious, unconscious, or subconscious elements that comprised the personality, was left to researchers and theorists.

Despite tons of texts, multitudinous manuscripts and uncounted verbal expressions about what makes an individual interact with others, it is my belief that the domain of human personality that we seek to explore and understand is so large and intricate that, as yet, we have just begun to penetrate its borders.

Among the various therapeutic and treatment services there are divisiveness and conflict; and within each one there are internecine struggles which testify to the primitive level at which they are in approaching some solution to the enigma of what and how each can contribute. I am willing to accept these contra-active forces, because I believe that it is necessary for the process of differentiation, integration, consolidation and separation to take place before growth, maturation and eventuation can occur.

These views of the nature and magnitude of the problem with which we have to deal, the various areas with which we have to cope, the limitations and problems that have to be dealt with and the inter and intra professional obstacles that have to be overcome represent only a beginning phase in the treatment of offenders.

There is no person who, in the present, in his historical past, or in his anticipated future, existed in a vacuum. For the offender, whether he is designated as a criminal, delinquent, juvenile or adult, or asocial person, various influences have played some part in contributing to what he has been and is. In order to know what and why he is as he is today, it is vital to have some concepts and knowledge of formative influences.

The knowledge, understanding and utilization of the formative influences that contribute to the making of offenders is something that the therapeutic, or treatment, person, repetitiously and constantly, has to bring into the helping relationship for the process to move toward the ultimate goal of bringing about "the change for the better" which is the sought-for end. Because the limitations of time and space do not permit examination and evaluation of all formative influences, and since our focus is upon familial influences only, we must curtail our observations to this aspect.

For every person his family has been a part of his past, is now a part of his present and will certainly be a part of his future social reality. The influences that the family exert are multiple, because the total family constellation, as a unit, and the individual members, as entities, have distinctive effects. The unique contribution that the family *in toto* makes to influence a person has been and is one area of inquiry and research. To synthesize the mass of accumulated information on just this subject is, indeed, a herculean task, but we can highlight some of the aspects that have emerged from this realm of investigation.

Of necessity families come within specific categories which can be briefly described. One of these is the natural family in which the relationship of the person to the family unit results from the normal procreative process. Another category is the *de juro* adoptive situation in which, through a legally prescribed procedure, a person is publicly declared a member of the unit. A third of these is the *de facto* adoptive status that arises when, by simple practice, without legal sanction, a person and a family unit establish a parent-child relationship. In another situation, that is negative in nature, a person may never have any interaction with others who have a status of *in loco parentis*. There can be variations on these basic relationships. Illustrations of these are when one or both parents have been divorced, or widowed, and natural issue result from the subsequent marriage; established families legally adopt another child; the child of deceased relatives, friends, or a completely strange child is simply "taken in" and treated as a family member.

It cannot be concluded that any one of these situations is desirable, nor can it be predicted that, because a certain status exists, a definite result will ensue; because it is not the status, *per se,* that creates whatever influences occur, but rather the combination of those forces which find expression and become involved in the interplay between the person and whatever the family unit is. Since every offender is primarily a person, what we know about the interaction between an individual and his family must be understood and integrated into the helping process, whether it be therapy or treatment, to move toward the emotional change and growth that is the objective of our purpose in dealing with the offender.

Regardless of whether or not his family is a natural one, or a *de juro* or *de facto* adoptive one, the perception of the offender regarding what his family is to him, his ability to differentiate, integrate, consolidate and separate himself with respect to it and interact through his understanding of the relationship to him that is of the most significance. The role of the professional person lies in aiding and encouraging the offender to surrender his defenses, to understand and give up his rationalizations and to take back his projections, so that he can respond in a constructive and creative manner to the factual, basic, reality of what actually exists. In other words, one part of the helping experience is to aid the offender to recognize the familial influences that impinge upon him, to understand the significance that they have for him and to react toward them in the most mature and responsible manner of which he is capable. Through the support given him, the clarification provided and the interpretation made to him, the offender is enabled to come to terms with this part of his social reality.

An essential of life is that quality to move from a status of being, through a process of becoming, to the attainment of accomplishment. This phenomenon is growth and it is one that has been experienced by everyone who has eventuated into what he is at a given point in time of his existence. The parts of the whole individual, his psychological and biological parts, interacting with other individuals and/or environmental factors culminate in his being what he is. Whether or not, at a given period, an individual is classified as a psychotic, neurotic, or an asocial offender, he has experienced this growth phenomenon in his eventuation.

The total impact of his milieu, consisting of individual persons, with their unique and distinctive differences and familial constellations, with their specialized characteristics, contributed to influencing and affecting the offender, to some extent, for him to become what he is.

These comments about the contributions of other individuals and environmental factors are not to imply that the role of the offender is passive and results wholly from his being acted upon. The process of living and growth, the quality of viability in being, emerge from active participation in relationship. The very fact that, to acquire the status of being an offender, the person has had to either do something that was of itself socially unacceptable, or do something that might have been acceptable, *per se,* but in a socially unacceptable manner, attests to the self-motivated element involved in the individual's experiencing the phenomenon of living growth and change.

Because the professional helping services have devoted so much thought and effort to why certain things "are wrong and constitute problems"; have promulgated numerous theories and devised many techniques to cure and correct "what is wrong," or solve "what is the problem"; and have dedicated themselves to "making a change for the better" through their scientifically-based methods of therapy and treatment; there seems to be justifiable criticism that one of the most important aspects of what is entailed has been negated, disregarded or forgotten. This is the person with the greatest stake in the progress of the relationship, whether it be therapy or treatment, the offender. It is his investment of himself in the relationship and his acquisition and use of the benefits derived that are of paramount importance.

Despite the unique traits and characteristics of the individual in his interpersonal relationships, regardless of the nature of the family constellation of which he was a part and notwithstanding the environmental factors with which he had to interact during his process of becoming what he is, the actuality has a different significance and value to the offender than it should and must have for the person proffering the helping service. The etiology, history of onset and development pattern are of vital importance to the therapist, or treatment person, for him to understand the nature of the difficulty he is undertaking to "change for the better," to know if this particular problem is within the area of his special competence, to determine whatever tentative goals his specialty can seek and to prognosticate, to a limited degree, the eventuality of making his skills available for the subject. For the offender, it is his conceptualizations of the why and how he finds himself in the status that he is now in, his acceptance and understanding of the significance of this status to him, and his choice and selection of the possible courses of action, within socially acceptable limits, that will change his status, which is of paramount importance to him.

I do not wish to criticize any method of seeking to effect a "change for the better" in the status of a person, I do not advocate that any particular philosophy, theory, or "school" of therapy and treatment is superior to any other, nor do I imply that there is a panacea for the intensive, extensive and complex problem of crime, delinquency and asociality. The contributions of every helping service are of equal value and efficacy when they are made available and utilized by those persons with problems who come within the province of the service that is best equipped to deal with their problems.

It is of vital importance and inestimable value that inter and intra professional differences exist, because differences are the incentive for interaction and interaction is the basis for theorizing, inquiry and investigation. The practice of recording experiences, along with presupposing, questioning and seeking, constitutes the field of research, through which the dissemination of the information possessed is made, the areas in which information is needed are defined and clarified, and the discoveries that contribute to filling in gaps of knowledge are made available.

To get some concept of how and why a given individual attains that status of requiring help, either therapy or treatment, whether or not he has been institutionalized for it, or referred for it, without surrendering his participation and motility within the larger community, there are two broad situations in which he finds himself that cause the person to "break" from acceptable modes of behavior and acquire the status of being either "sick" or socially unacceptable.

In one of these situations there is something within the individual himself that causes him to perceive other individuals, in his interpersonal relationships and his environmental associations in a distorted manner. Because he so misperceives and distorts his interpersonal and environmental relationships, he develops anxieties, fears and frustrations which cause him to behave in whatever way he can to find surcease from the conflicts and tensions he feels as being imposed upon him by the other persons, or the environmental situation in which he is. As long as he cannot alter and amend the persons or situations to which he is reacting, or remove himself from what he feels as their influences, regardless of difference, his conceptualization of the "truth" to him and the factual "reality," the basis for his sickness, delinquency, or asociality, persists. Many texts and periodicals have delved into the internal causes of what makes offenders to such an extent that a wealth of source material is available. Because of limitations of time and space, I suggest the contributions of August Aichorn, Franz Alexander and William Healy, Franz Alexander and Hugo Staub, Kate Friedlander, Sheldon and Eleanor T. Glueck, Roy R. Grinker and John P. Spiegel, Robert Lindner, Paul Tappan, Henry Thurston, Rosa Wessel and many others for further enlightenment of this aspect of the offender becoming and being what he is.

The other broad situation is one in which the person himself is essentially not responsible for his status, but is truly the victim of the instability, frustration, confusion, or "sickness" of other persons in his relationships, or his environment. He is that category of person about whom it could be said that, if anyone had to live with the persons and situation in which he was involved, they would probably end up in trouble. Everyone who is knowledgeable, to some extent, of the development of delinquent and asocial patterns, understands the impact of the conflict between different cultures, or major and minor cultures, upon those persons subjected to this kind of pressure. In the field of fiction such novels as "A Stone for Danny Fisher," "Native Son," "No Down Payment," "The Catcher in the Rye," and similar themes dramatize the affects of inter and intra cultural relationships. With respect to the role of parents in having an influence upon the creation of offenders, Beatrice S. Reiner and Irving Kaufman have published, under the auspices of the Family Service Association of America, a series of case histories which illustrate how the personal of one or both parents contributed to their child becoming an offender. In addition to the environmental and parental influences that play a role in the creation of offenders, there are reports too numerous to list, which indicate how siblings, natural, step and adoptive, can be significant in a person eventuating to the status of being an offender. As we look at the extensive sources that are available on this aspect of how externals contribute to the evolutionary development of offenders, sexual differences and age contrasts seem to be of little significance. The vital importance of how sibling A was affected and influenced by siblings X, Y or Z lay in the relationship that existed between them and the active or passive role that sibling A took in his relationship to the others.

With the degree of understanding that we can extract from the foregoing about the causes, affects and influences that create offenders and contribute to the existence of the major social problem with which we dedicate ourselves to deal, let us consider the roles, functions and participation of the helping services, as catalytic agencies, in effecting a "change for the better" in the subjects of their services.

It is my conviction that the primary step to be taken is clarification of the principal problem involved; next, a determination of the area of special competence within which the problem lay must be made; then, after bringing the helpee and helper together, collaboration and cooperation among all available professional disciplines should be integrated toward the goal of achieving the "change for the better" that would prove beneficial to the subject.

As a Social Worker, whose scope of special competence is in dealing with those social realities that impinge upon and affect the conscious behavior and attitudes of the client, I would be averse to becoming involved with intra-psychic conflicts and the unconscious motivations underlying the perceptions, attitudes and activities of anyone. This is not to say that those Social Workers who are interested and specially trained to do so cannot and should not, under competent supervision. When this does occur, it should be clear that those individuals who chose to do this are not engaged in the practice of Social Work, but have adopted another function. I merely wish to say that the sphere of Social Work operation is clear and limited, is so defined and professionally responsible in its functioning.

There is a great deal more that can be examined about the realms of the various helping services, but this is neither the place nor the time to indulge in a consideration of these problems. Suffice it to say that an inter-professional difficulty exists that, hopefully, will be clarified through experience, research and an ultimate clarification of roles.

To continue with the dynamics of the helping process, I wish to present one point of view that, I emphasize, is not to be taken as definitive or final. I do feel that experience and documented practice give a basis for a conviction about its efficacy and value to provoke growth and creative living.

There is no way for an individual to relive his past so that any physical or psychological elements which were missing, or existed to an excessive degree in his development, can be brought into balance with any idealized concepts of what should and might have been necessary for his growth. The actuality of what has occurred is past and unalterable, but it is of inestimable importance to have a partial understanding of how and why the present situation exists. It is vital to know the causative elements of the familial and environmental roles in an offender becoming what he now is. Of greater importance, however, than the knowledge of how, what and why any contributions were made to the present formation of what a person has developed into, is his acceptance and understanding of the relationship between his "truth" and the actuality of "reality," regardless of its nature.

As he, through his current relationship with a helping person, can begin to truly accept the reality about his family and environment, he can start to understand his relationship to it, discover his own likenesses and differences from it, then make his own choices about whatever active role he can take in this relationship. Instead of being a mere "thing" upon which individual and environmental factors, or a combination of these, act to wreak their wills and desires, he will discover a quickening within himself of his own wishes and motivation to assume greater responsibility for his becoming and being different. It is at this point that all externals take on new meaning and a shift in his relationship to these results. Instead of the outer being the actor and he the helpless acted upon, his sense of selfness enables him to accept and understand the reality of being acted upon, but, in turn, he becomes an active reactor to the outer influences. In short, the relationship becomes one of mutual interaction.

Any incentive to change must arise from some dissatisfaction within the person with what the current situation is. It is usually some major immediate dissatisfaction with his perception of his "truth" that impelled a person to act in the manner that resulted in his becoming an offender. As he can take into his conscious awareness the knowledge, acceptance and understanding of the individuals and circumstances as acting upon him; then assume, in turn, his own reacting to them, the fact of what has occurred in the past, the methods through which it has happened and the reasons for which it is developed will diminish with respect to the role he can now play to uncover his own satisfactions, discover his own motivations and

266

utilize his own manner of living the life he desires within socially acceptable limits.

Regardless of what we now know and can measure about the capabilities of people, despite what we understand and can prove about external and internal influences which contributed to their being what they are, to utilize our skills, knowledge and understanding to effect any goal, it is essential to accept and realize, with real humility, that the incentive, motivation and willingness to become engaged in the effort of effecting a "change for the better" lies, to a major degree, in the hands of the person to whom the service is offered.

Notwithstanding the quantity of scientific knowledge amassed about the factors involved in the formation of individuals into problems of status and being; despite the numerous skills, techniques and methods of providing ways of alleviating these problems; regardless of the desires of dedicated people to erase these problems from human existence; and in spite of the efficacy with which this information and understanding is utilized; little of any permanent value can eventuate from the relationship to provide help without the fullest participation and acceptance of the helpee. If we eliminate the existence of organic, or bio-chemical, factors as contributory to the becoming and being of problem personalities, a phase of the question at hand that I am neither desirous nor qualified to comment about, I believe that the most important, significant and vital concept about human behavior is that each person possesses within himself the force of life and growth that helping services, whether they be designated as therapy, treatment or any other title can, when properly utilized within their specific limits, awaken, stimulate and nurture toward maturation.

X

THE FUTURE OF COURT PSYCHIATRY

WILLIAM H. HAINES, M.D.
*Director, Behavior Clinic of the Criminal Court of
Cook County, Illinois*

The year 1956 marked the twenty-fifth anniversary
of the Behavior Clinic of the Criminal Court of Cook
County, Illinois. It came into being in 1931 at the
instigation of the Chicago Medical Society, the Chicago Neurological Society, the Institute of Medicine,
the Chicago Bar Association, and the Chief Justice
of the Criminal Court, who at the time was Judge
John P. McGoorty.

The primary purpose of the Behavior Clinic was
to examine defendants charged with crimes who were
unable to hire private psychiatrists, so that the poorest
defendant would be able to secure the same psychiatric examination and testimony as the wealthiest defendant. The services of the Clinic were to be offered
to all defendants, regardless of ability to pay. The
report to court was to be submitted in triplicate so
that the State, the Defense, and the Court each would
have a similar copy of the findings.

The secondary function of the Clinic was to examine those who were being considered for probation, and to advise the Court as to their mental condition, prior to probation. However, this latter function
was soon found to be impracticable due to the large

number of indictments in the Criminal Court and the limited facilities of the Clinic. The efforts of the Behavior Clinic were then confined to the mental condition of defendants prior to trial.

We are approaching our 9000th examination. I have been the Director since 1941. I am called to testify in court approximately 150 times a year, either at the request of the Defense or the State—occasionally by order of the Court. The greatest number of our requests to testify come from the defense attorneys. The Behavior Clinic does not examine defendants, nor do I testify in court, unless a court order for the examination has been entered. Occasionally the strategy of the defense attorney is to enter an order at the time of the hearing, and I will be called to testify. I will testify that I did not examine the real defendant and the defense will then ask a hypothetical question, or I will be used as an expert witness. In a few instances my testimony has been limited by the Court to the legal definition of sanity at the time of the trial or hearing.

In Chicago we have three Psychiatric Court Clinics:

1. The Family Court, formerly the Juvenile Court, has a Psychiatric Department which examines approximately 750 a year.

2. The Municipal Court has the Psychiatric Institute, which examines approximately 4000 cases a year.

3. The Criminal Court of Cook County has the Behavior Clinic, which examines approximately 500 a year.

As mentioned above, the Behavior Clinic examines only upon order of Court. The request must come from the defense attorney, as under the law in the State of Illinois neither the Court nor the State's Attorney has the right to order a mental examination of a defendant after indictment, prior to trial. If the Court had that authority then its psychiatrist in the eyes of the jury would be the only impartial psychiatrist in the courtroom.

If the defendant comes in the courtroom insane, that is, if he is an escapee from a mental institution, or has otherwise been adjudicated insane, it is then proper for the State to request a sanity hearing, for the purpose of finding the individual legally sane, so that there will be no question as to the individual's sanity at the time of impaneling the jury for trial on the indictment.

A restoration must be held on every defendant before the Court who has ever been committed as feebleminded or insane (mentally ill), in order to prevent a reversal of the sentence at some future time. This must be before a jury of twelve.

Cook County returns approximately 3000 indictments a year. At the present time there are around 2300 in the County Jail awaiting sentence or serving sentence. The jail was originally built for around 1200. One can readily see how emotional difficulties will occur under such overcrowded conditions.

Our report to court is presented in triplicate so that the Judge, at his discretion, may give a copy to the Defense Attorney and the State's Attorney. We are not permitted to mention in the report any previous incarceration in penal institutions, nor are we permitted to refer to, or comment on, the offense for which the individual is being tried.

The examination consists of the following:

1. A physical examination.

2. A psychological examination, with the impression of the examining psychologist. One must always remember that the I.Q. is not lower than that obtained, but may be higher, depending upon the desire of the patient to cooperate, or to be found insane by reason of feeblemindedness.

3. A resume of the social history.

4. A resume of the mental examination.

5. The conclusions:
    (a) A medical diagnosis.
    (b) The legal terminology of sanity at the time of impaneling the jury for trial or the sanity hearing. This is mainly—does he know the nature of the charge and he is able to cooperate with his counsel. If either of the last two are answered in the negative it is a notice to the Court that the individual is insane. It is then mandatory that a jury of twelve be impaneled and a sanity hearing be held.

If there is a sanity hearing, then the hearing is quasi-criminal and the rules are that of a civil proceeding, i.e., "A preponderance of the evidence," or a slight tipping of the scales. If it is insanity at the time of the offense then the rules are according to the Criminal Code, i.e., "Beyond a reasonable doubt," or a complete tipping of the scales.

In Illinois one may be:
1. Insane at the time of the offense but sane at the time of going to trial.
2. Insane at the time of the offense and insane at the time of going to trial.
3. Sane at the time of the offense and insane before going to trial.
4. Sane at the time of the offense and become insane during the trial.
5. Sane at the time of the offense and become insane before sentence.
6. Sane at the time of the offense and become insane before execution of sentence.

The State of Illinois has special tests to establish insanity (responsibility) of an individual at various stages of the trial:

At the Commission of a Crime: When an accused person is put on trial for a crime on misdemeanor, the correct test as to insanity is whether or not the defendant is capable of knowing right from wrong as to the act in question, and is capable of exercising the power of choosing either to do or not do the act, and of governing his conduct in accordance with such choice.

Before Trial: He is not considered a lunatic or insane if he is capable of understanding the nature and object of the proceedings against him; if he rightly comprehends his own condition in reference to such proceedings, and has sufficient mind to conduct his defense in a rational or reasonable manner although upon some other subjects his mind may be deranged or unsound.

Before Judgment: A person who becomes lunatic or insane after the commission of a crime or misdemeanor shall not be tried for the offense during the continuance of the lunacy or insanity. If, after the verdict of guilty, and before judgment is pronounced, such person becomes lunatic or insane, then no judgment shall be given while such lunacy or insanity shall continue. And if, after judgment and before execution of the sentence, such person becomes lunatic or insane, then in case the judgment be capital, the execution thereof shall be stayed until the recovery of said person from the insanity or lunacy. In all of these cases, it shall be the duty of the Court to impanel a jury to try the question whether the accused be, at the time of impaneling, insane or lunatic.

Before Execution: The defendant before execution is to be regarded as sane and not lunatic, when he has sufficient intelligence to understand the nature of the proceedings against him, what he was tried for originally, the purpose of his punishment, the impending fate which awaits him, and a sufficient mind to know any facts which might exist which would make his punishment unjust or unlawful, and sufficient of intelligence to convey such information to his attorney or the court. When he has not such intelligence and mental ability he is to be regarded as insane or lunatic by the verdict of the jury, if so found, and his execution stayed or delayed.

The same tests apply for feeblemindedness and insanity in Illinois, that is, one must not be able to distinguish between right and wrong, and must not be able to cooperate with counsel.

Considerable interest has been shown recently in the Durham decision in Washington. In Illinois we are influenced by the M'Naghten Rules, which were responses made by fifteen judges in England in 1843 to five questions put to them by the House of Lords. Our own Illinois Supreme Court opinions are based on these rules.

Roughly, the M'Naghten Rules are: A person is not criminally responsible for an offense if at the time the act is committed he is mentally unsound as to lack of knowledge that the act is wrong. This is called the "right-and-wrong" test, and is law in all but two of our states. It is the sole test of irresponsibility in England and in twenty-nine American states. The wording of the rule varies considerably: in at least half the cases it is stated that to be excused the defendant must be so disordered as not to know the "nature and quality" (sometimes "nature and character," "consequence," etc.) of the act, or if he did know it, that he did not know it was wrong.

Since 1843 in seventeen of our states will power enough to resist the impulse to commit a crime has been added to the knowledge that the act is wrong.

To repeat, twenty-nine states base criminal responsibility on knowledge of the so-called "right-and-wrong" test: seventeen states and the District of Columbia add the second test of irresistible impulse. In these latter jurisdictions a person is excused if he is incapable of knowing the wrongfulness of the act, or even though he does know it is wrong, if he is incapable of controlling the impulse to commit the act.

273

In New Hampshire the Court has rejected both of these tests and has a rule that there is no legal test of irresponsibility by reason of insanity: "It is a question in fact for the jury in each case, whether the defendant has a mental disease, and if so, whether it was of such a character or degree to take away the capacity to form or entertain a criminal intent."

In Rhode Island the Court has never passed upon the question of a legal test of insanity.

In Nebraska feeblemindedness and mental disease have been held grounds for mitigating punishment.

In Illinois if a defendant is found insane he is committed to Illinois Security Hospital until such time as he is "totally and permanently recovered." He is then returned to the custody of the Sheriff to stand trial on his original indictment.

The Illinois Security Hospital is a hospital of maximum security. It is about sixty miles south of St. Louis in the town of Chester. The hospital has a population of about four hundred and is under the jurisdiction of the Department of Public Welfare. Transfers may be made to it, from the other State Hospitals, of homicidal patients, escapees, behavior problems, etc., upon departmental order.

The prison system has the Psychiatric Division, which is a walled institution within the Illinois Southern Penitentiary, on property adjoining the Security Hospital. The Psychiatric Division is for insane criminals, sexual deviates, behavior problems, etc. It has a census of about six hundred, and is under the jurisdiction of the Department of Public Safety.

One example of a trial on the indictment after hospitalization is the case of a general paretic who was examined by the Behavior Clinic and found to be insane at the time of the impaneling of the jury, many months after the crime. I had seen and treated this individual as a patient, in the Neurological Dispensary of Rush Medical College, many years before.

274

After a period of seven years in the hospital he was found to have recovered his sanity and was returned to the court. I was subpoenaed by the defense attorney to testify as to the mental condition at the time of the alleged crime. My testimony was limited by the Court to my own personal mental examination. I did not make the physical examination, so I was not permitted to testify as to the fixed pupils and the neurological findings. I was not permitted to testify that he had syphilis, in that I did not draw the blood and run the serological test. I was not permitted to testify for which disease I had treated him in the Central Free Dispensary of Rush Medical College, as I again did not draw blood and determine the serology. It was all hearsay evidence. I was permitted to testify that I had given him a prescription, and the name of the medicine I prescribed. The Court ruled that inasmuch as my mental examination had been performed many months after the commission of the crime, I should not be permitted to give an opinion as to his mental state at the time of the crime. The defendant was sentenced to forty years in the penitentiary.

Frequently claims of insanity are used by the defense to delay a trial, to tire out the witnesses, etc. A case may be ready to go to trial when the defense brings before the Court the issue of insanity. It is then mandatory for that issue to be disposed of before the trial can proceed. When the defense attorney can provide no other defense he can always claim that the defendant was temporarily insane and has now recovered, so that he would not have been responsible at the time of the commission of the crime. We had one patient who claimed to be insane after three o'clock in the afternoon, at which time the jail was closed and we were not able to observe him in his so-called periods of insanity.

If the prisoner is facing the electric chair one must

be suspicious of malingering. We had one patient, charged with murder, on whom we were about to report to Court that he was unable to cooperate with his counsel, based upon his mental examination. However, a letter which he attempted to pass to his wife during a visit was intercepted by a jail guard. This letter read in part: "I am not supposed to be aware of anything, as I am supposed to be crazy. I want to impart some information to you which you in turn will give to the lawyer representing me. Don't you realize that my life hangs in the balance, that everything depends on you, as I put my trust in you? So please, for God's sake, heed my words. Don't you realize that they want to make an example of me and put me in the electric chair, even though they may not be able to do it if I go to trial? It is too late to turn back now. I have gone too far and they are mad at me because if I am pronounced insane it will spoil the State's case and they will have to commit me to the Psychiatric Division until I am cured, and then I will come back to have a chance to beat the rap, because I can contend that I was not responsible for my actions. After you have copied the information burn this letter. I want you to volunteer this information of your own accord because you naturally know all about my life." He then gave a list of friends to call upon to testify that he gave the impression of being "unstable, irrational and unsettled"; that he would always lose interest in things he was doing; that he would begin a conversation and suddenly stop in the middle of it and start roaming; that he would sit and stare into space for long periods of time, and he would pay no attention to those about him. He advised that all his friends be informed of this and then that they be subpoenaed to testify in court. In a twelve-page letter he outlined the steps one by one. Confronted with this evidence his behavior changed immediately. He submitted again to a mental examination and no overt signs of mental disease were elicited.

We have had individuals come to court acting in a very bizarre manner and the jury would find them insane. As soon as they leave the courtroom their behavior would be normal. One, charged with murder, entered the courtroom in a disheveled fashion, and during the court procedure threw his shoes and socks around the floor. As it was in wintertime and the stone floors were cold, it was noted that he attempted to reach his socks with his feet, in order not to touch the cold floor. His sister was an excellent witness in his defense, collapsing on the stand. Later it was learned that she had taken dramatic lessons to prepare her for her court appearance.

We have had many interesting cases. Fear plays a large role in many instances. I have seen a man drop dead after leaving the witness stand; another attempt to dash through a barred window before going into the courtroom, although his offense was a minor one and probation had been assured him. Some attempt suicide and are successful. Others become panicky, others mute, some combative, some have epileptic seizures, others faint or have heart attacks.

Our greatest difficulty is with defense lawyers in cases of psychoneuroses and psychopathic personalities. Anyone who shows the slightest deviation in behavior from normal, or who was retarded in school, is considered by his counsel to be insane in order to avoid the consequences of his acts. If the charge is serious and the individual has previously been com mitted as feebleminded or mentally ill, the defense tries to avoid the legal tests and attempts to have him committed civilly. This is especially true in the borderline mental defectives and veterans receiving compensation.

Our Civil Code for commitments does not apply to those charged with crime.

The question is often raised: Just what type of patient does the Behavior Clinic examine? To answer that I have taken referrals for a month in the not too distant past. The total examined was forty-seven, six of whom were under 21 years of age. During the month I testified in court thirteen times, either at the request of the State or for the Defense. The charges were as follows:

Crime vs. Children	2
Crime vs. Nature	1
Contributing to Delinquency of a Minor	7
Indecent Exposure	1
Abortion	1
Manslaughter	1
Attempt to Murder	1
Murder	6
Larceny	3
Burglary	3
Robbery	12
Arson	2
Forgery	1
Narcotics	1
Disorderly Conduct	3
No complaint (one witness and one writ filed by an inmate of an institution for the mentally defective)	2

One of those examined was a female.

Thirty-one were referred by the Criminal Court; seven from the Municipal Courts; one from the Family Court; three from Justices of the Peace in outlying districts, and there were five writs from institutionalized patients asking for their release. Forty-one had previously been arrested for various charges. Thirty-four gave a history of excessive alcoholism. Nine out of forty-seven were, or had been, using drugs. Ten of the forty-seven were found to be insane and were committed to Illinois Security Hospital. Five were examined to determine whether they were sexually dangerous persons. Those found to so classify were committed as wards of the Director of Public Safety under the new "Sexually Dangerous Persons Act."

It is alarming to note the increase in pornographic literature and pictures. One of those arrested had a stolen camera. When the police came to his apartment to investigate they found a huge collection of obscene pictures. One series involved bestiality. This defendant stated that he had been collecting obscene pictures for many, many years. He had been overseas in India and the Far East. He made many copies of these for the officers. He stated that he had huge albums of pictures when he returned to the States, but that these were stolen from him soon after his arrival. He told of a certain drug store in the south side that would rent the pictures for party purposes. He would take the pictures, go home and promptly make reproductions of them.

Another who was arrested for indecent exposure stated that he had made obscene pictures for a "fast buck." He hired couples for $3.00 an hour to pose in various sexual acts. He took pictures with a Polaroid camera and then sold them. I was recently told of a new procedure of one company that sent such pictures through the mail. The recipients of the pictures knew the procedure, which was to open them in the dark and expose them to certain solutions. If the packages were opened by the postal inspectors or the police, the exposure to the light would destroy the picture.

In the "Sexually Dangerous Persons" group we had one who denied the present charge. However, he had been examined by the Behavior Clinic in 1941, at which time he readily admitted sexual involvement with children. Another in this group would kidnap young boys for sexual purposes. One murderer under the influence of alcohol killed his victim and literally chewed off parts of her body. Another diagnosed as a sexually Dangerous Person was employed by the City supervising and teaching young children. He made it a point to meet the families of the children and gain their confidence. He then would take the children out for immoral purposes. Of late he had been working on the 3:00 p.m. to 12:00 midnight shift, so that he would not be on the streets when children were coming home from school.

One, on a charge of contributing to the delinquency of a child, had young boys beat him with a rod in order to excite him, at which time he would masturbate in their presence.

Of those examined, one was a witness who had motoraphasia, the result of being struck and shot during a holdup. The Court ordered the examination, thinking that he might be intoxicated at the time of his appearance as a witness. Another had epilepsy. One of the two arsonists had been examined by the Behavior Clinic several years ago and his behavior was repeated under alcohol. In other words, under the influence of alcohol he would set fires. The other was an 18-year-old boy who readily admitted setting several hundred fires in his life. He denied any sexual thrill from setting the fires. He had served time but had not profited by his past incarceration.

Suicidal attempts are frequent in the County Jail. Occasionally an inmate succeeds. If he has ever attempted suicide the defense attorney, if he has no other defense, frequently calls this a form of insanity to disclaim responsibility. Of the forty-seven, one had attempted suicide in the County Jail which, from the description appeared to be a genuine attempt. He was facing the habitual count. Another attempted suicide at home, but his mother waited until late the next day before she took him to see a doctor at a psychiatric clinic. He was certified to the Cook County Psychopathic Hospital, and was admitted. Again, anyone charged with crime cannot be committed civilly, under the laws of the State of Illinois. This young boy had been involved in some robberies and was removed from the Psychopathic Hospital to the County Jail. He did not later try or attempt suicide while in the jail.

What is the future of Forensic Psychiatry in the State of Illinois, and how can it be improved?

My recommendations for the future improvement are:

(1) To create a building under the supervision of the Department of Public Welfare in the northern section of Illinois, or possibly on the grounds of Chicago State Hospital, to house those from the entire state where after indictment the question of insanity has been raised. Now we have a Behavior Clinic which functions for courts in Cook County, but outside of Cook County the State's Attorneys must rely upon psychiatrists who are willing to come to examine and later testify. In some counties they have no psychiatrists. As I understand it, one county in Illinois has only one physician, so that it is necessary to impanel juries for commitments in civil cases. The Mental Health Act requires two doctors in a county to act as a commission for civil commitments. A Forensic Diagnostic Center could perform a complete physical, psychological and mental examination. The doctors could also testify when needed in various counties of the state. Possibly a wing of the Cook County Jail could be set aside for observational purposes, the State to reimburse the County for the expenses involved.

281

(2) Legislation should be enacted to provide for a panel of psychiatrists to be appointed by the Court and made available to both sides. The psychiatrists testifying in court should have access to ALL information held by both sides, to avoid partiality. Their fees should be paid by the State.

(3) The hypothetical question should be abolished.

(4) The psychiatrist should be permitted to testify along medical lines so far as it is humanly possible to do so. He should not be limited to the rigid interpretation of the M'Naghten Rules. As it is now, he is not permitted to express his opinion in court, except on evidence which has already been introduced. A pretrial conference of psychiatrists would be of value in that they could discuss their findings and reach points of agreement.

(5) The sanity issue should be abolished. The defendant could be tried on the offense charged and then, if guilty, psychiatry could be used to assist or aid in the disposition.

(6) The newspapers should not glamorize crime.

(7) Many lawyers expect the psychiatrists to determine the guilt or innocence of their client. Psychiatrists should concern themselves only with the mental condition of the accused and not sit in judgment. Legislation should be enacted so that the examinations could be considered as a privileged communication.

Reprinted with the permission of the American Academy of Forensic Sciences. Dr. Haines' article originally appeared in the January, 1957 issue of the Journal of Forensic Sciences, Vol. 2, No. 1.

INDEX

283